Life In the Balance

Life In the Balance

The Life and Work of William Edward Hipkins

To David,

Best wishes

Andrew P.B. Lound

authorHOUSE®

AuthorHouse™
1663 Liberty Drive
Bloomington, IN 47403
www.authorhouse.com
Phone: 1-800-839-8640

First published by AuthorHouse   09/08/2011

ISBN: 978-1-4567-9800-0 (sc)
ISBN: 978-1-4567-9801-7 (hc)

Printed in the United States of America

Contents

This book is dedicated to

Janet Pickard

William's closest living relative
whose help made this book possible.

Foreword

In the hectic world of business, the focus is always on future growth—and rightly so. However, it is worthwhile to take time to look back, to see where a company like Avery Weigh-Tronix came from, and to establish how the name of Avery became synonymous with weighing. Any article or book written about a company is a great tribute, but to read a biography of Avery's first externally recruited Managing Director is particularly pleasing, as it demonstrates an understanding and appreciation of the efforts of an individual who never sought recognition for his work at Avery.

Over more than 250 years of history, the name Avery has been associated with quality and service and, as such, remains one of the world's most iconic names in weighing. Achieving such a level of recognition requires a great deal of work and development over many decades.

By the end of the 19th century, many well established firms were closing. Companies which had been family concerns found they could not compete with demands of a modern industrial and commercial world. To survive, firms had to be radical in their approach to management and working practices, while still remaining socially responsible. William E. Hipkins came to Avery's at a point in the company's history when the firm could have disappeared entirely. Through his radical and at times dynamic approach, the firm grew to become the world's largest weighing machine company.

Hipkins' efforts to standardize working arrangements and rationalise manufacturing may have become commonplace in today's industry, but at the end of the 19th century they were revolutionary. He was responsible for kick-starting the expansion of the Avery business globally, as well as having a significant input into improving standards for workers, industry and weighing itself.

Business leaders, like all people, are products of their time; William Hipkins, however, would fit neatly into the modern age, being able to respond quickly and effectively to the challenges brought by the changing economic climate. His dedication to the task is a great inspiration to all who strive to drive industry forward. He never wavered from his aim to make the name *Avery* the foremost weighing machine company in the world, and was one in a line of Managing Directors that have helped the company to achieve the status we hold today.

Mike Scott
Managing Director, Avery Weigh-Tronix

Acknowledgements

No matter how good the researcher, there is always the need to acknowledge the help and assistance given by those who have specialist knowledge, archives or offer useful advice. A detailed listing of those who have assisted is listed in the bibliography. However, I feel it is important to make special mention here of those whose assistance during the last twenty years has been invaluable. Former Curators of the Avery Historical Museum, Howard Green and John Doran have given freely of their time to find unbelievable quantities of material hidden in old filing cabinets. Especially for the access I was allowed on September 10th and 11th 2001when I virtually emptied eight cabinets of historical material. I feel more indebted to them, as my research eventually led to me to become the Curator of the museum on John's retirement! Fiona Tait, and the staff at Birmingham Archives and Heritage, have as always been patient in finding and retrieving countless documents. The staff at Collindale Newspaper Library, Family Record Office in London, Maritime Archives at Liverpool Maritime Museum, Lambeth Palace Library, Coventry Library, and the Library at the University of Wisconsin have all assisted me in locating material. Michael Horne has once again offered valuable advice on engineering matters, in particular taking me through a crash course in casting and tool making. He also read through and checked the engineering descriptions. The Hipkins family were noted corkscrew makers, and I am grateful to the advice supplied by Don Bull, Bertrand B. Giulian, and Fletcher Wallis. These men introduced me into the world of corkscrew collecting, for which I have too small a bank balance! To understand the nature of being a managing director of a large company I am grateful for the advice of Martyn Vaughan who was at the time Managing Director of Alstom Transport at the old Metropolitan Cammell works in Birmingham. Another director at Alstom was Brigitte Over who gave generously of her time to give me her appraisal of William Hipkins' managerial style. I am grateful to Hugh Barham Carslake for taking the time to explain Bertha Hipkins' last will and testament. My dear friends John Forbes and Regina (Forbes) Schraut assisted greatly in the history of Boston, Massachusetts. I am indebted to Dr. Barbara Smith whose incredible study of the history of W. & T. Avery Limited, led me down many useful paths, and pointed me towards other material. A number of local history societies have offered great assistance, and in particular Handsworth, Quinton, and Smethwick Local History Societies, and the Cradley Then and Now Group for producing former Avery employees who shared their knowledge and reminiscences. Professor Carl Chinn of the University of Birmingham has been a constant source of encouragement and along with a number of presenters at BBC Radio WM has broadcast appeals for information. Max Hipkins, of Australia has been tracing the Hipkins' family trees and I am grateful for his generosity in sharing his findings. Another researcher in the southern hemisphere Keith Houghton kindly shared his knowledge of the Houghton family with me. My first real boss, Harry Seabourne, deserves a mention. As far back in 1981, it was his advice to me to contact the Titanic Historical Society that led me to discover the name 'William E. Hipkins.' Over the last twenty years there have been a number of managers at Avery's that have allowed me free access to archive material. Tory Manning gave me great assistance in not only supporting my research but by inviting me to speak at Soho Foundry about William Hipkins. Support she continued when she became my boss! Also at Avery Weigh-Tronix, John Garner, Helen Fisher and Laura Wilks have offered support, and advice that has been more valuable than they could image. I am also honoured that the current Managing Director at Soho Foundry, Mike Scott who agreed to write the foreword. Members of my own family have given a lot of their time and assistance; my late father drove me around the country seeking out archives and locations associated with William Hipkins. My mother has offered valuable opinion and advice, particularly on Hipkins' family life. Finally two people who have given much support: Janet Pickard, the closest surviving relative to William Hipkins, who provided photographs and an artifact of William's. Her reminiscences were of great value especially regarding Bertha Hipkins; and Linda Waite whose expertise in genealogical research, archive hunting and clarity of thought resolved a number of issues. Linda also gave of her valuable time to proof read the book and suggest changes. Photographs of the Hipkins family has been kindly supplied by Janet Pickard; images from W. & T.

Avery is by courtesy of the Avery Historical Museum; images of Hipkins' advertisements are by courtesy of Birmingham Archives and Heritage. I have tried to include everyone in the bibliography and I apologise if anyone has been inadvertently missed.

5

Preface

Over the years many books have been written about the history of Birmingham. In all of them attention is paid to the individuals who through their drive, enthusiasm, vision, and in some cases genius, led Birmingham to become, at the beginning of the 20th century, the world's leading and most diverse industrial city. The likes of Matthew Boulton, James Watt, William Murdoch, Thomas and William Avery, and Joseph Chamberlain, along with a dozen others rightfully hold their places as the leading figures in Birmingham's history. There is however a name missing from the list of esteemed and recognized people, and it is not due to the fault of local historians. It is in part the fault of the man himself and to the tragic circumstances of his untimely death. Birmingham's forgotten son is *William Edward Hipkins*.

It all began for me, when I started my first job. My boss Harry Seabourne had an interest in the *Titanic* disaster and referred me to the *Titanic Historical Society*. This organization publishes reproductions of documents relating to the ship, and one proved to have dramatic consequences for me. Exhibit B of the US Senate Inquiry report into the loss of the 'Titanic', one line reads:

> Hipkins, Mr. W. E. . . . Avery Scale Company,
> North Milwaukee Wis.

Being a resident of Birmingham I am familiar with Avery's and wondered what the connection was between this Mr. Hipkins and Birmingham. Thus began the search for the life of an extraordinary man.His story is a fascinating one, but it has not been an easy one to obtain. Considering the positions he held and the impact he made In Birmingham at the turn of the 20th century, the absence of printed information is surprising. More intriguing is that there are no memoranda or business letters of his existing in the W & T Avery Limited archive, where he was Managing Director.

Clues to his life emerged from a memorial book written and published by Avery's Glasgow manager, George Allinson. This book was only a starting point. As the years passed a story emerged of Hipkins' connections with the great, the good and the not so good of Birmingham business. I found a network of business connections that controlled a large amount of the metal trade in the city and a small group of men who decided who would sit on the boards of companies.

As a businessman at the turn of the 20th century he was one of the first of a new generation taking Birmingham industry away from the undisciplined and casual practices of family concerns, to the more professional and organised commercial ventures that one is familiar with today. His life links together the past history of Birmingham with the large-scale developments of the Victorian era, and in some of his speeches we see a very familiar tone in regards to British industry as a whole. Tracing the life of William Hipkins was impossible without tracing the history of Birmingham and seeing how his development was not coincidental to the time but was partly formed by the time, and indeed Hipkins himself contributed to the development of Birmingham's industrial and economic life.

The search to seek out William's life has been long and arduous, but well worth the effort and offers an insight into a time of great change for Birmingham and the world. It is not complete, many mysteries remain. His wife Lavinia Ellen remains elusive. Her origins and how she met William, is still unknown; and if any reader knows anything of this lady I would be grateful for them to contact me. For although this book is written, the research will continue.

Introduction

Although it was technically summer, it was difficult to tell whether the Spring had been extended into June, or that Autumn was coming early. The sky was gray and over-cast, little drops of rain had begun to fall. In the centre of Birmingham, on this melancholy afternoon, life went on as normal; businessmen hurried themselves across the city, office workers were dashing in and out of shops during their lunch break, and the never ending supply of students were engaged in a variety of academic—and not so academic activities. With all of this hustle and bustle no-one noticed the 35 year old man speeding his way across the city heading for the taxi ranks next to the ramp that leads to the Palisades shopping area.

He was in a hurry because he was on his lunch break, and had moments earlier stepped off a bus that had brought him from Washwood Heath and his place of employment. Now he needed more transport to take him to his final destination. The line of black cabs sat expectantly, and without even waiting to see if the driver was ready he climbed into the back and called out the destination. "Warstone Lane Cemetery." The driver duly started the engine and although the request would at first seem strange, especially as Warstone Lane Cemetery was now more of a curiosity than a place of remembrance, the driver asked no questions of his rather excited passenger.

Through the city they drove, the passenger ever more excited the closer the cab got to the cemetery, and then at last it stopped. The passenger hurriedly paid the driver and got out, walked a few feet to the small wall that rings the cemetery and simply stared. The wall had a gap leading to a small winding path that led into the heart of the cemetery itself. He walked carefully taking in every moment of the small journey as if exploring a new land unseen before by any man. The noise of the traffic behind him on the main road was loud and the occasional outpouring of road rage added to the atmosphere of a 20th century city; but the 35-year-old man heard none of it, his mind was far away, and as the rain fell onto his un-coated frame, he walked with increasing excitement. He followed the winding path and stared around him, the hundreds of gravestones marking the place of a person who had long since departed this world, a person who had lived, loved, felt joy and sadness and now the only reminder of their existence was a cold gray stone. In his mind the man could see the sequence from the movie the *Good, the Bad and the Ugly* where Eli Wallach finds himself in a cemetery needing to find just one grave out of the thousands, Eli runs around looking at each in turn. This man also needed to find just one grave, he knew it was here he had found the entry in the Warstone Lane Cemetery index in Birmingham Library, all he had to do now was find it.

He spun round not sure in which direction to start, he followed the path a little way more, coming to open section that split off into three routes. "Which way?" he said aloud. To the left was a set of benches; on one of them were two people down on their luck sipping from bottles. Forward the path led deep into cemetery and on his right . . .

He walked slowly to a large black rectangular monument. It was much bigger than he had expected, the words at the bottom were hard to read but he could make them out:

George Frederick Hipkins

He walked closer falling to his knees and getting a better look at the inscription, he ran his fingers through the carving. "I found you" he said aloud.

For a few moments he just remained there looking at the words, the rain still falling. He got up and walked around the monument and found a second inscription

Rebecca Hipkins

He then realized he hadn't looked on the top of it, so he stood upright and looked over on the top face of the monument and there picked out in white were the words:

Lavinia Ellen Hipkins
William Edward Hipkins
Bertha Hipkins

He fell prostrate onto the monument closed his eyes and simply savored the moment.

After years of research he had finally found the Hipkins' family plot, it was as if finding a lost family, it was like making a physical contact with the people he had been tracing for so long.

That 35 year old man was me. I didn't realize it at the time, but it was the beginning of the final phase of my research into the life of *William Edward Hipkins* a man who had simply appeared as one of the 1,500 plus people listed as "Lost on the Titanic." A man as it turns out who was far more than a simple statistic. A man whose business methods had created the greatest weighing machine company on Earth. A man who was to herald in a new era of working practices that would be copied across the nation. A man whose name never appears in any of the books on industrial history, a name that has been lost as the likes of Cadbury, Lucas, Austin, Dunlop, Chamberlain and Docker courted publicity.

It is time to tell the story of William Edward Hipkins, Birmingham's forgotten son.

Andrew Lound May 2011

CHAPTER 1

THE IRON MEN COMETH

Let the path be open to talent

—*Napoleon*

The sky was grey and a little drizzle fell, the air was chilled but it was by no means unpleasant. John Leland rested his horse on the dirt road and considered his position. In the near distance black smoke was rising into the grey sky and he could just hear the sound of metallic hammering. He headed on, and the closer he got the louder the hammering grew until when he reached the town itself he could distinguish the sound of numerous hammers crashing down on anvils, echoing like an uncoordinated symphony of iron. This was *Birmingham*. He trotted up the road, crossing the bridge over the River Rea and entered the market town. On either side of the road he saw numerous open smiths inside the largest of which four men worked, each taking a turn to hammer on the anvil. With the air filled with hammering, the smoke rising and the red and orange glow from the fires in the smiths, it resembled a scene from a mythical world. One must wonder if Richard Wagner knew of Birmingham's smiths when centuries later he wrote *The Ring Cycle* depicting the *Niebelungen* hammering away, as the Birmingham of old certainly had the feel of mythical ironworkers.[1]

Birmingham and the surrounding area had begun life, like so many towns, as a farming region with strong emphasis on pasture farming but with the changes in economic and population conditions the region evolved and changed with the times. The natural resources of wood and water were a great asset in developing industries of all kinds and helped fuel the town's development. The farming industry slowly changed from pasture to arable, and in many places it gave way to textile production with the energy of the rivers and streams being utilised with the building of mills. The availability of iron and coal from Staffordshire to the North had

1

fuelled the developing trades of ironwork, with a furnace for melting and casting iron being set up in 1615 in the local parish of Aston.[2] The pervading economic pressures resulted in much of the land being abandoned and becoming absorbed into existing farms. For newcomers to the region there was little land available and with the general farm production centred on beef there was little work. Many of the iron workmen, having no acreage of land to themselves operated from small buildings creating a *cottage industry*. The slow but gradual process that converted the region into one of iron working, one which created employment and wealth had begun.

With the wealth came the need for bigger and better housing and new buildings to accommodate the influx of workers. The organisation of labour in the metalworking field became a vital part of the growth as at this time cottage workers not only made the goods but also took them to the market to sell. A clutch of such metalworkers sprang up along *Digbeth*, the main road into the town from the South; at the north end of the road was Birmingham's Corn Market, which was an ideal place to sell the finished goods. As the number of ironworkers grew the workshops began to spread all over the town and a new type of tradesman appeared—the ironmonger.

Ironmongers supplied a number of cottage workers with raw materials and received the finished goods, which they then sold on. This was far more efficient than the ironworkers doing everything themselves, they could now concentrate on production alone. This arrangement offered an opportunity for entrepreneurs like John Jennens, who operated from his own iron production facility in Aston, selling a host of iron ornaments in London as well as the local markets. The business was a family one with John passing it down to his son Humphrey. Other ironmongers, although not as wealthy, were just as enterprising and Birmingham began to grow as the efficient system attracted more workers from all parts of the country, bringing with them a wide variety of skills which inexorably led to a wide variation in the products being produced. Guns were produced from the late 17th century, and by the 18th century every type of household item was being made. The wealth generated from the trade resulted in more people having spare money to spend, which in turn led to a demand for a greater variety of luxury goods such as metal ornaments. Such a trade in various metal items became known as the 'Toy Trade', and Birmingham became the 'Toy shop' of Europe as the workshops not only supplied products to various cities and towns in Britain but also exported products around the world.

Traditional methods of manufacture as employed by the workman of the cottage industries were still prominent in the 18th century as it was cheap and practical, but with the demand growing higher and the need to produce more quickly to meet this demand, mechanisation began to take a foothold. The water mills that had sprung up to support the textile industry now began to be converted for use as rolling mills and machines for stamping out small items en masse were introduced enabling a fast output of items. Not only iron but copper and brass items began to be produced in large quantities, along with steel in the 19th century, which became popular for toys as it resembled silver yet was a fraction of the cost. Careful organisation brought with it a great deal of specialisation with various workmen concentrating their efforts on buttons, buckles, door furniture and domestic utensils etc. The situation became ripe for someone to make a lot of money by organizing industry to meet this ever-growing demand. John Taylor took the bull by the horns and set up a factory with what appears to have been a flow line process in the production of items such as buttons. He produced large quantities of material, although the quality left a lot to be desired helping Birmingham gain a reputation for shoddy or *Brummagem* goods—although the cheap mass produced goods met a particular market. People soon began to demand far better quality, and if the Birmingham metalworkers were to meet this demand then something even more radical than Taylor's factory was to have to come about. The new radical idea came in the form of Matthew Boulton.

Boulton had served his apprenticeship in his father's buckle making business eventually becoming a partner. He had an ability to improve existing products (especially a rather good buckle which had helped his father's business to prosper). On his father's premature death in 1759 he took over the business, but found that it was too small to meet his great ambitions, (which were at the time to be a great silversmith producing high quality products). In 1762 he formed a partnership with John Fothergill and set up a manufactory at Soho in Staffordshire a little to the north of Birmingham town centre. In this manufactory he brought together highly skilled craftsmen to produce very high quality goods in an efficient organised manner. With Boulton being manufacturer and merchant it enabled him to control the whole of the business with his workmen producing quality goods to suit demand. In 1774 Boulton's business friend, John Roebuck, handed over his interest in steam engines which were being produced by a Scotsman called James Watt. The steam engine and its manufacture would change forever the course of manufacturing and the manner in which technology was used to improve the quality of products. The mills would no longer rely on water to drive the machinery; a manufactory could operate for 24 hours a day all year round if need be. Boulton and Watt (and it must be added William Murdoch) became the driving force behind the mechanized industrial revolution that would place Birmingham at the epicentre of world manufacturing (although steam power did not appear in many of the smaller workshops of the town for many years).

Boulton was not simply a man to herd a mass of workers into the world's largest manufactory and then take the profits. Like many of his day he was a social reformer and offered excellent working conditions including sick benefits and pension arrangements. Indeed his humane treatment of workers was so good that other employers in the town complained that they had trouble holding on to theirs, as everyone wanted to work for Boulton! In 1795 Boulton and Watt built the *Soho Foundry* in Smethwick

> *". . . in order to obtain the desired degree of perfection in their manufactory of steam engines."*[3]

It was here that high quality steam engines were produced for a whole variety of uses, especially in the developing area of steamboats.

With the Soho Foundry churning out steam engines and the Soho Manufactory churning out endless quantities of quality products, the whole region had become the world centre for metal work of all kinds. Birmingham attracted countless workers from all parts of Great Britain (and indeed Europe), for if one had a metal working skill, the place to be was Birmingham.

William Hipkins was a man with such skills and he moved from his native Staffordshire into the town to seek work, and although he had the skills, Birmingham was a highly competitive town. By 1801 the population was a little under 61,000 and William was just one man trying to make a living. With his wife Margaret they set up home in Bread Street on the north side of the town, at the back of which was a workshop where he and several others set to work making a variety of small household items, including corkscrews, nut crackers etc. The hours were long and conditions were harsh with smoke constantly choking the men, and William often took on extra work in the evenings to supplement his income. William's particular skill was in spring making with a specialism in making corkscrews. The spiral of a corkscrew is, essentially, a very strong open spring which has to be strong enough to allow quite a force to be applied, yet have enough spring in it to take the strain without breaking.

Corkscrew production became a major industry from the first quarter of the 18th century as most bottles containing liquids were sealed with a cork. The inventiveness of people throughout history can in fact be demonstrated by the development of the corkscrew. When corks were first used to seal a container there was no tool designed to remove them and it is thought that a farm implement (which was more of a spike) was used to enable a person to sample the delights of the container. Over time a *steel worm* was developed to remove the corks eventually becoming known as a corkscrew.[4] With the development of moulded glass bottles and the mass production of wines, spirits, beers and bottled water feeding the ever-growing industrial towns, there had to be a practical and plentiful supply of implements to uncork them. The first patented corkscrew was by the Reverend Samuel Henshall in 1795 who had them manufactured by none other than Matthew Boulton at the Soho Manufactory near Birmingham.[5] Since then over 300 patents have been taken out in Great Britain[6] from straight forward pulls, to rack and pinion systems, levers, levers with rack and pinion systems in fact every conceivable method to remove that little cork appears to have been considered, with Birmingham workmen playing an important role. Edward Thomason, who had worked at the Soho Manufactory, patented the corkscrew known as the *Ne Plus Ultra* in 1802 producing over 130,000 examples in fourteen years. For a period of time it was seen as 'the' standard for the big houses, and at a guinea a piece only those in the largest houses could afford them![7] Cheaper corkscrews came in a variety of materials and styles with most being made of steel with steel, wood, or ivory handles. Some were very ornate for use in hotels or big houses, William Hipkins, however, produced fairly straightforward corkscrews usually to the Henshall patent.

William was able to establish himself and in 1812 Margaret gave birth to their first child, a boy they named William Edward, and he was followed three years later by another son, James Bradford. The children were bright and active and it was not long before Margaret was with child again. However soon after the news, James Bradford aged only 8 died.

Their youngest son George Frederick was born on September 30th 1818 at their home in Bread Street, William was pleased, it was important to have sons who could learn the trade of their father and, when old enough, they could assist in the workshop. A common feature of iron-working in Birmingham was that fathers would employ their sons as additional help, the older ones receiving a wage paid by their father from what he earned from his employer, and the younger ones earning pocket money. William Edward was bright and learned the trade well. By the age of 13 he was helping his father in the workshop, and in his spare time was taking lessons on how to read and write. The family kept growing, William and Margaret had a daughter Margaret Ann in 1823, and with the extra mouth to feed it was important that the two boys worked hard to help bring in extra money.[8]

As would be expected there were great strains associated with the day to day existence in a large town with overcrowded houses and a smoky atmosphere. The sewerage system left a lot to be desired and illness was all too common. The Hipkins had done quite well, the quality of their work was good and there was plenty of demand. For whatever reason, or combination of reasons, sometime around 1835 William and Margaret became estranged from each other, with Margaret moving away to Upper Windsor Street in Ashted on the east side of the town. Their eldest son William Edward left home obtaining a job as a clerk, and soon thereafter he married Lydia Wood in Harborne and moved to 29 Great Hampton Row. George Frederick stayed with his mother and began work at Samuel Cotterill's, a corkscrew maker located in Duke Street Birmingham.[9] Cotterill had been in business since at least 1821.[10] His son Edwin took over the business in the late 1830s and soon the firm began to expand. By the 1840s he was turning out a variety of corkscrews, champagne nippers, boot and buttonhooks, horse pickers and tweezers etc. supplying a number of ironmongers in Birmingham and London, catering to all market levels. George fitted in well and began learning the iron trade.

His brother William Edward was also doing well. He had set up home in Birmingham and was overjoyed when his wife announced she was pregnant. On 17th January 1838 a baby girl was born but the joy of the new child was short lived as his wife, Lydia, who was never a strong woman grew ever weaker and ten days later she died of exhaustion. She was only 29. The baby girl, named after her mother was also weak and William Edward's mother helped nurse the child. The effort, although valiant, was in vain, and she died eight months later of consumption. William Edward was distraught. His life had been shattered in just a few months and he decided that he needed to leave Birmingham and make a fresh start. He moved to London and got a job with the firm of *Thomas Lund* based at Cornhill and Fleet Street. Lund's had been established in 1796 and produced a variety of household items such as cutlery, kitchen utensils, dressing tables and portable writing desks, employing a number of highly skilled workmen. The quality of work was high targeting the high end of the market for most of their products (although some smaller items were also produced for general sale). William Edward joined the firm as works foreman at the Fleet Street facility under William Lund using his expertise in corkscrew manufacture and product design, and making an immediate impression upon his employers as an excellent organizer. The new start suited him well and in 1844 he married his second wife, Mary Ann Trew, and with the births of Annie Mary in 1847 and Emily in 1850 he began to raise the family he so much wanted.

Although doing well in London he did not cut himself off from his mother, sister and brother in Birmingham; when he could he visited them to ensure they were doing well. His father, William, had died of pneumonia in 1841 which made William Edward the senior figure in the family and he felt a responsibility to his siblings. George Frederick had grown into a hardworking but physically weak man. Rather thin and always looking as if he needed a meal his thin face was hidden by a spectacular beard and moustache. His employer Edwin Cotterill had expanded his business even further and had a growing reputation as an inventor and developer of new products. In 1846 he had taken out a patent for door and window furniture which featured locks, latches, springs etc. and the business boasted the manufacture of latches of all kinds. This development coincided with his move to better premises at Henry Street in Ashted. Cotterill's patented lock was causing quite a stir. An American locksmith Alfred C. Hobbs had made a name for himself in England by challenging lock makers to produce a lock that he could not pick. Jeremiah Chubb, a very well known lock maker looked on in dismay as Hobbs successfully opened one of his locks that he thought was pickproof! Arrangements were then made for Hobbs to attempt to pick the famous *Bramah Lock*. Joseph Bramah had a shop in Piccadilly, London and in the window he displayed his patented lock and a challenge.

The artist who can make an instrument that will pick or open this lock will receive two hundred guineas the moment it is produced.[11]

Well this was too good a challenge for Hobbs to turn down and thus he set to work. Hobbs worked on the lock under supervision for 44 hours over a period of 10 days. In the end the lock opened and Hobbs was able to relock and unlock the mechanism repeatedly. Hobbs was seen as 'the' tester of lock mechanisms and he stated that:

". . . wherever the parts of a lock which come in contact with the key are affected by any pressure applied to the bolt, that lock can be picked."[12]

The lock trade was given a boost by his enterprising activities and lock makers across the country vied each other to produce locks that Hobbs could not pick. It was not long after Cotterill's patent that the Birmingham lock maker's mechanism was given to Hobbs. Hobbs failed to open the lock and Cotterill's reputation as a lock maker was established beyond doubt.

George had become an excellent spring maker under Edwin Cotterill and his foreman Edward Hudson. Hudson was a little older than George and the two of them were highly regarded by Cotterill who had more plans to expand. He wanted to add new lock designs and increase the range of products in the light steel toy side of the business. Cotterill's ambitions would mean that opportunities would present themselves for his best workers. Cotterill encouraged those that had worked for him to further develop themselves by setting up on their own and manufacture his designs, thus in essence setting up satellite workshops. George and Edward were both keen to have a piece of this action. Apart from the business opportunity, George had other reasons to become a business owner. He had met and married Rebecca Houghton, a handsome woman strong in build and character with a gentle yet determined nature.[13] Rebecca came from Norton in Worcestershire and little is known in detail of her origins save that she was illegitimate and her grandfather was a carpenter. Her mother Sarah lived off a private income possibly left by her father or Rebecca's father.[14]

Edward Hudson set up a business of his own specialising in making Cotterill's patent door springs in Ashted Row just a couple of minutes walk from Cotterill's. In 1849 George went into partnership with Hudson and thus made the first step towards his goal of becoming a manufacturer. The partnership specialised in producing door furniture of all kinds (knobs, knockers, hinges etc) as well as door bells.[15] George had good reason to feel that life for him, like his brother in London, was on the up, Rebecca was pregnant with their first child and the timing of his move to Hudson's was perfect. Birmingham was still growing rapidly and the town's reputation for the wide variety of manufactured items had spread the world over. There is no doubt that by 1850 whatever you wanted and no matter how many you required, someone, somewhere in Birmingham could produce it for you, and George was just one of many fighting to obtain orders. For every successful brassfoundry three or four would fall by the wayside and the competition was fierce and growing. The town's success was attracting ever increasing numbers of people from all parts of the country to find work in the manufacturing industries. By 1852 the population of Birmingham had risen to over 200,000. This influx of people all requiring work, accommodation and feeding had been a strain on the small town and radical measures had taken place to meet the growing needs of the people. The inner town areas were becoming overcrowded and the once green areas of the suburbs of the town were now changing, Ashted being a prime example. Ashted had been one of the first generation of Birmingham suburbs, named for Dr. John Ash, Birmingham's famous physician, who had been the force behind the founding of the *Birmingham General Hospital*. From the late 1780s professional people had moved in from the town centre to get away from the smoke and fumes of the factories and small brassfoundries. A number of marvellous Georgian houses had been built along Ashted Row and the area became known for its wealthy inhabitants. With the constant development of Birmingham the industrial activities of the town began to spread out with manufacturing units and cheaper housing being built in the surrounding areas including Ashted. By 1850 a whole variety of trades had moved in to the once green suburb including corn merchants, breweries, tobacconists, blacksmiths, brassfounders, carriage builders and a dozen other trades. The previous immigrants from the smoke moved out to other areas such as Edgbaston (that had been protected from the building of industrial premises). Many of the Georgian houses in Ashted had been bought by entrepreneurs such as William Wallis who ran a number of steam mills, having had some of the houses extended at the rear to fit workshops and stores. Wallis let some of these properties as business premises, 203 Ashted Row was such a property situated on the corner of Ashted Row and Dartmouth Street having William Wallis' Steam Mills as next door neighbours along with corn merchants, small brassfounders, mills, and countless single room workshops. All of these industrial units were conveniently located to roads that led into the town centre. A couple of minutes walk to the south of Ashted Row stood *Curzon Street Railway Station* which handled goods traffic of all kinds enabling distribution of materials in an efficient manner. A little further along was *Vauxhall Station*, (Birmingham's oldest) which handled passenger traffic and was within easy walking distance of the premises.

The main house at 203 was three stories tall plus an attic and basement. There was ample room for Edward Hudson and his family of wife and daughter plus two house servants (who used the rooms in the attic). A room on the ground floor at the rear of the house served as the works office, with a door that entered the cobbled yard that in turn led to a long brick building which acted as the workshop. This workshop, although two stories tall, had only one level with small windows in two lines along its full length. The interior was typical of a brassfounder's workshop with the Pattern Shop and Pattern Room separated by a thin partition. The pattern room was lit mainly by large skylights fitted into the roof and the two rooms together were only about 35 feet long and 12 feet wide. The wall space of the pattern room was taken up with shelving which held numerous patterns for use in the workshop. Next to these were the moulding and casting shops, the dressing room, finishing shop, a dripping and colouring room, and a lacquering room. Opposite this long building were stores and a warehouse and in between the buildings was a cobbled yard which ran to a pair of large wooden gates that led to a small passageway shared with Willis' steam mills which was used for the delivery of materials and the distribution of finished items to the various ironmongers in the town and beyond. The workshops were staffed by 10 men (2 in the pattern room, 4 in the casting shop, 1 in the finishing room, 1 in the colouring room and 1 in the warehouse along with a boy). All of them had to double up their duties to keep the fledgling firm producing and Hudson himself was often seen on the shop floor working away.

The working conditions in the workshops of Birmingham were at best unhealthy, many were appalling and dangerous, and in most cases it was not just the workmen who were affected. With the living accommodation attached to the workshops, more often than not all of the family members were exposed to fumes containing a mixture of chemicals that would damage lungs and increase lead and zinc levels in the blood. The moulding and casting shops were particularly noxious with vats of molten lead used for tempering steel producing fumes that slowly poisoned the workmen. The furnaces of the shops were sunk below floor level with the pit for the removal of ashes being covered by hinged iron gratings. The domed covers for the furnace top were constructed of cast iron, and inserted in the flue was a damper that regulated the draft. These furnaces were fuelled by hard coke and in summer time the conditions were appalling for the men working in the moulding rooms. No matter how many vents were added the heat always seemed to remain trapped in the building, which is more than can be said for the fumes as at certain times Hudson's house would find itself engulfed by smoke! Workmen in the brassfoundries often suffered from *Brassfounder's Ague*,[16] an intermittent fever brought on by the inhalation of the fumes from deflagrating zinc. The effect of the conditions on workers in brassfoundries was not always immediate. Workers in general enjoyed good health until the age of about 45 when there was a sudden increase in the death rate of such workers, usually from lung decease.[17] George, however was fortunate. He lived away (although not too far away) from the Ashted works in rented accommodation in Bloomsbury Street. Living away from the works did not guarantee better health; soot and smoke particles were forever in the air, sanitary provisions were of poor quality and with most of the population living in close proximity, disease spread rapidly. Birmingham suffered greater than some towns from cholera, diphtheria, dysentery and diarrhoea and had nearly twice the national death rate in these diseases taken as a whole.[18] Children under 5 years often suffered from bouts of chronic diarrhoea which led to severe dehydration, and in many cases death. The infant mortality rate, although high, was a way of life in the big industrial towns and Birmingham had the lowest infant mortality rate of the major towns[19] and was overall healthier than most other large industrial towns.[20]

Rebecca gave birth in March 1850. The child was very weak. The Hipkins were fortunate that they could afford a doctor and not simply rely on a local woman to administer medical attention as was common with the working class community. Their physician Thomas Swain of Newhall Street felt the child might hang on to life and gave what support he could. The worried parents named the boy George Frederick for his father and George now had an heir, someone who could keep the business going after he had retired. The boy seemed to be doing well but like so many others he became ill with diarrhoea, and on October 19th 1850 George Frederick Junior succumbed to the all too common complaint. The little body was laid to rest in Key Hill Cemetery near Birmingham's Jewellery Quarter. William Edward came down from London to console his brother and his wife, but in the Birmingham of the 19th century there was little time to mourn, life had to go on.

The partnership with Hudson had worked well, but it was only a temporary measure, Hudson found it hard going and he wanted to sell up and take his family to a cleaner environment. George Hipkins had spent two years learning the business and with the help of his wife's dowry, and his brother, he bought out Hudson and Birmingham had a new brassfounding firm—*G.F. Hipkins*. He entered the premises at 203 Ashted Row and felt the tingle that it was now his to do with as he saw fit. The equipment in the workshops he had bought was in fine condition and some of which were quite new. George wanted to establish himself in a branch of brassfounding that concentrated on door and cabinet furniture and general brassfoundry, but he also wanted to diversify as a locksmith and bell hanger utilising the skills he had learned at Cotterill's keeping the close relationship with Edwin Cotterill.

A large proportion of the manufacture was contained within the Ashted works with some elements being sub contracted to local firms. George wanted to concentrate on the products he knew well from his days at Cotterill's—door springs. The production of Cotterill's single and double action door springs, patent latches and various types of bolts was inherited with the purchase of Hudson's. These products were produced for sale in ironmongers with the springs being sold by the dozen, and the price varying from around 6 shillings for the lighter springs and 15 shillings for the heavy. George was keen to diversify and to develop his own products and not just manufacture items patented by others. On 18th July 1855 he, jointly with his friend and colleague John Britten applied for and received a patent for *Applying springs or weights for the purpose of closing doors or resisting shocks, strains or pressure.*[21] This mechanism will be very familiar to those who have worked in offices and watched as some doors close slowly and others slam like a rat-trap! The mechanism is fitted to the top of the door on the hinge side and a bar mechanism controls the speed of the closure of the door. This is an ideal feature where a door is in constant use. The specification for the patent is a hefty document of 22 pages, plus drawings and attempts to describe as many variations of the theme as possible.

His diversification included a venture into bell hanging and this required more than simply making the parts; it involved dealing with the customer face to face taking orders and then visiting the residence to fit the bells. In the days before electric operated door bells, the most fashionable way to announce one's presence was to pull on a door bell lever. The bells were rung by means of highly elaborate wires, pulleys and rods. George's facility produced most of the components used in bell hanging, namely: levers, slides, quadrants, sunk bell pulls, push and pull levers, check springs and steel bell springs all of which combined to give motion to the wires and operate the bells. In most houses the arrangement of the bells and wires was straightforward; however in larger houses (especially those in the wealthy suburb of Edgbaston) this could be far more complicated, especially when the system was used in combination with ropes and ribbons to operate the bells. This top of the range system featured not only front door bells but also servants' bells and a tradesmen's entrance bell! This complicated arrangement involved mortise, pillar, leader, drive and purchase cranks driven into walls with spikes, or fitted on plates to suit internal and external angles, along with drive wheel and chain cranks to enable the whole system to function effortlessly. It was not always a simple task to set up either. The owners of many of the larger houses did not want to see the wires and levers fitted to the walls, so tubes would be inserted into the walls to act as conduit for the wires.[22] George actually knew most of the customers professionally as many were owners of medium to large manufactories, some of which were in Ashted. When an installation was to be done he would arrive at the home with two men and ensure that the work was started on time. He would return a few hours later to ensure everything was going smoothly and would then inspect the work on completion.

According to the famous Birmingham writer on the Midlands Iron Trade, Samuel Timmins, the manufacture of articles of cabinet brassfoundry lay at the root of the brass trade in Birmingham. The cabinet side of George's work was in places a variation of the door furniture, with handles, hinges, bolts, latches and doorknobs all being made. The whole carpentry trade was catered for with the production of casters, table fastenings, hat and coat hooks, window fastenings, picture rings, hooks of various uses for guns, lamps, sconces etc. A large number of improvements had been made to the quality of such items as originally, articles made for cabinets were very functional and not ornate. By the middle of the 19th century people wanted and expected to be able to purchase elaborate and fancy drawer knobs and the numbers of styles developed was staggering. The down side of this requirement was that in producing such items they became less robust and were more susceptible to wear and tear. It was with this in mind that prompted George to produce his second patent application, this time for the *Construction and attaching of knobs and spindles; and in connecting knobs to doors, drawers and other articles.*[23] His design aimed to prevent the unscrewing of a knob while in use; a problem we have all encountered on various types of furniture! As a supplement to the door furniture, bell hanging and cabinet brassfoundry work he also produced more general brassfoundry items such as washers, bottle openers and simple corkscrews all produced using techniques of casting, stamping and piercing. George avoided some of the much larger items such as railings, fireguards, balustrades for staircases etc.

With such a wide product range he soon found himself supplying a large number of ironmongers in the midlands and London. This wide selection of products also meant he was heavily dependant on other firms supplying him with some of the components he needed as the Ashted works was not large enough to enable every item to be produced. The economy in the 1850s was, on the whole, a good period of growth although, as at any time, businesses could run into financial trouble by over extending in a boom period. Some ironmongers did just this and as a result some of Hipkins' customers were struggling to meet payments to him. Some of the home owners in Edgbaston were also slow at paying the bills for the bell hanging work which in turn meant that George had problems meeting payments to his material suppliers and sub contractors. On December 5th 1855 he voluntarily applied for bankruptcy under the Bankruptcy Act 1842 in an effort to sort out the problems.[24]

Thomas Bittleston of Waterloo Street, Birmingham was appointed the Official Assignee and took over the financial affairs of the business. George was scheduled to attend the *Birmingham District Court of Bankruptcy* on December 21st 1855 and January 11th 1856 where he had to make a full disclosure of his estate and effects. Evidence also had to be provided as to George's conduct as a trader both before bankruptcy and during the bankruptcy process. His brother, William Edward, came down from London to assist him in drawing up plans for the future of the business, they were in no doubt that the situation had resulted from the failure of customers to meet their payments.

The January hearing went well with George being granted a public sitting for the allowance of a certificate under such petition for adjudication. The granting of a certificate would enable him to start work again, however his creditors needed to attend the sitting to make any objections. On Valentine's Day 1856 at the District Court of Bankruptcy, George Frederick Hipkins was granted a Certificate First Class with no objections from creditors.[25] This certificate was granted as it was seen that George had been placed in the position by no fault of his own and that he should be allowed to continue running a business.

The decision to be granted a certificate without any objections from creditors was helped by his brother who provided a vital lifeline by arranging with his employers (Lund's) for George to manufacture corkscrews patented in 1855[26] by William Edward Hipkins and William Lund. These patent corkscrews came in three forms; the first comprised of two steel pillars with a central rack and pinion system and would retail for around 11 shillings; the second was a two piece lever corkscrew and the third was a pocket corkscrew. The corkscrew side of his business was now to be a major element and not just a secondary item to the door springs.

Birmingham had its fair share of corkscrew makers and a number bore the name *Hipkins*[27] thus competition was fierce. With Lund's patents George could cater for the higher quality user such as hotels, bars, restaurants and of course the big houses in Edgbaston. He dropped the bell hanging side of the business altogether but continued to produce door springs and general brassfoundry.

It had been a turbulent time and many small businesses often failed to survive such events but not G.F. Hipkins. The icing on the cake was that a couple of months later Rebecca announced that after 6 years of trying she was once again pregnant.

CHAPTER 2

THE BIRTH OF THE COMMANDER IN CHIEF

I Consider in my army there are no princes. There are men, officers, colonels, generals; and there is the commander-in-chief who must be more capable than all the others, and who must stand far above them.

—Napoleon 1805.

On New Year's Day 1857, the cold weather had not in any way dampened the enthusiasm of those wishing to welcome in the New Year with a glass or two of warm beer. Birmingham, the epicentre of world-wide manufacturing was taking a partial break—only partial because some workshops were working away as normal. The workshop at 203 Ashted Row was silent; the small business of George Frederick Hipkins was closed until the 2nd, partly for the New Year and partly due to the fact that George's wife Rebecca was in labour. Her screams, a mix of pain and anxiety echoed around the walls of the three-storey house, they reverberated through the empty workshops and carried the short distance to the steam mills next door. All went silent, and then the un-mistakable cries of a new-born baby, much louder than the cries of the New Year, announced to the world his arrival. Doctor Thomas Swain took the child—a boy—and wiped his face. He was very light, and Swain quickly wrapped him up to keep him warm. Rebecca was exhausted; she was no weak woman, well built with soft gentle features that often belied a tough and determined personality. She had to be, seven years before, her first son had died at only 6 months old and she had wondered if ever she would conceive again. The parents' joy on the first day of 1857 at having a new son was soon to be dampened as Dr. Swain explained that the boy was not well; he was underweight, pale, and he would do well to survive the winter.

Throughout that winter Rebecca wouldn't be separated from him and George kept a roaring fire burning. The January of 1857 had fortunately been mild and, in fact, the previous December had seen temperatures rise somewhat giving an almost spring like feel.[1] Rebecca would often sit rocking the baby gently in a wooden cradle, the fire burning bright and her clear eyes reflected the flames as her mind drifted. She thought that after everything they had been through surely now, things would go well. She was staying at the house in Ashted Row for the time being, although the family normally lived on the Coleshill Road having moved there in late 1851. Rebecca spent most of her time trying to keep the newborn warm, and in an age when infant mortality was high, it was becoming likely that Thomas was right and the boy would not see the winter out. In fact, so alarmed were his parents that George had delayed registering the birth, but from somewhere deep inside the boy there was a strength that made him overcome those early months of life. Rebecca had added to that strength by supporting the boy, talking to him, and encouraging him. By the summer, he was doing well, still a little under weight but at least feeding and slowly developing. In July 1857 George and Rebecca took William Edward to St. Phillips Church in Birmingham to have him christened. The church is one of the most beautiful buildings in Birmingham and many Hipkins traditionally had their children christened there.[2] The Italian style architecture with the fabulous dome topped tower was a sight that made a deep impression upon all those that gazed upon it, here in the deep industrial town was a building of such beauty. Its interior was no less spectacular with two galleries running on either side above the pews. Columns and arches adorned with decoration, large windows to allow in plenty of light with everything pointing towards the apse with its splendid triple-decker pulpit. J.M. Aston performed the service and attending with the parents were George's brother, William Edward, after whom his son had been named, nine year old Annie Mary Hipkins (William Edward's daughter), and Rebecca's mother Sarah. It was a very proud moment for George; he was hoping that here in this boy would be the future of the business, a boy who would continue the Hipkins line. What future lay in store for him? Would he marry? How many children would he have? What sort of businessman would he make? Only time would tell and George was in little doubt that the future would be a good one for the new William Edward, with the help of the guiding hands of his parents. William Edward would need more than simple guidance, as it was clear that as he began to grow he was physically weak and his eyesight was not good; in many respects his fragile frame resembled that of his father.

In 1859 when William was two, Rebecca gave birth to her third child, a girl they named Bertha. Bertha was a strong fit healthy baby—quite a contrast from William. With the two children doing well Rebecca moved to a Victorian house at number 3 Copeley Hill, a nice quiet little side street a mile and a half from Ashted where conditions were better for bringing up children. With the business doing well there were enough finances to support the help of a domestic servant, 21 years old Miss Esther Bladen. She had come to the big town from Salop to gain experience in house keeping and Rebecca was glad of the extra hands. As George was spending ever more time at the works he didn't have as much time to spend with his young family as he would have liked.

The young William had an inquiring mind; he was quiet, a little shy and preferred to sit quietly playing on his own. Rebecca found this very satisfying; she referred to William as 'Willie' and Bertha as 'Beadie' and spent as much time as possible with them. Rebecca was keen to keep both children amused and enable their minds to always remain active and alert. In the afternoons she would play the piano and sing to them. Willie showed an interest in the piano and Rebecca would hold his little hands on the keys, tapping out some notes. Usually, by the time George got home, the children were asleep in their beds.

George had to keep an eye on the ironmonger market and the demand for highly polished steel goods was growing. The Ashted works had a small steam engine but it was rather temperamental and not up to the task of running the ever-increasing number of machines rigged to it by a tangle of belts and pulleys. It needed to be replaced, but to do so would also mean some building alterations so in order to keep production going he hired a small factory unit at *Bullock's Steam Mills* in Cleveland Street where he carried out steel polishing. With this facility he was also able to take sub contract work polishing steel toys for other manufacturers. By 1862 the business had expanded further from simply a small brass and iron founders centred on door fittings to the more diverse toy trade. As already mentioned the 'toy' trade of the 18th and 19th century referred to a trade in small personal trinkets such as vinaigrettes, coasters, salves, tureens, etc. As well as his stock in trade products of double and single acting door springs, G.F. Hipkins began to specialize in corkscrews, steel snuffers and fire-iron ornaments.[3] George now entered into a market in which Birmingham had developed a high reputation, thanks in the main to the work of Matthew Boulton. It was also a very competitive market and only the very best quality for a good price would survive. Birmingham's newspapers every day carried lists of small businesses that had been called before the bankruptcy courts, something of which George knew only too well. As 1862 came to a close George Frederick Hipkins saw the future as a bright one for his business and his young family. As was becoming of such a family, the 'in' thing was for him to take the family to a local photographer to have their portraits taken. Willie looked splendid in his old fashioned soldier's uniform, the musket being taller than he was! The photographic record of the Hipkins family had begun.

It was only a couple of months after the photographic session that the first sign that something was not quite right appeared. George started to experience regular headaches; they were mild at first but began to occur more often. Over several weeks the severity and regularity increased and Rebecca had grown concerned. She noticed that George had become more irritable of late and was not paying the attention to business as he used to. This was out of character entirely, he had been a hard working and conscientious businessman, and the change was startling, George had even started to grow impatient with Willie and Beadie, and even Esther complained that George was becoming very short with her. The Hipkins sent for the family doctor, Thomas Swain, who examined George. It was not un-common for brassfounders to suffer from headaches and Thomas treated him in the standard method for the day with sulphate of soda and taraxacum along with a specific diet to tone his general system. One night in March 1863, Rebecca was awoken by the sound of George being violently sick; he seemed to be very ill. She sent Esther for Dr. Thomas Swain who made all haste to the house. He entered and went up the stairs to where George was laying. Esther was placed in charge of the children and a rather fearful Rebecca waited as the Doctor examined George. Swain noticed just how frightened Rebecca looked. George was lying in bed, he had been sick once again and his pale colour almost matched the sheets. With the limited resources available to a physician of the middle 19th century, Dr. Swain produced drugs to relieve the headaches and to try and stop the vomiting. The treatment was varied with mustard foot-baths, and croton oil on the tongue used to help stop the convulsions, and his bed was positioned near an open window so that he could breathe pure cold air.

After several days George seemed to be getting worse, a whole catalogue of symptoms began to show themselves including lethargy, abdominal pain and he had begun to slip in and out of consciousness. Dr. Thomas' diagnosis was as vague as it could be—a *cerebral disease* and that George should remain in his bed and essentially let the disease take its course. The whole family pulled together, George's brother William Edward raced up from London with his daughter Annie Mary to help Rebecca. Rebecca's mother, Sarah, moved in with her, and Rebecca's sister would spend the odd weekends and sometimes whole weeks at a time at the house. George's brother, William Edward, took control of the business and Annie Mary helped Rebecca in the house. Rebecca set to the task of nursing her husband, who was suffering more with terrible headaches and convulsions. Dr. Swain maintained a careful watch on George's progress and Rebecca kept administering everything imaginable to try and help her husband. These included croton oil enemas, doses of caster oil and opium, sulphate of magnesia with sulphuric acid, camphor, and even hot sulphur baths. When George ran a fever Rebecca would dab his brow with cold water and wrap a cloth soaked in water and eau de cologne around his head.

Young William and Bertha were more and more in the care of their aunt Annie Mary as their mother spent long hours at George's bedside. William Edward kept the business functioning well and the workers did what they could to assist and to make that extra little bit of effort. George went through periods where he seemed quite well, but would fall back into severe bouts of sickness. Dr. Swain did what he could, but there were so many symptoms, so much to treat and all he could go on was how George described how he felt. Rebecca made a variety of healthy meals for him including restorative soups, brandy and egg, gruel, beef tea and even lime water and milk![4] It seemed to make little difference.

In the last week of May Dr. Swain became a regular visitor to the house and on June 3rd he had the unenviable task of informing a mother of two young children that her husband was dying. There was nothing that he could do, save for trying to relieve some of the pain. Rebecca was heartbroken. All the dreams, the plans, the life that they had worked for now seemed to be in tatters. In order to ensure that Rebecca and her two children were financially secure, George made a will from his sick bed, bequeathing all of his goods, tools, stock in trade, furniture, properties and effects to his wife. Thomas Swain and Annie Mary Hipkins acted as witnesses. Six days later on June 9th 1863 George passed away in his bed, he was 44 years old. Willie was only 6 and Beadie 4. It was a devastating blow to Rebecca, it seemed that after the initial hard work of setting up a business and starting a family, fate had intervened. Rebecca would have gladly followed her husband to the grave save for the fact that she had two young children to look after; they were her absolute priority now.[5]

It was a very pathetic sight to see Rebecca dressed in black, a thin veil covering her pale face flanked on either side by her two children, standing next to the grave of her husband in Key Hill Cemetery. It was a cool day for June with the temperature in the middle 50s Fahrenheit. The Sun had tried to force its way through the clouds, but it was struggling, and soon the rain began to fall. The shower grew forceful and Beadie held out a hand to catch some raindrops. Rebecca had chosen some simple words for the stone:

In affectionate remembrance of George Frederick Hipkins,
who died June 9th 1863 aged 42 years (sic).
The memory of the just is blessed.—Proverbs X verse 7.[6]

Rebecca had to be encouraged to leave, and steadily she walked, hand in hand with her children down the small path leading to the entrance of the cemetery. She never faltered, and maintained a very brave and neutral demeanour.

Rebecca inherited effects to the value of around £1,500 plus the business and the property in Aston.[7] Nothing however could replace the loss of her husband, but at least she was financially secure. George had left Rebecca the option of doing whatever she saw fit with the estate and it would have been the easier option for Rebecca to sell up, but Rebecca was not a woman who gave up. She decided to continue the business herself with the help of her brother-in-law William Edward, and with her niece Annie Mary she could bring up Willie and Beadie. It was clear (to her), that if she was to provide the best for her children then their future financial security was a priority and that lay in the business. It was difficult adjusting to the change in circumstance and Annie Mary although only 16 years old was a tower of strength. Rebecca had to be strong for Willie and Beadie, they were too young to understand what had happened and although he did not know it, the future prosperity of the family would ultimately fall to George's son. His uncle and namesake was working long hours but the business was carrying on as normal and after three weeks the Hipkins were coping well. On June 26th William Edward developed a cold which quickly developed into bronchitis. Dr. Swain treated him accordingly with croton oil, beef tea and bleeding! He was sent to bed for rest with the air in the bedroom moistened by steam—Rebecca placing a pot of water over the fire. William Edward had suffered from asthma for a number of years and this had led to him taking up smoking tobacco, which was thought at that time to be therapeutic! Suddenly on July 4th William Edward had a violent asthma attack, on top of his bronchitis he found himself in great distress. Rebecca's sister Louisa sent for Dr. Swain but no matter how hard he could ride across the town, he could not reach the house in time to save him. William Edward died in the arms of his daughter Annie Mary. One can only imagine the feeling in the house as another family member passed away so soon after George. Annie Mary was devastated and now Rebecca had to be a tower of strength for her.

On a sunny day in July, William Edward Hipkins was laid to rest in Key Hill cemetery, the Hipkins' stood by the grave side still numb with the shock of the events that had unfolded before them over the last four weeks. It would take every ounce of inner strength of both Rebecca and Annie Mary to move forward, but what choice did they have? Two young children were depending on them. Rebecca took a fresh look at their situation and decided to consolidate her assets by letting the house at Copeley Hill go, and continue renting the business premises in Ashted at £35 per year.[8] The family would occupy the house at 203 in much the same way as George's old partner Edward Hudson had done with his family essentially living over the shop, which was the most economical and practical course of action for Rebecca. Conditions were not however easy, the noise from the neighbouring steam mills and brassfoundries could at times be overpowering, and the lunch time drinking sessions at the local pubs such as the *Parliament House* and the *Swan with Two Necks* just a few doors down the street did nothing to make the area attractive for bringing up a family in the manner that Rebecca expected. Ashted was however an ever-developing industrial area with an odd assortment of private dwellings and factories but this did mean that local shopping facilities were excellent. Just a few walking paces from 203 Rebecca could find a butcher, grocer, fish monger, tailor, boot maker, chemist, furniture dealer, brush maker and a draper![9] Even so given the right opportunity

Rebecca would wish find more suitable accommodation elsewhere away from the business.

As far as the business was concerned the existing workforce would simply continue as before, and as she was already familiar with the general running of the firm, it would have to be business as usual. Contrary to popular belief, it was not uncommon for women to run businesses in the middle of the 19th century. With many men dying young due to diseases contracted from the workplace many women were widowed quite young and their only means of support was to continue in business trading under their late husband's name.[10] Rebecca therefore was not exceptional, *G.F. Hipkins* continued in business as before.[11] Rebecca was all too aware that she would not be able to court any special favours from other businesses who might have taken pity on her circumstance. Business was business and she had to either sink or swim in the manufacturing ocean of Birmingham. She set for herself a distinct goal and that was to prepare Willie for the day when he would take over the business, for this was not only his legacy but it was also the family's future. To this end she set about to keep the firm ticking over, not taking any risks and keeping the financial side tight.

Although Rebecca had to pay a lot of attention to the business Willie and Beadie did not want for lack of attention. Their aunt Annie Mary took day to day control of them; she was reasonably educated, could read and write and therefore could give the children basic lessons. Schooling in Birmingham was a hit and miss affair with working class children mostly missing out altogether. Parents preferred their children to start work as early as possible and the only education they might receive was from Sunday school. Middle class children were often sent to private classes and this would have been expected for Willie and Beadie however Willie was deemed far too fragile by Rebecca to attend the rough and tumble of a school and he was thus kept at home. Annie Mary acted in many ways as a second mother, she took them out on trips to parks and the town centre for shopping in the Bull Ring market although these trips were very limited as Rebecca's concern for Willie's health was paramount.

Ashted may not have been the ideal area for children to grow up, but it wasn't the dullest area either. Willie and Beadie were often taken to visit St. James the Less church located on the corner of Barracks Street and Saint James Street only a few minutes' walk away from their house. The church had originally been the home of Dr. John Ash the founder of the General Hospital; it had been converted for use as a chapel in 1789 and had been greatly enlarged in 1835. Built of plain red brick, rectangular in shape with a semi-circular projection on one side it could hold 850 standard (or free) seats with a lesser number of shareholder seats. An ornate rectangular tower rose above the semi-circular protrusion that gave the building a unique appearance. The building sat in a small grassy area with trees and the small site appeared like an oasis in the district. Nearby was the St. James Church School open to all for a small fee and a Working Men's Reading Room where the average workman could go to learn to read and write. The church and its grounds was a peaceful place to visit; across the way on Barracks Street was a place which offered a young boy a great deal more excitement—the Calvary Barracks. This military facility had been erected between August 1792 and summer 1793 in order to have stationed in the town a permanent garrison of soldiers who could be called upon to quell any civil disturbance. Birmingham like other major towns had seen its fair share of civil unrest. The Birmingham riots of 1791 had been the reason for the building of the barracks. The riots had lasted three days and had begun as a protest against a dinner being held to support the fall of the Bastille during the French Revolution. The dinner was attended by supporters of radical political and non-conformist religious ideas who offered strong criticism of the British Government and the King. The supporters of such ideas included the members of the *Lunar Society* such as Joseph Priestley and James Keir. It was Priestley who the mob (protesting outside the hotel where the dinner was being held) wanted to vent their anger. He was not actually at the dinner but his political and religious views echoed the sentiments of the so-called radicals. During the riots his house was burned to the ground along with his laboratory and scientific papers spanning a quarter of a century. Houses of other prominent men were destroyed, including the house of the historian William Hutton (as well as his library), along with a number of chapels and meeting houses. With Birmingham's own special constables overwhelmed by the rioting an appeal was sent for troops. Three days later two troops of Dragoons arrived to relieve the town. The riots of 1791 had a profound effect on Birmingham with the authorities drawing up plans to protect the town's inhabitants against any further uprisings and these plans included the building of the barracks. As for the members of the Lunar Society and others who had radical views, they felt less able to speak publicly of their political and religious beliefs and Joseph Priestley himself left Birmingham eventually to emigrate to the United States.

No single regiment was based at the barracks instead different units would take a tour of duty in the town usually a Calvary regiment which would be able to sweep all before it, always ready to respond to any crises.[12] Willie liked to see the soldiers, the Calvary especially, the order and discipline appealed to him and just like all little boys of all time periods he played with his toy soldiers and fought imaginary battles, always victorious under his generalship! He could dream of such glories but he could not enact them in war games with other boys, his health would not allow it. Annie Mary would see that he and his sister were able to play in fresh air. Not too far from home a triangular patch of green formed Adderley Park situated just outside the industrial buildings of Ashted which was a favourite location. On special occasions they would go to Aston Park somewhat further away which had the added attraction of a lake and on these excursions they would be joined by his grandmother Sarah Houghton. Willie was naturally spoiled somewhat by his aunt and the run to the local shops could provide a treat or two as next to the butcher's was the confectionery shop! At home Rebecca was ever attentive she was a keen pianist and she taught Willie how to play some simple pieces. For Willie this was a joyous discovery, for here in music he could relax and allow time to simply flow by. As he grew he became proficient enough that he would hold a weekly recital for his mother and sister, and even when he missed the odd note both of them would applaud and support him, although to Willie a mistake was a mistake and he would play a piece right from the beginning again until he got it right.

Willie's very early childhood was therefore closeted from much of the happenings in Birmingham; he was surrounded by caring if a little overbearing women who spoiled him. Both Rebecca and Annie Mary had lost their main male influences in their lives and the young Willie received their undivided attention. For Rebecca to give so much attention to Willie was remarkable because she had the running of a business to contend with although greatly helped by her existing workers and by Edwin Cotterill who often checked to see that all was well. What seems more remarkable by a modern perspective perhaps is the fact that she could run the business successfully even though she was illiterate. Illiteracy in the mid 19th century was very common for the working classes it would perhaps have been thought that a middle class woman would have had reading and writing skills.[13] Whatever the circumstances she was a successful businesswoman co-ordinating well the various elements that made for a successful brassfounding firm. She was helped greatly by the state of the British economy, the 1860s was a boom period and there was much call for the range of products that left the workshops in Ashted. After all that had happened it was some comfort that Rebecca did not need to worry too much about her financial position. She took every opportunity to point out to Willie the importance of the business and of dedicating himself to it; only through hard work could he achieve anything. The plenty of attention and deep affection shown to him made Willie quite an intense and sensitive child and in a home full of females he needed a strong male influence in his life. Rebecca knew this, but her own devotion to her late husband remained and she never considered remarrying she had to devote herself to the business and her children.

Rebecca had held off sending Willie to a school for fear of his health and thus the only alternative was to bring a tutor in to him (and Beadie). St. James the Less church in Ashted was to provide Rebecca with just the help she needed. With the church receiving official recognition (following parish reorganisation) the resident became a vicar and thus a curate would be needed. In 1867 he duly arrived in the guise of James Oliver Bevan, a 23 year old Welshman who had recently completed his BA at Cambridge University. He was already acclaimed as an interesting conversationalist having a variety of interests that included archaeology, history, education systems and prior to his theological career he had been trained as a civil engineer. He took a keen interest in the community around him and was eager to attend to the educational needs of the work-people. He was introduced to Rebecca after hearing stories from a variety of business owners of a woman whose husband and brother-in-law had died leaving her to run a brassfoundry. On meeting Rebecca he was immediately taken by her caring gentle nature, he was half expecting a tough aggressive woman, but he was surprised to find such a gentlewoman who spoke softly, albeit with authority. For his part the young Welshman also made a great impression, he was bright, intelligent and his educated Cambridge accent was coloured pleasantly by a Southern Welsh voice that made him sound older than he was. Rebecca asked if he would be tutor to her children and he readily agreed. Willie now had a male figure in his life just when he needed it.

With Willie being Rebecca's only son and a delicate one at that, it is perhaps not surprising that she doted on him somewhat. Bevan was able to put things into better perspective. Rebecca was often tied up in business matters and the help of Bevan must have been seen as heaven sent. Bevan carefully set out lessons for Willie with the object of improving his memory, to quicken his faculties, to increase his stock of knowledge and to test the correctness of his inferences. Bevan instilled in Willie the need to attend as diligently to small matters as to big ones and to master the first principles of any subject so as to obtain a good foundation on which to arrange his future stock of knowledge. Failure to do so would mean that he would ". . . *find it to be a most difficult matter to compensate for the defect afterwards.* "[14] Willie often became impatient at not being able to grasp some subject quickly but Bevan pointed out that his motto should be *"Slowly yet surely"* and that he should never be discouraged if his progress was slow. It was far more important to be certain that he actually knew the subject and not to fall into the trap of fooling himself that he did actually know it when in reality he had only read about it without actually thinking about what he was reading. Bevan's belief was that acquiring knowledge was about being able to connect several parts of a subject together, and by this a person gained knowledge that was of use rather than simply a recall of a text or facts. Willie became an ideal student, attentive, questioning and a stickler for perfection, something Bevan thought that he was a little too preoccupied with but none the less, Willie learned well at a pace that suited him.

As the months went by Bevan became a close friend of the Hipkins becoming virtually a family member spending many hours in the family home striking up a good relationship with Willie looking upon him more as a son than pupil, and Willie looking upon Bevan as a father.[15] Bevan's influence on the boy was as deep as any father's offering the boy much advice. He took pains to point out just how fortunate Willie was to have such a comfortable home and a mother that dedicated a great deal of her time to him. In other parts of the town the back to back houses were the homes of many children who had to work for only a few pennies. Bevan even took Willie with him when he visited the poorer members of the community, these people played an important part in the life of the town and they were people with just the same feelings as Willie. Bevan not only had a positive affect on Willie, Rebecca found she could confide in the young curate and when the affairs of business seemed to be getting on top of her she knew that James Oliver would be there to listen and to offer comfort and support. It was just the tonic Rebecca needed and the loneliness of the loss of her husband no longer seemed as agonising.

The young Curate was not the only male influence in Willie's life however, Rebecca wanted Willie and Beadie to have a good all round education and to this end she brought in other tutors on specialized subjects. Bevan had advised her on the program of education that Willie needed and this included the learning of French. Business links between Britain and France were strong and on the continent in general French was a language spoken by most businessmen. Rebecca did not just want any French tutor she wanted the best and in Birmingham the best meant *Achille Albites*.

Albites was born in Paris in 1808 and became Professor of French Language and Literature at the University of Paris. He was invited to come to Birmingham by Captain Basil Hall and duly enough in 1839 he became French Master at the *Birmingham and Edgbaston Proprietary School*. He soon developed a reputation as being an excellent tutor and his French class was one of the most popular in the school; for his large knowledge and teaching power and kindly manners made learning a pleasure rather than a task. He made French the language of his class-room with no English being spoken, thus the pupils unconsciously developed colloquial French. His devotion to his duties, his constant and intelligent care, his ingenious methods to attract attention and impress the memory, his kindly manners and personal enthusiasm won the hearts of his pupils. In 1856 he started a French class at the *Birmingham and Midland Institute* that had over a hundred pupils per term.[16] For twenty-five years Albites had a succession of pupils at his classes and in private tuition some of whom would become well known figures in Birmingham such as Samuel Timmins, P.L. Chance, M.A. Harold, R.F. Martineau, and Thomas Martineau.[17] He wrote several books including a land-mark French text book entitled *How To Speak French or French and France*. He formally retired in 1864 and returned to Paris much to the sadness of many in Birmingham who considered him less of a teacher and more as a personal friend. His absence was however a short one and following the outbreak of the Franco-Prussian War he returned to Birmingham where he continued private tuition. It was during his second stay in Birmingham that Rebecca was able to secure his services and Willie and Beadie visited Albites in his home in Edgbaston to learn French.[18]

The children soon found that Albites was not merely a teacher of the French language but also a devoted student of the literature and history of his country and he passed on his enthusiasm to his new pupils. Willie sat and listened to the Frenchman speak excitedly about the achievements of Napoleon Bonaparte, of his military victories, of his leadership and ability to win the hearts and minds of his soldiers. Willie was captivated and the stories told by Albites fed a mind hungry for more. He sought out books about Napoleon and one in particular he found inspiring, it was a small book of Napoleon's Maxims, the words of the Emperor himself. Albites had exercised a large and lasting influence in forming the tastes of his pupils and Willie proved to be no exception, the seed that the talented Frenchmen sowed would grow throughout Willie's life.

Willie's life between 1867 and 1869 was therefore an intense one education wise and he progressed steadily and strove to master the subjects he was given. He became an avid reader of many subjects but those that appealed most were military matters and he eagerly lapped up details of the American Civil War as they appeared in the newspapers. His eagerness to find just the details he wanted led him to develop a knack of hunting through the paragraphs of information discarding the irrelevant.

1869 was an important year for all concerned. Bevan had met a young lady Alice Williams the daughter of a clergyman in Saltley (Birmingham). Six years younger than Bevan she was kind and gentle and was a perfect match for the curate. Rebecca had been a great help to the Curate while his mind had been somewhat distracted from his usual interests and Bevan had found Rebecca an excellent sounding board. A few months later Bevan left Birmingham, being posted to the Sheffield Infirmary.[19] With his leaving, Willie lost an important day to day male influence in his life although Bevan did remain in contact with the family writing regularly and visiting every couple of months. A year later the Hipkins attended Bevan's wedding to Alice Williams at St. Saviour's Church in Saltley. It was a very happy occasion although Willie found it difficult to relax in a large gathering, he was still quite a shy boy and it was now perhaps time for Willie to take a step out of the protective walls of home and into the wider world. Willie was now old enough, (and it seems deemed fit enough), to begin formal institutional education, although with the introduction of the 1870 Education Act which stated that all children between the ages of 6 and 14 should attend school, Rebecca and Willie had little choice. In keeping with Rebecca's drive to ensure that for Willie only the best would do, there was only one school in Birmingham that he should attend—*King Edward VI*.

Known to most as simply the *Grammar School* it was founded in 1552 and situated in New Street right in the heart of the town. In curriculum terms it had a very modern syllabus which included English, mathematics, science, and drawing as well as ancient and modern languages. Entry to the school had been dependant on nomination from a Governor and being a member of the Church of England; however in 1864 under the guidance of the Chief Master Charles Evans, a number of pupils became eligible by passing an entrance exam. Bevan assisted Willie in his preparation for the exams scheduled for the 14th and 16th June 1870.[20] For Willie the prospect of failure was terrifying partially because he would see it as a personal failure but mostly because he felt that he would be failing his mother after all of the efforts she had made for him. He need not have worried he passed the entrance exams and on September 13, 1870 he began attendance at the *King Edward VI School*, the most prestigious school in Birmingham.[21]

With some 500 boys at the school the change from a rather closeted upbringing to the hectic and competitive world of such a school must have come as a shock to Willie's system. The building itself was an imposing Gothic structure designed in 1833 by Charles Barry[22] to replace an existing building on the same site in New Street. The view of the school from New Street was spectacular with seven great buttress separated windows two stories tall on the first floor with smaller windows with four-centre arches on the ground floor. The whole front was embattled with buttresses, diminishing as they ascended, overtopping the battlements with their coquets and finials.[23] Willie entered through the huge porch entrance on either side of which, stood a lion and a dragon on top of two pillars adjoined by a castellated feature. On passing through the arch Willie found himself inside a large vestibule, further forward to the right was a large staircase and dead ahead was the Lower Corridor—a rather dark wide passage with the only illumination being through some beautiful stained glass windows at the far end. Walking along the Lower Corridor Willie came to another staircase that was for the use of the boys that led to the Upper Corridor on the first floor. The lofty ceilings and grand open spaces of the open courts, the large rooms of the Grammar and English schools made a small boy feel even smaller.

Many of the boys in the school were physically tougher than Willie, his delicate nature persisted and he felt he had something to prove and thus he drove for success. No doubt the personal attention of a private tutor free from the usual distractions of school life had given him an excellent start in education. The school was no soft option, under Chief Master Charles Evans the regime was old fashioned and severe.[24] Evans would rush about making the best use of his time as possible, considering other diversions such as morning payers to be an intrusion into the day with caning being not only excepted but also seen as a necessity. Evans was however dedicated to improving the education of boys not simply in the school but also by improving the standards in Birmingham generally. He had become master in 1862 and saw that changes were required to bring the school into the modern age and that it needed to look to the future. He petitioned the governors to improve facilities by adding a lecture room, chemical laboratory and engineering room. It was clear with the developments in engineering in Birmingham that the future laid more with the sciences than with the traditional classics, and it was essential that the school moved with the times, especially if it was going to provide the young men equipped for the future business world. Financial considerations prevented the governors from acting upon the recommendations; however Evans was able to appoint a master to teach science in 1864. In mathematics the school was falling behind, although taught within the classical school no examination was taken at the end of the year and thus the subject was not taken as seriously as others. The Governors were not too keen on such changes and both sides remained locked in their views. Evans was able however to achieve the higher standards in mathematics he desperately sought when in 1869 he appointed Rawdon Levett as mathematics master. Levett would transform the teaching of mathematics at the school.

Evans efforts in pressing for the availability of some places in the school to be awarded via examination were a triumph. Although it had been heavily resisted Evans was able to show that this policy had the result of raising standards of education in the town generally as boys studied hard to enable them to pass the exams to attend the prestigious school. Willie therefore entered the school at a time when the school itself had been undergoing a great number of changes. It was alive and looking to encourage those to learn modern subjects in a modern way. This was the ideal arena in which Willie could learn about life. The masters were men of culture and Willie looked up to them for guidance as well as academic knowledge, the school porter Robert Turner was also a source of great support. Bevan had taught Willie well, and he was able to follow the rules without any hardship, unlike some of the other boys who found the change to scholarly life somewhat of a culture shock.

Willie began his formal schooling as a *Fresh Herring*[25] in the tenth class under the tutelage of Mr. W. Allen. His fellow classmates were typical examples of the school's intake at this period with the sons of builders, grocers, engineers and of course owners of small iron and brassfounders taking their places amongst the sons of wealthy gentlemen and widows. It was this mix of students that Evans was catering for, the boys who would eventually become business owners in Birmingham. By the end of the first term Willie had received nine prizes. His main rivals in the class were James Henry Corbett the son of a builder who was a little younger and had started a full term before Willie, and Frederick Bartleet the son of a grocer who had started at the same time as Willie. Bartleet had a lot to live up to; his father W. Bartleet had served on the Committee of the *Grammar School Association* in 1864 alongside some of Birmingham's most noted businessmen.[26] Corbett won ten prizes and Bartleet nine with these two boys being top boys in the class overall.[27] For the first time in Willie's life he had direct competition, there was no molly codling he was on his own. He found he could match most and better some, he did not stand out in the crowd save perhaps for the fact he was somewhat quieter and far more reserved, much happier to concentrate on his studies than to court friendships.

It was during this first term that Willie's great strength of character began to show through. In spite of his poor health (indeed maybe because of it) he took an interest in athletics and in particular boxing. The school itself had no athletics facilities, in 1866 the Governors had arranged for boys to attend the *Birmingham Athletic Club* gymnasium for two afternoons a week at a fee of 2s 6d each.[28] An attempt by the BAC to renegotiate the arrangement with the school in 1870 came to nothing.[29] Willie attended the club as a private individual an association that would last many years.[30] With him being rather shy and reserved his teachers encouraged this interest in sport and these sporting activities gave him a good outlet for any pent up tensions. It was at the BAC that he met Joseph M. Hubbard the Club's senior instructor. Hubbard was an ex-pupil of King Edward's and was a noted athlete excelling in all forms of gymnastics. Hubbard had made a name for himself in 1866 when at the age of 21 he gave a demonstration of his gymnastic skills in Bingley Hall. He so impressed those watching that he was invited to meet Clement Davies one of the founders of the Birmingham Athletic Club who invited Hubbard to become an instructor. Hubbard proved to be not just an excellent teacher but a fine leader paying strict attention to training the body to become fit and strong and training the mind to strict discipline. Hubbard had a marked influence on Willie, he helped him to overcome his physical weakness, and helped him develop a strong mental attitude one in which he could overcome many physical problems by shear will power. Hubbard along with E. Middleton taught Willie boxing as a way of strengthening his character as well as his physique and every Saturday evening between 8 and 9pm William would travel to the gymnasium to receive instruction in the fine art. This was also a time for Willie to learn to stand up for himself, and no doubt his ventures into boxing enabled him to protect himself from the more cruel school experiences. The quiet shy boy was seen at first as a soft target for the playground bully.

The following term saw that both Corbett and Willie had been promoted to the ninth class both winning nine prizes. For the third term Willie jumped a class and was promoted to seventh class while Corbett moved to the eighth. By July 1872 Willie had found the going slightly harder and although winning eight prizes he remained in the seventh. His final term in the latter quarter of 1872 saw Willie winning seven more prizes and reaching 4th in the class in French and perhaps a little disappointingly 14th in overall work.[31] The Winter term of 1872 was to be Willie's last at the school. His education was not however completed. The next phase of Willie's education was to be two tours, the first a tour of Europe with his sister Beadie, visiting the major Cities—especially Paris as Willie wanted to see the capital of Napoleon's Empire. The second tour would be of the United States taking in not only the sites but to see firsthand the manufacturing industries State side. The tours abroad could not of course be unescorted, Willie and Beadie were far too young and their tours were not a holiday they were educational with visits to tutors and planned excursions to museums and in Willie's case manufactories as well. The man to escort them was to be the Reverend Thomas I. Guest who had succeeded Bevan as Curate of St. James Church in Ashted.[32] Bevan had left some notes of advice for him and these included a suggestion to keep in touch with the Hipkins family. Guest had much experience in escorting young men around Europe and North America, and Rebecca hired him to broaden the minds of her precious children.

For Willie the time spent in Paris would provide some of his most happy memories. The culture, the artwork, the music all appealed to him, and most especially the life and works of Napoleon Bonaparte. Ever since Achille Albites had introduced the life of Napoleon to him he became a committed Francophile reading all he could about the Emperor. He saw in this man some similarities with himself. Napoleon had not been medically a well man, his lack of height was also a disadvantage, however Napoleon used his sharp mind and attention to detail to outwit his opponents firstly at school and then later on the battlefield and eventually in the political arena. Here was a man from history that Willie could identify with. Napoleon was his inspiration, always keeping with him a copy of *Napoleon's Maxims* which he often referred to, memorising many of them by heart.

Willie found it hard to contain his excitement as he with his sister and Thomas Guest stood on the platform at New Street Station in Birmingham waiting for the train to London. The New Street Station of 1873 was one of the finest in the world, its iron and glass roof which when built was the largest of its kind in the world. It was of similar structure to the spectacular Crystal Palace and the lighting effect as the rays of the sun beamed down through the 120,000 square feet of glass onto the platforms gave the suggestion of a cathedral of steam.[33] The steam engines were coming and going in this busy station and the steam from the engines' chimneys rose into the beams of light mimicking the summer sky of white fluffy clouds. Soon Willie was looking through a carriage window at the blue sky as the train raced southwards towards London. It was from London that the journey to Paris would start in earnest, transferring to Victoria Station, Willie, Beadie and Thomas boarded the 8.15pm night mail train to Dover for an overnight stay at the *Lord Warden Inn* near the port.[34] The next morning they boarded the steamer *Douvres-Calias* a boat much more comfortable than the usual mail steamers, which took longer to cross the channel.[35] They would spend a whole day in Calais taking in the sites of the large town. Thomas Guest naturally took the children to see the famous church built by the English described as *a fine early Gothic edifice.*[36] They stopped the night in a quaint little hotel and rose early to catch the 12.35pm express to Paris, a journey of five-and-half-hours. The trip was giving Willie and Beadie an excellent opportunity to try out their French, and it was good French too, colloquial French as only Albites could teach! The train passed through the beautiful French countryside and through the tunnel under the town of *Boulogne* and across the harbour entering the station on the opposite side. From here the train entered the Paris line and steamed away following the valley of the *Laine* and through more tunnels and the *Forest of Hardelot*. Soon the train sped past the wide estuary of the *Canche*, Willie looking out of the right side of the carriage saw two tall lighthouses in the decayed port of *Etaples*. The train gathered speed as it raced over the flat terrain to *Montreuil*, here the railway ran parallel to the coast eventually crossing the

Canche heading straight on; with, on either side a high range of sand hills. On past *Noyelles* and then past *Abbeville* and up through the valley of the Somme and across the fine meadow land towards *Amiens* station. Amiens was a major manufacturing town with countless numbers of waterwheels used to power the various manufactories; major use of steam power had not reached most of the textile trade yet. There was enough time at the stop for Thomas and the children to stretch their legs and take the air, and then it was back on the rails ascending from the valley of the Somme to the *Plain of Picardy* and then down towards the *Oise Valley* passing close to the towns of *Breteuil*, *Clermont* and *Liancourt* to *Creil*. As the train passed the Creil it crossed the Oise by a bridge, rebuilt after it had been destroyed in the war of 1871. Passing over two spectacular viaducts they entered *Chantilly* and crossed a highland and into *St. Denis* before making the final run into Paris, the train pulling into the *Station Du Nord*. Willie was at last in the City he had read so much about; here he would walk in the footsteps of Napoleon Bonaparte.

CHAPTER 3

THE EMPEROR'S EUROPE

Secrets travel fast in France

—Napoleon

Paris is a city that affects everyone who calls upon her. Mostly they fall in love with her and have to return to renew the acquaintance, but no matter how many times one visits the City it is always the first time that one remembers. Willie would remember his first visit for the rest of his life.

In 1873 Paris was a city with a population of over 1.8 million people and its recent history had been one of turmoil and violence. Only two years previously the city had been under siege which had only been broken when France surrendered and the Prussian soldiers marched in, camping on the *Place de la Concorde* and *Champs-Elysees*. The Franco-Prussian war had cost France dearly not least the internal chaos of Frenchmen fighting Frenchmen. The spiral into chaos began after the French had been defeated at Sedan and Napoleon III faced a revolt in the capital leading to the forming of a new republic. The Prussians had then marched on the capital and the siege began with the French eventually surrendering. This surrender split the country and Paris' National Guardsmen revolted forming the *Paris Commune* urging Frenchmen to continue the war. The Prussians responded by releasing 30,000 convicts and murderers from the prisons and arming them. Within two months the city was ablaze as the Versailles troops from the Commune torched public buildings. The Commune was eventually defeated and the French surrender was ratified with a new united Germany under Otto Von Bismarck claiming Alsace and Lorraine as German territory. Willie had followed the war closely with the able assistance of Achille Albites. It had been Albites' support for Napoleon III that had led him to return to Birmingham so soon after his retirement. Now Willie was standing in that great city and he wanted to see everything. His tour schedule was a punishing one, as it generally was for those middle class people wishing to complete their education. There was only one place that Willie wished to visit on the first day of the tour, the *Church of St. Louis* and the tomb of Napoleon.

Willie, Beadie and Thomas entered the church and were immediately struck by the number of flags hanging from the roof, trophies from Napoleon's battles.[1] The piers of the church bared memorials to Napoleon's generals interred on the site.[2] In 1801 the church had been used for the first inauguration of the *Legion of Honour* in the presence of Napoleon himself who was then First Consul. The nave of St. Louis was 220 feet long followed by a circular choir surmounted by a dome rising 310 feet from street level. Under this dome stood a circular marble balustrade surrounding a depression 19 feet deep in the centre of which stood the sarcophagus containing the body of Napoleon Bonaparte. The entrance of the tomb was very grand with two winding staircases leading down to the opening of the vault. Placed beneath and behind the high alter were the urns of Marshals Duroc and Bertrand two of Napoleon's faithful friends standing guard over their emperor even in death. The vault itself was closed by two bronze gates flanked by colossal statues in bronze. Over the entrance was inscribed an extract from Napoleon's will:

> *Je desire que mes cendres reposent sur les borsds de la Seine,*
> *au milieu de ce people Francaise que j'ai tant amie.[3]*

A wide corridor ornamented with ten marble bas-reliefs representing the signing of the Concordat, the establishment of the University and eight other important events of peace led to the bottom of the circular crypt. Twelve enormous statues supported the circular balustrade and a mosaic floor decorated with flowers and the names of the great battles in which Napoleon took part surrounded the tomb. The sarcophagus stood in the middle of this splendour made of a single block of polished granite from *Lake Onega* in Russia weighing about 13 tons. Napoleon's body was encased in a series of six coffins all placed inside one another like a metreshka. On the south side was a chapel in which Napoleon's sword, insignia and crown were displayed. Willie just stood and stared, here he was confronted with history, and here in front of him was Napoleon. He was very moved but did not show it although Thomas clearly understood.

In Willie's pocket was his trusty copy of Napoleon's Maxims, he took it out and read several out loud in the crypt.

Willie's fascination (which bordered on worship) of Napoleon became an ever growing characteristic of his life. For any given problem Willie would refer to Napoleon's work to seek inspiration and even a strategy. For him Napoleon was a genius yet still just a man because even the great Emperor had faults and made mistakes, but he never let errors of judgement stand in his way something that Willie would remember. For it was Napoleon's never faltering belief in himself and his ability to read a situation (both politically and strategically) that had led to his many successes, and successes in quick succession. Willie knew that his destiny was to take over the family business and he saw no reason why he could not use Napoleon's example for success. This viewpoint was not appreciated by those around him, James Bevan would have preferred Willie to become far more religious as he saw Napoleon as a degenerate, but it was Bevan that had encouraged Willie to think for himself, and this he did. Now he was finding his own way.

Following the visit to St. Louis it was time for lunch and then a visit to the Zoological Gardens. The following day they made a visit to the *Conservatoire des Arts et Metiers* (Academy of Arts and Trades) where collections relating to industry and engineering were kept. The Conservatoire was not merely a collection of artefacts it was alive with education and research with laboratories and lecture rooms attached. They entered the building by a vast vestibule on the right and to the left of which were collections of agricultural products such as seeds and fruit. Beyond this area they entered a hall known as the *Salle de l'Echo* a sort of whispering gallery. Beadie and Willie both had some fun here. Turning left they entered a hall containing a variety of weighing machines, here a brief but comprehensive history of weighing was on display with emphasis on French weighing standards. Willie noticed how amongst the many machines there were some from England, indeed from Birmingham, clearly marked with the name of *Avery*. Turning around and walking back through the whispering gallery they came to the hall dedicated to metallurgy with displays of metals and ores. Naturally with the Hipkins' business associated with brass, steel and iron this particular hall was of great instructional value. Willie was actually interested in the raw state of the materials and how they were fashioned into the materials used in the foundry back home. Beyond the Metallurgy Hall was the *Salle des*

Filatures containing models of looms and spinning machines of all ages and from all countries. Passing through this section they came to the hall dedicated to agricultural items before reaching the old Priory which formed part of the original building in which the Conservatoire was housed. Thomas was particularly interested in the priory and had visited the site many times simply to look at the gothic structure. Willie naturally was interested in the more scientific exhibits that the first floor offered such as the large collection of steam engine models showing the various types including those developed by James Watt in Birmingham. The models were used to show the wide and various uses of steam power in industry such as rolling mills presses, steam hammers and fire-engines. One of the most spectacular models was that of a large screw steamship along with a variety of marine engines with their separate parts clearly showing how they operated. This intrigued Willie, the transfer of power from a simple steam engine into the motive power for a large ship seemed a fantastic development, people could travel across the world's oceans more quickly and in much better comfort than ever imagined. He had followed the press reports of Brunel's giant ship the S.S. *Great Eastern* as it laid the Atlantic Telegraph Cable and was impressed with the huge size of the ship, and wished that when he crossed the Atlantic in a few weeks he could have been on her. The *Great Eastern* though was too far ahead of her time and Willie would never ride on what was then the largest ship in the world. Next to the standard steam engines were models of steam turbines, water wheels and workshops of different trades. These workshops were extremely detailed and Willie recognised the one that represented a brass foundry—just like home. The whole building was full of the most exciting exhibits, all housed in a building to assist in the education of all people and of course for those who attended the Conservatoire as students. Apart from the collections already mentioned the building housed astronomical instruments, clocks, tools, pottery, glass, an exhibition on the techniques of printing as well as a collection of 20,000 books and a patent library. It was the ideal environment for the would-be manufacturer.

Thomas had instructions (from both Bevan and Rebecca) to ensure that the tour was to be of cultural and artistic sites as well as the cold scientific and industrial ones. Through Albites Willie had already developed a taste for French art and Beadie had already developed a taste for art and music thus the Louvre proved to be a wonderful experience for both of them. Like all visitors to the museum the Louvre is somewhat overwhelming and needs to be savoured in small tender bites rather than gulped in one big meal. Thomas had set aside three days for them to explore the galleries. The magnificent Library of Art had been sadly destroyed by members of the Commune in 1871, but the rest of the museum had been spared. So the three had the time of their lives exploring the Greek, Roman, Egyptian, Assyrian and medieval treasures; gallery after gallery, hall after hall of exquisite work, history and beauty. The art galleries contained so many great paintings that even three days were not really enough to do them justice. The much-talked about *Mona Lisa* presented herself to Willie, and so to did the many religious works that Thomas found most inspiring. The naval museum in the Louvre was more akin to Willie's taste, the models of fighting ships, canon and the busts of celebrated commanders were to him as inspirational as the paintings of the crucifixion and the Virgin Mary were to Thomas.

Willie was bought a number of books while he toured, many of them reference works on art. Bevan had always stated that a love of art is acquired and not simply learned. Willie had to be given time to find the art that appealed to him which stirred emotion. The best way to encourage this was to expose him to as many variations and styles as possible. Thus the tour of Paris was as much to awaken Willie's senses as to improve his French and to stimulate his intellect. As the days turned to weeks the tour took in all that was great about Paris. They attended concerts at the *Conservatoire de Musique* in the *Rue du Fraubourg Poissonnaire* where they listened intently works by Beethoven and Haydn. Notre-Dame Cathedral one of the most celebrated cathedrals in Europe was given special attention by Thomas. There were trips on the Seine by steamboat, walks in the gardens and countless visits to cafés with their chairs and tables neatly arranged on the pavement. It was a magic time to be young and in Paris. The leaving of Paris to move forward into Belgium, Holland and Germany was to both Beadie and Willie a sad time, but their tour had to progress, and anyway Willie vowed to return to Paris someday.

The train from Paris to Brussels in Belgium left very early and the Sun was still low in the sky as the train passed through Northern France to Chantilly past the famous racecourse and on to Compiegne. It was here remembered Willie, that Napoleon welcomed his new wife Maria Louisa following his divorce from Josephine. The train raced onwards, the Sun ever rising as they passed through Noyon, and St. Quentin. The countryside was flat, heavily cultivated with long stretches of woodland

and small villages with their distinctive houses with red tiled roofs. The area had many relics of the Franco-Prussian war scattered around, Willie spotted these eagerly and imagined the armies moving across the land. The view was not all clear though; dust and soil disturbed by the train blew into air obscuring the view a little. The Belgian border grew closer as they passed the fortress of Mauberge one of the French frontier defence points. Willie was now travelling through the great coal fields of France clearly marked by the large number of iron works and trains loaded down with shiny coal heading back towards Paris to fuel the homes and workplaces of that great city.

The train pulled up at the frontier and all the passengers had to disembark and take their luggage for inspection at the customs station. The Belgian officials were particularly cold and officious marking each bag with a chalk mark signifying that it had been inspected—although none of the bags were actually searched! Many passengers complained that the whole process was a waste of time. Guest informed Willie and Beadie that they should simply follow the rules without complaint. The whole 'inspection' only took about fifteen minutes and soon all the passengers were back on the train and racing through the Belgian coalfields eventually reaching Mons. A brief stop and the train moved on to Brussels often known as a 'miniature Paris', Willie would have time to see for himself if this statement was justified.

Brussels was well laid out with boulevards, fountains, statues, monuments and parks set out neatly. New building work had begun in the city with the construction of a large Palace of Justice and the land was being cleared for the new Museum of Fine Arts. Willie however was taken by surprise not by the buildings but by dogs. In Brussels dogs were used as working animals, pulling carts, milk wagons, and turning spits. Dog teams chased around the city as regularly as horses in Birmingham! Guest took Willie and Beadie to see the sites of interest and a night's stay in the city was arranged. The next day would be another pilgrimage of sorts.

Willie awoke early; he had already studied a map of Europe in detail and marked upon it the places that were of importance to Napoleon. Belgium has often been called the 'Cock-pit of Europe' as so many battles had been fought on her soil. Willie knew that a few miles outside Brussels lay Waterloo, the final battlefield of Napoleon Bonaparte. Guest took them to the monumental mound standing two hundred feet high overlooking the battlefield. Guides speaking various languages told stories of the epic

41

battle in which Wellington defeated his French nemesis. Willie knew what had happened here and he carefully viewed the scene, noting where the Emperor would have stood directing his troops. The site though was not treated with any reverence far from it—it had become a major tourist attraction especially for wealthy Americans touring Europe. These tourists would be led around the battlefield being filled with stories of heroism and bravery, much of which had been invented to provide a good half-day's entertainment for the tourists. The guides choreographed their flock beautifully around the site ending close to the souvenir stalls where ancient looking bullets and pieces of muskets could be purchased—supposedly recovered from the fields. In reality the bullets and musket parts had been shipped to Waterloo from Birmingham in England![4]

From Belgium it was on to Germany passing through Liege with its many high chimneys belching smoke into the air, numerous workshops making firearms, cutlery and numerous metal items were scattered across the city. The image resembled that of the Black Country that Willie had left behind. The train rolled on leaving the dark smoky atmosphere for the rolling green hills of the Belgian countryside passing small villages until arriving at Herbesthal on the Belgian-German border where German custom officers boarded the train and inspected the passengers' papers. Unlike the Franco-Belgian border where the officers were frosty here at the German border the officers were polite and efficient and the process was speedily concluded with the sounding of a horn and the ringing of bells. The train moved on to Aachen.[5] To Willie this town had a special meaning it was the home town of another great European leader—*Charlemagne* and a visit to the cathedral and the tomb of the leader was a must. From Aachen the party travelled to Cologne in order to pick up a steamer on the Rhine that would cruise them up to Bonn. The town with its university had a timeless look about it, accents of numerous nations were abound and it more resembled Cambridge or Oxford than Birmingham. Beyond the town lay the *Siebenbierge*—the seven mountains including the *Drachenfeld* on the peak of which lay the ruins of a great castle. It is amongst these mountains where the cave supposedly exists in which Siegfried had slain the great dragon and released his future wife. Such was the poetic romances of the almost unbelievable beauty of the German countryside. The steamer cruised on passing the incredible fortress of *Ehrenbreitstein* brimming with batteries and containing a standard detachment of 5,000 soldiers. In the time of war it could hold up to 100,000 soldiers and store enough supplies to withstand a siege for 10 years! Over the fortress flew a large German flag testimony to the Kaiser's mastery of the Rhine and a reminder to all of the crushing defeat of Napoleon III. The banks on the stretch of water bristled with batteries and the Kaiser's forces were forever on watch for any French aggression. Europe may have been at peace but it was an uneasy peace.

The party left the steamer at Mayence and after two nights rest they carried on their tour by train, steaming south past Carlsruhe, Baden-Baden, Strasburg, Offenburg and Freiburg finally crossing into Switzerland; then on through the incredible mountain scenery stopping at Geneva spending three nights before moving on back into France for the last leg on the way back to the coast and finally the steamer across the channel to England.

Thomas Guest had taken his charges on a marvellous tour, a tour that had been taken by many before him and would be taken by many others throughout the 19th and 20th centuries. Such tours opened the minds of the young and for Willie (and Beadie) their minds had been opened to a much wider world full of art, industry, politics and beauty.

The European tour had been a marvellous adventure, almost a history lesson on a grand scale and Willie appreciated it much, but it was to be the tour of North America that was a revelation to him. If Europe had been a lesson of the past North America was a prediction of the future.

CHAPTER 4

ATLANTIC ODYSSEY 1873

*This accession of territory affirms forever the power of the
United States, and I have given England a maritime rival who
sooner or later will humble her pride.*

*—Napoleon 1803
(following the sale of Louisiana to the United States).*

Taking a tour of North America to broaden one's outlook was becoming
more and more common in the 19th century. A great deal of the continent
was still unexplored; only thirty years previously John Franklin's fateful
expedition had disappeared with little trace while attempting to find the
North West Passage. Civil war had ravaged the country which had resulted
in the unification of a large nation, a nation that seemed to see no limit to
what it could achieve. Many people from Europe were beginning to emigrate
to the United States in order to make a new life in the New World. The
Land of Opportunity was awakening and its international trading was just
beginning to make a major impact on Europe. Birmingham had close ties
with the United States, and in the 18th century Benjamin Franklin had been
a good friend of Matthew Boulton, Joseph Priestley and other members
of the Lunar Society, and such friendships did not suffer when the United
States broke away from Britain following the Revolution. Birmingham
even had other connections with the American Revolution being the new
home of the exiled *Lord Chief Justice of Massachusetts*, Peter Oliver, who
fled to the town in 1776 following the British withdrawal from Boston.[1] In
the 19th century a US consular office had been opened in New Street, from
which close attention was paid to the trade in industrial goods produced
in Birmingham and the Black Country which were then exported to the
USA. The ties were not just economic they were cultural too. One of the
US consuls *Elihu Burritt* was a tireless worker for international peace and

suffrage working closely with many Birmingham men such as Joseph Sturge and John Bright.[2] In fact the need for the United States to attract skilled workmen from Europe was heavily assisted by Burritt who in 1869 set up an *International Land and Labor Agency* in Birmingham in order to make the process of emigrating to the United States a lot easier.[3] United States industry had given some local businessmen cause for concern. The country's lack of skilled workmen had led to a greater reliance on machine tools and the technology was developing faster in the US than in Britain where there was a glut of skilled labour. Willie had a fantastic opportunity to see for himself what the New World was really like, but first he had to see a part of the Old World.

Guest and Willie would be starting their voyage to North America from Liverpool a town that had grown around its port and had a population of just over half a million people many of whom were terribly poor. The back slums of the town were:

> ". . . *scenes of wretchedness and vice of places where human life is reduced to a mere animal existence.*"[4]

Thomas Guest, like many other clergymen, was deeply concerned about the poor children in the large industrial towns. In Liverpool many of these children who were orphans or had been abandoned onto the streets of Liverpool were collected by Father Matthew Nugent, the Catholic Chaplain of Liverpool who gave them some basic teaching and was placing them on board ships to North America where they would find new homes and hopefully have a better prospect for a new life. It was another reminder to Willie on just how lucky he was. Father Nugent wasn't the only man organizing such transportation; some children were destined for *"Miss Macpherson's Homes"* in Canada. It was in 1869 that the shipping of children to the New World had begun under a program of resettlement of displaced children with a varying degree of success, with many of the children resettled in the New World (and Australia) finding themselves being seen merely as slave labour. All of this was a world away from Willie who need not worry about his future direction, but only in the manner on which he would accomplish his mother's hopes for him. Guest took time to show Willie just how bad things could get for some people, even though Birmingham had terrible slums the sight that greeted Willie was shocking and almost incomprehensible to a boy who had grown up in relative comfort.

The tour of Liverpool's back streets was brief and it was soon time to get down to the landing stage to board the steamship *Tarifa* of the Cunard Line. They had to be aboard by 4 o'clock in the afternoon of June 26th, with the ship sailing at 830pm;[5] the ship's master R. Cambell would not wait for late-comers. The two of them walked across the gang plank avoiding the piles of luggage and parcels placed haphazardly in the boat.

Willie looked about him keenly as he walked about the deck. The *Tarifa* had been built in just six months in 1869 by J & G Thomson and Company of Glasgow being 292 feet 6 inches long and weighing 2,058 gross tons. She was powered by a single screw oscillating geared engine with two cylinders with 60 inch stroke. This 280hp engine was fuelled by twelve furnaces. Although equipped with a steam engine she carried two masts with sails for use to assist the engines and make use of good winds making her maximum speed of around 10 knots. She had accommodation for 50 cabin passengers and 600 third class passengers.[6] On reaching the side of the ship the luggage and parcels were quickly lifted aboard and the passengers and crewmen made their way to their allotted places. Willie and Thomas Guest had then to sort the luggage that they required in their room from the luggage that the sailors could place in the hold, once they located theirs a crewman directed them to their cabin located at the stern of the ship.[7] Almost as soon as the passengers sorted their bags the dinner bell rang and it was time to savour the delights of the first meal aboard the *Tarifa*.

Willie and Thomas were escorted to the dining saloon located above the staterooms at the stern where the cabin passengers' meals were set. This room occupied a little more than a third of the after part of the ship, three rows of tables fastened securely to the floor ran down most of the length of the room with long benches for the passengers to sit on, no chairs of any description were used let along swivel chairs. It was best to get to dinner early or else you wouldn't get the best place on the end of a bench where one could quickly leave if they had an attack of sea sickness—which was all too common. The location of the passenger accommodation at the stern of the ship meant that every movement of the vessel was felt by the passengers—and for many this was a physically horrendous experience.

The outer rows of tables were lit by portholes with the middle row illuminated by a basic raised skylight which projected through the upper deck. Over the tables hung shelves or trays for wine bottles, glasses and the like. The tables were laid out for dinner in a basic fashion—no napkins, Cunard considered that passengers should supply their own sometimes reminding any passenger who questioned the quality of the service that going to sea was a hardship and the company considered it as such! Cunard ships although rough were considered the safest with an unblemished record, and it is perhaps for this reason that William went by Cunard and not another company such as the Ocean Steam Navigation Company (White Star Line) which was operating new liners with far better service and accommodation. Only a few months earlier the liner *Atlantic* bound for Boston from Liverpool had hit rocks off Nova Scotia sinking with the loss of 535 lives. Willie's mother may well have been mindful of this when consulting with Thomas Guest on which shipping company to choose.

The first order of the day after getting on board was dinner with the Cabin Passengers' menu being something to relish:

> *Breakfast—Mutton chops in mashed potatoes, fried soles, veal cutlets and ham, fried ham and eggs, Irish stew, cold meats.*
> *Dinner—Turtle soup, Turbot and anchovy sauce, beef a la George IV, saddle of mutton and currant jelly, calves' head and brain sauce, roast duck and apple sauce, boiled turkey and oyster sauce, cold ham, tongue, cold round of beef, fillet of veal and bacon, pigeon pies, tripe and onions, vol avent of lobster. Assorted vegetables.*
> *Puddings and pastries—Plum and vermacelli pudding, transparent jellies, Chester cakes, Italian creams, apple and rhubarb pies, maid of honour cakes. Assorted desserts.*[8]

The dinner was not the last meal of the day; a supper was laid on at 9 o'clock which usually consisted of boiled herrings and potatoes. There was never any danger of Willie and Thomas going hungry!

After dinner it was time to settle into the cabin. Most of the sleeping berths in the cabin section were doubles, although some were four person berths. These were generally ten feet square, lit by a porthole for outboard berths and by a skylight on the inboard berths along with gimbled candle lamps for use at night. On entering the berth, Willie was faced by a small wooden cushioned bench, to one side of which, was a small cupboard that included a small basin for washing. On the other side were the cribs, arranged one on top of the other with wooden boards fitted to the sides to prevent the sleepers from falling out. There was little free space to dress only an area about 4 feet by six feet, which meant that only one person at a time, could dress. These cabins were arranged in four rows two outboard and two rows of berths back to back inboard creating two access corridors. The conditions though were not exactly conducive to a sea voyage. There were only two toilets on the ship and these were also at the stern, no bath. Although there were stewards of a sort to assist the passengers there was no bell with which to call for assistance, so Thomas had to walk into the corridor and shout for a steward, who would then, after a time walk to the cabin.

Willie was naturally excited about making a long sea voyage on a steamship and he found it hard to settle in his cabin, he wanted to see so much, the deck, the bridge, the engines, everything! On board with them were many people of wildly differing backgrounds, businessmen making their umpteenth journey across the Atlantic, middle class people like himself making a tour for pleasure, some American nationals returning home. The steerage section had a large number of people emigrating to the United States, their conditions were not as comfortable as Willie's. The whole of the fore part of the ship was allocated to the steerage passengers with women and children being berthed in cabins that could hold up to twenty people arranged in tiers four wide; in essence this accommodation resembled hutches rather than cabins. The men had to sleep in hammocks suspended from hooks in the ceiling. Meals were served on tables set up in between the berths and underneath the hammocks. These tables were stowed away when meals were finished. The food for the steerage left a lot to be desired and it was often meagre rations; it was wise for the steerage to bring their own food—either way they had to cook it themselves on the three stoves provided. The steerage passengers had boarded the ship some five hours before the cabin passengers in order that a health inspector could ensure that they were fit for the journey. To Willie (and other passengers) this was done to ensure that the steerage passengers' needs were catered for. In reality the health inspection was by order of the United States Immigration Service that insisted all immigrants had to pass a health inspection before they were allowed into the respective countries. All immigrants underwent another health inspection on arrival in into the

United States and anyone who was deemed too ill would be sent back to Britain—at the expense of the shipping line. Thus the health inspection by Cunard Line officials was in the interest of the shipping company rather than the passengers. Willie lay in his bunk and felt the gentle swaying of the ship and his eyes slowly closed.

He awoke next morning and felt more of a movement in the ship, a strong wind was blowing but the morning was clear and bright and a beam of light flooded the cabin. Thomas was already up and on-deck taking the air. Willie got himself up, washed and dressed and found his way to the deck to find Thomas. The *Tarifa* slowly made a turn and entered into Queenstown Harbour. Willie noticed two other ships sitting off the harbour, the S.S. *City of London* of the Inman Line a three masted steamship that had been recently modernised, offering more capacity and comfort; the S.S. *Celtic* White Star Line's new Liverpool built 452 foot liner weighing nearly 4000 tons, part of a new generation of passenger liners offering better comfort for cabin passengers. Willie looked at the 4 masted, single funnelled ship and marvelled at its size compared to the *Tarifa*. Almost as soon as the ship was tied up it was greeted by numerous traders hoping to sell items to the cabin passengers. For those who chose to leave the ship to spend a couple of hours in Queenstown they had to run the gauntlet of many traders selling everything from flowers to caged birds! The ship loaded and unloaded mails, allowed some passengers to disembark, and replenish supplies. With the replenished supplies the ship's stores now carried 1,000lbs fresh beef, 2,500lbs salt beef; 2,600lbs salt pork; 900lbs Ling fish; 4,500lbs navy biscuits; 50 barrels flour; 900lbs Scotch oatmeal; 800lbs rice; 250lbs Scotch barley; 1,000lbs split peas; 3,000lbs sugar; 250lbs tea; 250lbs coffee; 100lbs mustard; 50lbs pepper; 30 gallons of vinegar; 400lbs molasses; 400lbs raisins; 1,500lbs butter; 100 barrels of potatoes; 100lbs of arrowroot; 50lbs sago; 30lbs tapioca; 200 tins of preserved soup and broth; 200 tins preserved milk and 15 gallons of lime juice.[9] The organisation to supply a ship with provisions for a voyage was all-important and Thomas gave Willie the problem of trying to calculate what would be required for a given voyage. A few hours later at 6.30pm the *Tarifa* pulled out of Queenstown and a short while were steaming around the Old Head of Kinsale and out into the Atlantic, the next port of call would be Boston.[10]

A sea voyage can be somewhat tedious; Willie's universe was now an iron box 292 feet 6 inches x 38 feet x 26 feet travelling over an ocean. The time was not spent un-wisely, the ship's library was stocked with minor novels and some of the classics, and Willie and Thomas had brought along with them reading material as Thomas had planned a series of lessons for the mornings. After luncheon Willie would have an opportunity to learn something about the ship and about travel. Thomas gave Willie some tasks to carry out on a daily basis such as checking the wind speed, monitoring the tidal conditions and making daily weather reports. Willie enjoyed the routine of making the measurements and entering them into his voyage diary. On the third day out the sky was beautifully clear and " . . . towards the horizon the sea formed a belt of ultramarine, deepening with intensity outside, and gradually melting down until it was lost in the light of the green sea."[11] The sea was perfectly calm and was as smooth as glass, the ship glided through the water effortlessly. The weather did not hold and a few hours later the ship was rolling, many of the passengers had taken to their bunks, some of the more well-travelled played cards in the lounge, Willie and Thomas read and talked. Considering Willie's fragile nature he did not suffer from seasickness and in fact the sea voyage was doing his health a lot of good.

The *Tarifa* arrived at Boston at 12 noon on July 10th, having made one of the longest runs of the season for a Cunard ship.

Willie's first Atlantic voyage had been a marvellous experience; he had seen all kinds of weather from dead calm to stormy, he had seen the mixture of humanity on board a small ship all living together as they made their odyssey across the Atlantic. In sixteen days Willie had broadened his mind and learned more about life in general than he ever had done in two years at school. The voyage on the *Tarifa* was just the beginning.

After stepping off the ship at Boston the passengers all went their separate ways. The steerage passengers were led to the buildings that housed the offices of the immigration officials. It was here that arrangements were made to find work for the new arrivals, and there was plenty of it, indeed there was far more work than workers mainly in manufacturing and in textile mills. The businessmen departed to catch trains and the tourists simply took their time to gather their belongings and to plan their explorations. Willie began his American adventure in Boston an important trading port with cargo ships constantly loading and unloading goods bound for every corner of the world. Willie and Thomas set about to explore the city that is hailed as the *Cradle of American Freedom*, but before they could appreciate the sights they came across a scene that shocked them both. On 9th November

1872 a fire had broken out in two buildings on *Summer Street* and raged out of control until the afternoon of the following day. The fire devastated the business district covering 65 acres and 76 buildings, causing damage in excess of $75,000,000. The landscape resembled the ruins of an ancient city like Rome. Rubble was piled everywhere and only the roads had been swept clear to allow carts to gain access to clear away the charred wood. In between some of the ruins were temporary wooden huts and tents being used as makeshift accommodation, and eighteen months after the fire some of these were still needed. Willie found that the people of Boston had picked themselves up and started to clear and re-build with vigour.

Willie had been looking forward to seeing Boston, the state capital of Massachusetts, a state that had much in common with Birmingham and the Black Country, for this was the state where the centre of the American manufacturing industry existed. Within the state there existed over 13,000 manufacturing establishments representing some 320 branches of the manufacturing industry. Output from these manufactories was valued at $550,000,000. The growth of industry in the region had been rising dramatically since 1830 as more immigrants from Europe settled; bringing with them the skills they had obtained in their home countries. The growth was continuous and manufactories relied more on machines than skilled labour, and American manufactories tended to upgrade to newer equipment much more readily than British firms. In the States, if there was a chance to improve productivity and keep the cost of the final product down then the manufacturers would take it. The American businessmen also had a more optimistic outlook than their British counterparts, and tended to take a long-term view of trading. This attitude encouraged innovation and as Willie saw from his visits to manufactories in the Boston area, the USA dominated the machine tool trade. Prior to 1850 the world machine tool industry had been dominated by the lathes, planers, slotting and shearing machines developed by the likes of Nasmyth, Maudsley and Whitworth. American manufacturers had a need to make highly accurate components that were interchangeable with others, thus they needed machines that could produce such items with a constant level of quality. This level of quality could not be done cheaply by several skilled workers, or produce the quantities of material required to make the ventures profitable. The solution came in the form of the *Turret Lathe*. The idea for this ingenious device was brought to the United States by immigrant craftsmen from Britain, and the Americans took to the new machine like ducks to water.

The turret was a round or hexagonal block that rotated about its axis with a hole in the middle of each side, into which tools were inserted and brought successively into contact with the work. The automatic version of the lathe enabled the mass production of many small components all perfectly identical. These components could then be transferred to the assembly room where even unskilled workers with only basic training could assemble the finished product. In 1865 Charles Churchill, the son of a New England engineer, began exporting American machine tools to Britain. British industry had at best sat on their laurels remembering, perhaps, the days when Matthew Boulton's manufactory in Soho had been the world's leading establishment. Willie was impressed by this *'go for it'* attitude, there seemed to be no limit to what American's felt they could achieve.

Boston and the whole New England region had a very British feel to it. Boston itself was an old city and it wasn't arranged in the modern block system like New York and Washington. The streets were intermingled; some rough, some good, and buildings of various shapes and sizes, and constructed from various materials lined these streets, giving Boston the appearance of a British town. In the city there were many reminders of Britain's past presence. The *Old State House* stood proudly at the head of State Street. This red brick building with a white tower holds a special place in the history of the United States; it was outside this building that the infamous *Boston Massacre* took place when British soldiers shot dead five Boston citizens. From the State House balcony the *Declaration of Independence* was first read. The State administrative function of the building had been transferred to the *New State House* a magnificent building with a golden dome that mimicked the Sun on bright days. When the corner stone was laid in 1795 the ceremonies were conducted by none other than Paul Revere, the man who rode through the streets waking up the locals declaring that the *"British Are Coming!"* The British were still coming, in droves!

Willie and Thomas made their way down to the Boston Harbor and en-route they stopped to take a quick look at *Faneuil Hall*. This very impressive building was a meeting place and market donated to the city by Peter Faneuil in 1740. The building was the scene of theatrical entertainments staged by British troops ridiculing the American patriots. Soon thereafter the building staged the meeting between the citizens of Boston and General Gage as they discussed the terms in which the

British could leave Boston, taking with them Peter Oliver who fled to Birmingham. More recently the Hall had held a breakfast for the survivors for the steamship *Atlantic*. Willie like so many others before him and so many that would follow, was moved by the sense of history. They walked down by the harbour and for a few minutes they simply looked out at the boats moored nearby. Much of the city had been reclaimed from the sea an amazing undertaking and as the two Englishmen enjoyed the scene, Bostonians were planning the next expansion of the city, and young men freshly arrived off ships from Europe prepared to live the *American Dream*. Boston was however just the first stop on a whistle tour of the States. They headed to the station and board the train to race along the 65 miles of track to Fall River where Willie and Thomas would catch the ferry boat to New York.

To call it a 'ferry', as the service from Fall River to New York implied was to totally understate the boat. It was 400 feet long, 60 feet wide, and was fitted with every convenience imaginable to make the passengers feel at home. Five decks rose above the water, on the first were mounted the engines of the beam or Cornish pumping type. These drove two 60 foot diameter paddle-wheels which would push the boat along at up to 30 miles per hour. The exterior of the boat was painted white with detailing picked out in gold. Two funnels rose high above the deck. These were mounted side by side across the deck with the top of the beam engine mounted in between them. The interior of the boat was a sight to behold. The great saloon was 150 feet long by 35 feet wide, richly carpeted and illuminated by a fabulous set of skylights during the day, and a series of beautiful gas lights at night. Running along the sides of the room were a number of private state rooms. Around the top of the saloon there was a gallery furnished with sofas, loungers etc. A band played music as one ate or explored one of the several stores on board. A fully equipped barber's shop was available which offered a range of services. Waiters were on hand to take orders for drinks of any description one chose. The steamboat voyage to New York was an experience of comfort and service undreamed of for a 'ferry' service in Britain. On arrival at the ferry pier the travellers took the tram to New York, a city whose character was very familiar to Willie with many manufactories taking advantage of the natural deposits of zinc, iron and copper in the state. Iron production alone in the state had reached 60,000 tons per annum.

The city of New York was like none other on the planet. Hundreds of people were scurrying about, horse and carts trundled along and tram-cars raced around constantly. Railway lines ran down every street all, it seemed, linking to the lines that fed the piers. A railway ran overhead so that to enter a carriage one had to be on the second or third floor of a building. The noise of the city was deafening; bells ringing, people shouting, carts rolling; it was a fantastic sight. New York had a population of around 950,000, and Willie could be excused for thinking that all of them were on the streets at one time. Navigating around the city was relatively simple as the whole network of streets was designed on the block principle with straight roads interconnecting with each other, and what streets they were! Some of them were 100 feet wide! Willie could feel the life of the city; New York was a living breathing place, and the energy generated by the people of the street was as exhilarating as the energy generated by the Niagara Falls. Thomas took him to see *Castle Gardens*. It was here that immigrants to the USA landed; steam ships entered New York Bay directly from the sea, and passed between *Long Island* on the right and *Sandy Hook* on the left. The ships then entered the narrows which are called the *Gateway of the Western World*, a very narrow stretch of water under a mile in width, and on either side of these narrows fortifications and batteries had been built. On entering New York Harbour the ship passed several small islands, all of which had been converted into a fort. The ship then approached the southern point of *Manhattan Island* known as *The Battery*. The old fort situated there had been converted into an immigration depot. The depot was very lively as hundreds of thousands of people arrived having made their way across the Atlantic to begin new lives. Back in Birmingham, the US Consulate in New Street was doing its utmost to encourage skilled workers to make the journey to Castle Gardens. Skilled workers were beginning to take up the opportunities offered in the New World. With 3,787 mechanics arriving at Castle Gardens in 1872, Great Britain was one of the main countries losing workmen and women to the United States. Over a fifty-year period, over 1,156,000 people took their skills out of Britain. Ireland had a bigger problem, over 2,700,000 Irish men and women left the emerald isle for the hope of a better future. Many emigrants had found success in New York such as Mr. A. T. Stewart. He had arrived from Ireland a poor man. A short time later he inherited a small legacy and invested it in cloth. By 1874 he owned the largest store in the world, eight stories high with a total floor area of fifteen acres. The store was divided into various departments each selling a particular type of clothing such as coats. Willie found the store amazing, there was nothing like it in Birmingham and from it he purchased a pair of gloves for his mother.

New York's vibrancy had stimulated Willie, but it was time to move on. Willie and Thomas arrived at Manhattan to catch a large steam ferry to cross the Hudson. On either side of the river for about three miles there were lines of landing stages. These pier-like structures protruded out into the river for some distance enabling them to admit the largest trans-atlantic liners. The New York side of the river had between fifty and sixty of these piers protruding a good 250 yards into the river. Each pier was numbered and appropriated to some particular railway, ferry or line of packet steamers enabling persons to go direct to the point they wanted. A tram-way ran past the front entrance of the piers enabling passengers to reach the pier they required or leave the pier and travel to the centre of the City in an efficient manner. The large ferry pulled into one of the piers and Willie and Thomas found themselves ready to leave.

The next leg of their journey would take them from New Jersey City to Cincinnati by train passing through Baltimore and Philadelphia on the way. Cincinnati presented Willie with a very familiar sight; on arrival the city was clouded in a dense bituminous fog. The smoke from the chimneys of factories and from the steamers on the river made finding one's way terribly difficult. One would enter the street nice and clean but after only an hour one would be so black from the particles in the air it would appear that one had been working in a mine! Local mothers were known to mark their children before sending them out in the morning, so that they would easily recognise their own in the evening!

From here Willie took an excursion to Washington which was very much a history lesson. The city had been arranged in fifteen large avenues, each of which being some miles long in dead straight lines crossing and re-crossing each other being from 120 to 160 feet wide. Dotted all around were buildings of elaborate and imposing construction. The capital city of the USA had been purposely laid for the honour. Willie visited the *Capitol Building*, the *White House*, the *Senate Building* and *the House of Representatives*. He was very impressed with the buildings that seemed to be more akin to buildings he saw in Paris; certainly the Senate and the House of Representatives' Chambers appeared to have been modelled more on the *Corps Legislatiff* rather than the *House of Commons* in

Britain. What surprised him was the fact that all of these buildings were easily accessible to everyone whereas in Britain high fees were required to visit some of his own country's national buildings. The pace of the tour continued as Willie headed to St. Louis. On arrival at St. Louis station, Willie and Thomas were confronted by a large number of omnibuses ready to take all passengers to wherever they wanted to go in the city. Willie was constantly impressed by how well organised the transport systems were in the United States. It seemed that waiting for every train and ship were omnibuses and people, ready to take new arrivals to their hotels. St. Louis was a city with many social problems; drunkenness was rife with men laying in the streets, some conscious some not. Bars were open to the roads and many fights were in progress as Thomas and Willie drove past quickly, thankful that they were not on foot. Poverty in this city's back-streets was equal to anything Willie had seen in Liverpool. Willie may have been glad to leave St. Louis behind, but Thomas was pleased that he was seeing a wide contrast of living conditions and behaviour in North America. Willie needed to learn that people everywhere were people.

From St. Louis it was on to Chicago passing through some of the great prairie lands of America where successive crops of rotted grass and other vegetable matter had piled itself many feet high extending over hundreds of square miles and which required the plough or the rake to convert it into the richest soil for the growing of corn crops in the world; this busy city had a population of just seventy in 1830. Forty-four years later the city boasted a population of over 365,000! The rate of growth of US cities was something that Willie found incredible. He, like many, thought that British towns like Birmingham had grown quickly but compared to the scale of growth in the USA it seemed quite ordinary. Chicago was well known throughout the world, but not because of its growth. In 1871 a great fire swept through the city leaving tens of thousands homeless, and the value of damage caused was in the region of two hundred million dollars. It had started in a barn on the west-side of the city on the evening of October 8th 1871, and with the majority of buildings in that part being made of wood the fire spread quickly. A very strong south-west wind fanned the fire, and it roared on devouring everything in its path travelling at around 65 acres per hour. At one point the fire burned completely out of control as the water supplies were cut when the Chicago Pumping Works was overcome by the flames. Incredibly, only around 150 people were killed. Willie and Thomas walked through streets where once stood tall buildings, and even after two years the scorched remains of houses and offices remained as silent reminders of the horror that had overwhelmed the city. The city was being rebuilt in these areas, the fire may have destroyed timbers but not the heart of the people. Indeed, Chicago was still growing; ten railway lines ran into the city enabling a person to leave Chicago and venture to any part of the huge country. To Willie it was a great inspiration to see the energy of the people ever looking forward.

From Chicago it was on to Detroit in the state of Michigan; a fast bustling city with horses and carts loaded to the very limit of the carts' strength with fruit and vegetables of every description. Michigan was essentially an agricultural state with mechanised industry forming only a small part of the state's income. Information about the state and the city was readily at hand, the United States' authorities were highly efficient at gathering data about the commerce, population, medical and social aspects of the country. Willie saw efficiency he had not expected, it seemed a far cry from the stories of the 'Wild West'.

Detroit would be the last excursion on Willie's education odyssey. He would head back along the rail lines back to Boston, passing through cities and towns developing at rapid speed. As the train rattled from Fall River to Boston he felt sad that soon he would be leaving the United States. The Americans had shown him great courtesy; they had assisted him in all he wanted to know about buildings, history, industry and about the people themselves. Although the country was a mix of nationalities they all seemed to be pulling in one unified direction. Novel and new ideas were welcomed and encourage; a country where those who wished to work hard had a good chance of making good. There was a down side; those who did not work would fall by the wayside with little hope of recovery. Unlike Britain where social reformers encouraged a change to people's habits such as drinking and gambling, the USA used tough legislation such as the *Maine Liquor Law* introduced to prevent drunkenness in the streets, and adopted so eagerly by the City of Boston, with mixed results. It was a lesson of life for Willie, how people who spoke the same language (more or less) had found an alternative way to organise a nation. The most important lesson Willie learned however was that the future of world trade lay in the hands of the United States.

Willie and Thomas boarded a homeward bound steamship at Boston and the final leg of Willie's tour was about to start. A little under two weeks later the ship steamed up the River Mersey and he was back in Britain. The train put on a full head of steam as it raced southwards to Birmingham with Willie sitting quietly in the carriage. Thomas sat reading, he was satisfied that he had opened a young mind to the world. It was a changing world and Willie would, if he took the opportunities laid before him, be one of the driving forces of change.

The train pulled into New Street Station, the magnificent glass and steel canopy sheltering the platforms glinted in the late afternoon sunshine. Willie was home.

CHAPTER 5

LEARNING THE TRADE

Whatever may be the position in life of a parent, it is his duty to share his crust with his children.

—Napoleon.

Rebecca had worked tirelessly since the death of her husband to secure a future for herself and her children. It hadn't been easy but she had proven to many that she was an astute businesswoman. Suppliers were treated toughly, but fairly, customers were treated with courtesy.

The works at Ashted had been in production since 1848 but by 1871 the facility was looking somewhat tired. It had been a large domestic dwelling converted for use as a brassfoundry and it had suffered accordingly. The premises were let by William Wallis who was not of a mind to carry out additional work to upgrade the buildings. The alternative for Rebecca was to move to better facilities but that could be expensive. Rebecca was happy to wait until William was installed in the firm but an opportunity arose. Ashted had already gone through a period of change when many of the dwelling houses of the area had been converted into small workshops. Now in the 1870s a new stage was beginning as firms moved in buying up several properties, demolishing them and constructing large purpose built facilities. One such firm in need of new land was *Tompson, Berry and Tompson*, vinegar brewers. The three partners had come together to combine their talents to run a quality vinegar brewery. Arthur Berry had been a wine maker, John Tompson and John Tompson Junior had for many years operated out of Heanege Street, with John senior being a maltster and hop merchant with his son being a dealer in patent malts.[1] Arthur Berry took on a very keen and enthusiastic chemist named Edward Collens. Collens had been manager at the *Swann and Company Vinegar Brewery* in Stourport but had found the firm unadventurous for his liking. Thus, in

1869 he joined Tompson, Berry and Tompson. Collens had big plans that centred on constructing a large facility to house a state of the art brewery. Collens wanted to buy several properties, demolish them and build his new facility he named as *The Birmingham Vinegar Brewery*. Collens had his eye on a number of sites but the Ashted Row/Dartmouth Street corner offered much in the way of land, access and importantly a good supply of water from artesian wells. William Wallis was in agreement to sell but, of course, that left the sitting tenants such as Rebecca. Collens was keen to purchase numbers 202 & 203 Ashted Row, and he was also keen to add number 201 but Thomas Cattell, the tenant, was not particularly keen to go. Rebecca on the other hand wanted better facilities and the brewery wanted the land, so if they could come to some sort of arrangement such as paying her 'relocation' money, she would end her tenancy with Wallis and move out leaving the facility available for the brewery. All three parties were happy with this arrangement, and Rebecca made it known in the trade that she was on the lookout for a new works. The vinegar brewers were also keen to help her find somewhere new and it wasn't long before she found some. 107-108 Lichfield Street in the town centre were up for sale by James Denison. Denison was a property owner who rented business units/houses. The works at 107 Lichfield Street had been occupied by Samuel Nichols a stamper and piercer; and 108 had been occupied by Allen Ordoyno, a wood engraver, and Miss Marg Renton a tobacconist. The two properties were substantial with a domestic house, manufactory, warehouse, shopping, a steam engine and a variety of little workshops. More centrally located than the Ashted works they were only a few yards away from the Old Square. However, it was an old part of the town and the street had developed a reputation as being a haven for crime. The buildings were ideal for use as a brassfoundry and were far better laid out than the old Ashted works. Rebecca was not interested in renting, she wanted to buy outright, and with the money from the deal with the brewers she purchased 107 & 108 together with some equipment. She moved the works in 1871 in a gradual fashion which enabled some production to continue ensuring that plenty of work was prepared for the dressers and finishers allowing the pattern making, moulding and casting shops to be transferred over to Lichfield Street. Then as new castings were being prepared, the rest of the works was moved over. Production levels did not drop. Willie was naturally impressed by the way his mother had organised such a move, and she took time to explain to him her methods and reasoning for each stage of the transfer. Tompson, Berry and Tompson moved into Ashted Row in 1872 with the Hipkins still in residence in the living quarters, although the works had been transferred to Lichfield Street. A new chapter was to begin for the Hipkins and little did they know that a new chapter in the history of Birmingham industry was to begin as for the next eighty years the Birmingham Vinegar Brewery would be one of the most well known names in the town.[2]

Rebecca had shown clearly that she was a very shrewd businesswoman although it had been hard balancing family life with the business. When Beadie turned 16 she had more help with the house and Willie, for although Willie was 18 he was still prone to illness. He was attending the Birmingham Athletic Club once a week in order to remain fit. He had developed a habit of reading late into the night although never falling asleep with a book in his hand his mother had to encourage him to put it down and rest. Beadie being fit and healthy, had been given the task of helping her brother, almost acting as a nurse and sometimes sleeping outside his room to ensure he was alright in the night. Rebecca had told her that their future depended on Willie and every care should be taken with him. She well remembered her husband's symptoms several weeks before his illness was diagnose; she also recalled her brother-in-law and how he slipped away and now she was worried for Willie. It was time for him to start work in the family business, and he was taken on as a virtual apprentice to learn every aspect of brassfounding. Up until now she had done well to keep him away (as much as possible) from the choking smoke. She never showed her fears to Willie but she could once again rely on the Reverend James Oliver Bevan for support. Bevan had left the Sheffield Infirmary in 1874 and returned to the region as Head Master of *Castle Bromwich School* and Curate of Castle Bromwich. This was only a short-term post and soon thereafter he moved to the *Aston Union Workhouse* as Chaplain.[3] With Bevan being in very close proximity the whole Hipkins family had a loyal friend to turn to and Willie especially was pleased that his most trusted friend was at hand. Rebecca had also hoped to one day move the family's home away from the works; in late 1873 she was able to do so. Business had been good and she had conserved her money well and could afford to rent a house in Calthorpe Road, Edgbaston. Edgbaston the suburb protected from the industrial expansion of Birmingham; the very same suburb that her husband used to visit to fit door bells, the suburb where Birmingham's great and good (and no doubt not so good) resided away from their factories and workshops. The family was joined by a cook and a housemaid both of whom lived-in. Rebecca had a reputation among housemaids, they were treated almost as family rather than simply a servant and where possible Rebecca would take on a woman who was connected in some way with the family. The new home was now a refuge from work, and it was filled with books, music (the piano playing had never ceased) and happy family meals. Willie would need a place to escape the rigours of the day which would be spent at Lichfield Street.

Willie was well known to the workmen at Lichfield Street (they were the same people who had worked at Ashted Row), although he had not mixed with them a great deal, partly because of his shyness and partly because Rebecca had sheltered him from the business until she felt he was ready. He was now ready in her eyes so when he entered the workshop to meet the foreman, it was no longer as the owner's son, it was as a new worker, and although the foreman knew that this young man would one day be his boss, it did not change in any way the manner in which he would treat William (as he was called by the workmen). William's task was to learn the whole process of the business from pattern making to selling the product. For the next five years he would spend as much time as was possible learning the business and doing his fair share of lifting and carrying. His weak disposition could have made this a difficult task. However, he was receiving physical education once a week and this helped tremendously; he felt that he had to demonstrate to the workmen that he could hold his own. For every task he was given, including the cleaning, the sweeping of the works and the washing down of the yard, an explanation was supplied as to why the particular task was done. It was made clear that everyone in the works had to do their job right in order to be able to produce the products, everyone was important. The cleaning of the furnace was a really dirty job and William neither relished nor dreaded it, it was simply a task that had to be done to enable the furnace to function correctly. Like all the tasks he was set he insisted on perfection and left no corner untouched by the brush and cloth, in fact when the furnace had been cleaned to meet his exact standards he cleaned the ash pits and the gratings that covered them. Like most young men he was enthusiastic and eager to please. The older men, as usual, had some fun at William's expense and being the boss's son he knew he would be in for a rougher ride than most. His saving grace was his attitude. He accepted that the old hands knew a lot more about the business than him and he always bowed to their greater experience; this made him quite popular with older hands. He was moved from department to department learning all that he could studying the techniques used both from a standard text such as the *Brassfounders' Mannual*[4] and the practical work gaining an understanding of what was actually involved, learning techniques that no text book ever describes.

The key to a successful brassfounding establishment was the pattern shop. Modelling and Pattern Making were distinct branches of the business and seperate from that of the brassfounder. The models were made using pipe-clay for the ones that would require substantial work and stucco for straight flat models that could be finished off quickly. The pipe-clay was decomposed feldspar and made into putty with water or glycerine to prevent it from hardening too quickly. The clay was placed on a circular table and on this table the clay was modelled by hand and with a variety of wooden tools in much the same way as a potter. William watched and listened carefully as the senior model maker set about his task describing the methods he employed as he worked. He made it look simple, but he had tens of years of practice to perfect his art. Although working to drawings, or in most cases general sketches, it was his eye-hand co-ordination and his instinctive feel for the material that was all-important. Models could not be made dead size as an allowance had to be made for shrinkage and finishing as quoted:

> *Models, made either in clay or wood, and which are intended for immediate use, require to be made larger than the size given, by one quarter of an inch for every foot . . . Should it be required however, to make a metal pattern from the clay or wood, then the shrinkage will be double, and the model will require to be made half an inch per foot every way. The real shrinkage is only three-sixteenths, but the other sixteenth is allowed for finishing.[5]*

Special measures were constructed taking into account the need to make the models larger, these saved time on making calculations. Wooden models were a more complex affair. A high degree of skill was required to complete them and errors could result in the total loss of the material, whereas with a clay model the clay could be reformed. From the model a crude pattern was produced and a cast taken from this pattern which was then turned or filed-up to a high degree of accuracy which could then used to make the permanent pattern. The permanent patterns could be wood or metal with the wooden patterns taking a considerably longer time to produce often being turned on a lathe and finished off with file and rasp. Wooden patterns also had to be varnished or painted so as not to absorb any moisture. All patterns (metal and wood) had to be coated with black lead; this allowed them to be freed more easily from the sand after moulding. Once a pattern was ready moulds or casts could be taken.

The Lichfield Street works had its own casting facility, albeit small, and it was where the furnaces were that William had to clean. It was more common for small brassfounders to contract out casting work and, indeed, on some occasions Rebecca had used specialised casters to complete some work, but for the majority of items prepared in the workshops the casting could be done on site. The process began with the filling of the lower half of a moulding box with sand; when filled the patterns if flat were simply laid on the surface, if rounded they were driven in to half their diameter. Dry parting sand was then dusted all over the surface of the box (this would enable the two parts of the box to separate more easily).The top half of the box was then dropped onto the lower half and held in place by dowels. The sand was then filled in and beaten down. A moulding board was then placed on the back, the two halves of the box were separated and the pattern removed leaving behind the impression of the pattern in the sand. Connections between the impression and apertures in the side of the box were cut out; it was through these connections that the molten metal was to be poured. The mould was then dusted over with *bean flour* and the two halves joined together again and held closed by clamps. Molten metal was then poured into the mould through the apertures and all being well a perfect copy of the original pattern was produced. In fine casting the mould was dusted with *loam* or fine sand followed by wood charcoal powder. It was then placed over the pattern again and beaten. The fine sand and charcoal powder copied sharply all of the fine detail in the pattern. A more complicated cast system called *Cored Casting* was also employed when a hole or opening was required in the casting. A piece of baked sand the size of the hole required was inserted into the mould thus preventing the molten metal from filling the space. If the casting was to be of an ornamental nature then a number of false cores would be added. These cores were only inserted part of the way into the mould to create the effect required such as fluting. One of William's earliest tasks in the moulding shop was to make cores using the pre-formed core boxes and mixing the core material.[6]

The mixing of Copper and Zinc to form brass (like all alloy making) has often been seen as a *'black art'*. Although many text books existed most small brassfounders had only basic equipment and relied heavily on the experience and skill of the casters. It is for this reason that many specialised casters set up businesses of their own to cast patterns to order from small workshops. William enjoyed casting; the whole science and art of it fascinated him, the bringing together of two metals in a crucible was like man controlling and forming the natural world around him. This appealed to William greatly. Yet it was the caster's instinct that dictated the quality of the metal. Copper had to be at 1996 degrees F. to melt and Zinc 773 degrees F. The zinc, therefore, had to be added as the copper cooled and just before the pouring of the molten mass into the mould. However, the specific gravities of the metals played a vital roll as the greater the difference between them the greater is the difference between the composition of the upper and lower portions of the casting. Thus, timing was critical. The caster might also add small quantities of lead or tin to vary the sharpness and hardness of the cast. The casters could also produce other metals for casting such as Bronze and Bell Metal.[7] The level of urgency during the casting (whatever the metal) was clear from the shouting of the senior man, resembling in many respects the surgeon in the operating theatre. The speed of getting the liquid metal into the crucible and then into the mould box was critical. The crucible was lifted by long tongs and the hot liquid was poured carefully into the mould vertically. The metal had to be at the stage when it would cool quickly after pouring or the casting would be discoloured or sand-burned, which would result in additional work in the dressing and finishing rooms. It was not a place for the faint hearted!

With the metal poured and cooled the moulding box was opened and the cast tapped out; it was then ready for dressing. If the mixture of the metal was good, the casting process carefully controlled, and the mould was of good quality, the amount of dressing work was reduced. In the dressing room any rough edges were removed or *fettled*. William spent a lot of time doing this work getting a feel for the physical products produced. The castings were then sent for finishing where any additional work was carried out on them such as the drilling of fixing holes. The cast would then be smoothed and polished. Depending on the product it may also be burnished to give it the highest possible finish. It was then sent on to be annealed by heating the product over a charcoal fire until it glowed red, then allowed to cool slowly for two hours. The annealing process removed oils and any impurities, but with workmen handling the product it might require further cleaning in which case it was cleaned by boiling it in potash water. After annealing it was then pickled in a tank of nitric acid and water, before moving on to be dipped for an instant in pure nitrous acid to give the product a bright surface. The product may then be coloured to give the impression of being old, or give the illusion it had been made from a different (more expensive) material before finally being sent for lacquering. Lacquering was the process of varnishing the product to protect the colour, and was usually carried out within an hour of the dipping or colouring. If the products were simple stand-alone items they could then be packaged and shipped, but if they were components of a larger assembly they would then be sent to the assembly shop where they would be placed in boxes ready for the assembly workers to fit together to make locks, boxes, nut crackers etc. All the components of a lock, for example, did not need to go through all of the stages described above, so knowledge of what parts needing which process was vital. After numerous castings the patterns needed repair work, and on items that were required for larger assemblies problems often arose as the casts were no longer as true to the original that had been created some months previously.

Small items were often stamped-out using hand presses, and finished off with a file which gave a good degree of consistency for simple flat items. Other items could be turned on a simple lathe—the turret lathe had not found its way into the works although for the work being churned out the existing lathe was satisfactory.

The variety of corkscrews being produced by Hipkins gave an extra twist to the production line, which was the making of the screw or *worm* as it is known. Depending on the design of the corkscrew, the handle was a cast item with the worm being made by heating a steel rod and twisting it around a forming tool. This forming tool was a rod with grooves cut to the pitch suitable for the worm required. Once the worm had been made it was quenched in water or salts and then tempered by soaking it in a vat of molten lead. The longer the worm was left in the vat the softer it would become, so again it was the experience of the workman that was all-important. He had to know just how long to leave the worm in the vat to give the worm enough spring to be an ideal corkscrew. This tempering was second nature to most of the workmen at the works. George Hipkins had been a door spring maker at Cotterill's and the tempering of steel was part and parcel of that trade. The molten lead gave off noxious fumes and although Rebecca may not have been aware of it, her husband's death may have been attributable to his tempering of steel worms and door springs.

As William learned the practical side of the business he realised that it did not always match the theory, and a deep understanding of the materials involved helped greatly. The steel rods used for the corkscrews were bought in from local steel wire firms with Hipkins buying high quality steel which made the quality of the corkscrews superior to many on the high street. It was the corkscrews that were the best sellers for Hipkins, and ironmongers were more than happy to place repeat orders.

William had been working hard for three years. He had been through the workshops and was now learning something about the business side attending with his mother meetings with suppliers and customers. January 1st 1878 heralded his 21st birthday, he had come of age. A celebratory dinner was held in his honour and surrounded by his family and closest friends he felt relaxed. His mother had a special gift for him and she announced it at the dinner table. Now that William was 21 he was to be made a full partner in the business, and from henceforth the business would be known as *G.F. Hipkins and Son*.

George Frederick Hipkins in 1862
(Courtesy Janet Pickard)

Rebecca Hipkins in 1862
(Courtesy Janet Pickard)

William aged 5 with Bertha
(Courtesy Janet Pickard)

Emily Hipkins
(Courtesy Janet Pickard)

Annie Mary Hipkins
(Courtesy Janet Pickard)

William in school uniform
(Courtesy Janet Pickard)

William in 1873
(Courtesy Janet Pickard)

**S.S. "Tarifa" the ship on which William sailed with
Thomas Guest to the U.S.A. in 1873**
(Author's collection)

G.F. Hipkins' Advertisements 1862, 1876, 1882

(Birmingham Archives & Heritage)

Sansome, Teale & Company Advertisement
(Author's collection)

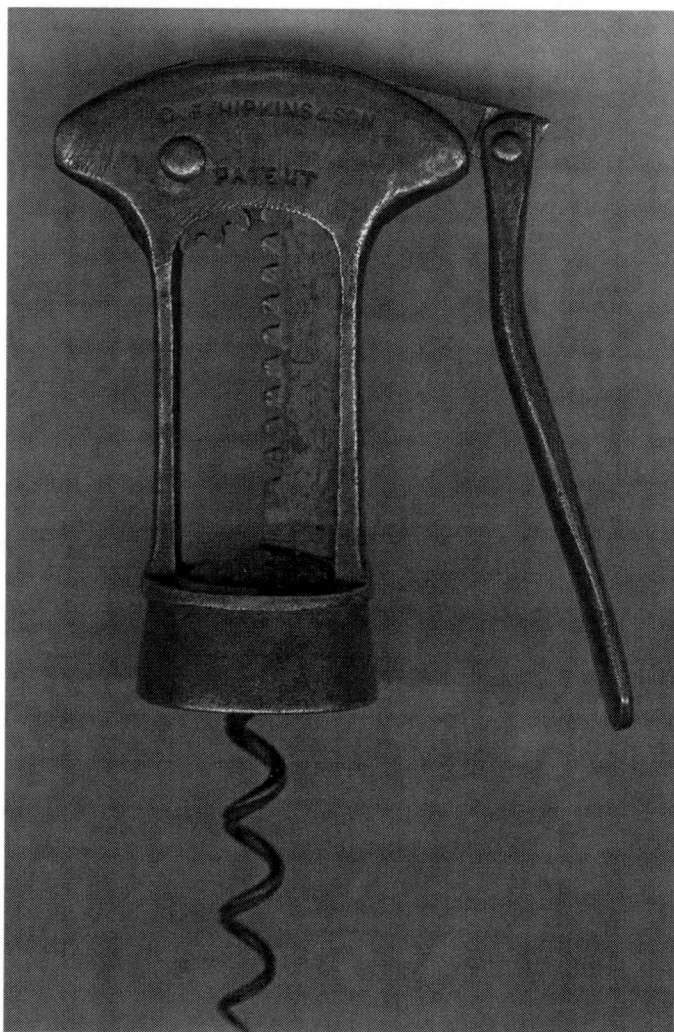

Corkscrew patented by William E. Hipkins
(Author's Collection)

Arthur H. Gibson, William's loyal friend
(Avery Historical Museum)

CHAPTER 6

G.F. HIPKINS AND SON

My business is to succeed, and I'm good at it, I create my Iliad
by actions, create it day by day.
— *Napoleon in conversation with*
Pope Pius VII at Fontainebleau 1804

William may have been a fully-fledged partner, but he was still learning the trade. After moving around each of the different workshops he spent much time at the lathe learning the skills of a tool-maker and machinist until moving in 1879 to the drawing office. Here he was to apply his acquired knowledge on how the products were made to the designing new patterns and new products.[1] On August 6th, 1879 he followed in his father's and uncle's footsteps by applying for a patent. His patent for *Improvements in Corkscrews* described a corkscrew that is *Simple in construction, compact, and efficient in use.*[2] The corkscrew had a single jointed lever capable of folding about the frame of the corkscrew. This was connected to the worm via a rack. The worm was screwed into the cork of the bottle as normal, which at the same time raised the lever. The cork was then removed by depressing the lever. A year later he took out a second patent, this time *for Syphons for Drawing off Champage &c.*[3] These patents were as much of an exercise in design and drawing as a serious attempt to change the world of corkscrews and champagne siphons. On his completion of work in the drawing office he was made Assistant Manager with his first task to be the relocation of the business.

While William had been completing his education, Birmingham had been growing and great changes were afoot. Joseph Chamberlain had become Mayor in 1873 and the town had erupted into life. Chamberlain had arrived in Birmingham at age 18 in 1854 and began work at the firm of *Chamberlain and Nettlefold,*[4] a screw manufacturer utilising new

American machinery. Joseph also had political aspirations, cutting his teeth at the *Edgbaston Debating Society* and the *Working Men's Institute* of his Smethwick firm. He was elected to the local council in 1869 as a Liberal and immediately he stamped his mark on the town reaching national status with his efforts for the *Education League,* and after only four years of being a councillor he was made Mayor! A year later he retired from business life so he could concentrate all his efforts into his civic responsibilities. He led by example giving money to start major projects, and encouraged successful businessmen in the town to do the same. In many respects he had an American outlook; dreams could be achieved with effort and hard work. Chamberlain wanted to improve the lot of everyone in the town. The back-to-back houses, the slums, the poor drainage, inadequate roads, the lack of a decent public transport system were all issues that were not just important from a social point of view, but were important from a business point of view. The improvement of Birmingham by clearing away the slums was a high priority but it would cost lots of money, so Chamberlain took control of the town's gas and water supplies. Gas was the first utility he municipalised, with the profits from gas sales being ploughed back into the town for the social improvement schemes. Birmingham was to be run on business lines for the benefit of the people. The water supply had been taken under control on the grounds of public health. The *Public Health Act of 1872* had led to Birmingham appointing a full-time medical officer who reported to the Council on the state of health of the town. Suddenly, after years of indifference, streets were being cleaned up, there were food and milk inspections and plans to tackle disease were drawn up. In only three years Chamberlain had shaken the town and a new pace could be seen in the streets. William saw that Birmingham was starting to look like one of the American cities he had visited in 1874. Birmingham was about to show the world that it was a force to be reckoned with. Chamberlain's improvement scheme took advantage of the *Artisans' Dwellings Act 1875* which allowed local authorities to place compulsory purchase orders on buildings in insanitary areas, with a view to demolishing the slum housing and make preparations for building anew.

Birmingham's growth had been impressive, but in order to house the growing population the town centre had become clogged with buildings housing numerous families and little workshops. The whole town had become a rabbit warren of dark alley-ways where crime and drunkenness was rife. Thus the improvement scheme was designed to clean up these areas, and to this end the council obtained over 43 acres of land in the town centre. Building work began in August 1878 with plans to cut through the town a long wide road called *Corporation Street,* that would run from *New Street* and head north cutting through the town and linking up with *Aston Road* at *Pritchet Street.* This new thoroughfare would mean the removal of a number of streets and the cutting in half of many others; Lichfield Street was one of those for the chop. This meant that G.F. Hipkins and Son would have to move.

The progress of Corporation Street was painfully slow and Hipkins' works did not need to be relocated until 1883. Rebecca and William were paid the going value of the properties which in reality was slightly higher than what Rebecca had paid for them. They relocated to 88-89 *Lombard Street* on the corner of *Moseley Street* next to the Baptist Chapel in the Digbeth area of the town. The Digbeth area was the original main entrance to Birmingham. It was here that John Leyland and William Camden first cast their eyes on the little cottage workshops. In 1883 the area was still a hive of workshops formed into small courts. Many of them were substantial with some of Birmingham's most highly regarded firms plying their trade in the narrow streets such as *Hoskins and Sewell Brassfounders,* and *W. & T. Avery Scale Makers.* William was in charge of the relocation putting into practice just what he had learned from his mother. The Lombard Street works was structured in much the same way as the Lichfield Street works save for the fact it was bigger, had a far better steam engine and more efficient furnaces including a furnace for steel casting. This was a far more sophisticated workshop than Hipkins had before on site; previously the Hipkins had large steel castings produced by a sub contractor. William had become something of an expert in the casting field spending long hours in the evenings reading as much as he could about the subject. With the superior casting facilities at Lombard Street the business started to produce heavier steel toys and tools including a cast steel machine forged hammer.

There was a big market for quality tools and it was the United States manufacturers that were dominating the market, even in countries of the British Empire, especially Australia. Hipkins, however, was able to break into this lucrative market obtaining orders in the range of fifty dozen.[5] The reasons for this were two-fold. Firstly quality; William had installed new American made machine tools including a turret lathe, and he utilised American techniques for producing tools and heavy steel toys. The second reason for the success in breaking into a hitherto American realm was the uniform discount William offered to merchants. The up-front discounts per given quantity offered potential customers firm deals and contracts could be agreed upon very quickly without the need for drawn out discussions. William wasn't the first to do this, but for the size of the business it was a very bold move and one that essentially wiped out several rival brassfounders who couldn't compete with the discounts offered for the quality of products. In many respects William's approach to business was similar to that of the firm of Nettlefold and Chamberlain. They had introduced American equipment and techniques both in manufacturing screws and in their business practice, and had laid all before them naturally causing much resentment among the traditional manufacturers. William provoked a similar response from other brassfounders although at first he was ignored, after all, the little firm churned out quality corkscrews, nutcrackers etc and had a fair share of the market but it was nothing out of the ordinary. The changes at the works were not simply in equipment. Although William was *Assistant Manager,* his mother had essentially withdrawn from the business and he was calling the shots. He began to surround himself with people of the mental calibre and drive that matched his own. He had a new accountant, Arthur Henry Gibson of *Gibson and Ashford* in Birmingham. Gibson had been active in business accounting specialising in converting old family businesses into limited companies. William used Gibson to take a fresh look at the accounts at his business and to make recommendations. This was the beginning of a long association with Gibson being William's loyal lieutenant. The general re-organisation resulted in little change to the working practices. The Hipkins' had always run an efficient and loyal workforce, but the manner in which debtors and creditors were handled was changed; less informality more business orientated relationships were created. William was also less informal with his workforce and his management style was somewhat different to many local brassfounders, forming more on the lines of a much larger concern. He spent less time in the works and more in the office delegating the day to day running of the shop-floor to his foreman. Unlike his father he did not have a personal relationship with his workforce. He was more distant and made decisions based on the needs of the business regardless of any personal considerations. This gave the business a distinct advantage over many of his rivals and he prospered. The methods seemed to work. After the boom of the 1870s the economy had taken a down turn yet G.F. Hipkins and Son were doing extremely well.

It was in 1886 when William formally became the manager of the business and his mother went into official retirement. Rebecca felt gratified that all her efforts had paid off and William had matured into a successful businessman. They were living in a spacious house in Edgbaston[6] and their futures if not wholly assured were certainly looking comfortable. William's success as a businessman had come quickly and he may have been forgiven for feeling that he had the magic formula for success. His ambitions were large. He had already expanded the firm and was exporting to Australia, the United States, and several countries in Europe, but he was very much aware that success could easily turn to failure. As the century entered its final quarter technological developments were changing the face of engineering world-wide; market trends were much more variable and new products were appearing all the time. Any business that wanted to survive had to keep pace with these developments. All three areas of change were encompassed in a product that was slowly becoming a global fad—the bicycle.

In the 1880s bicycles began to grow in popularity and the need to produce many machines on a large scale meant production methods had to be improved. It was once again the American machine tool industry that would spark a revolution in mass production of bicycles. William could see the potential of the bicycle becoming a commercial boom. With more workmen being unable to secure accommodation close to their places of employment a cheap alternative to the carriage and tram would be sought, (although the numbers of people using public transport was becoming so large people preferred to find an alternative). There was also a trend for fitness that included cycling. Hipkins had become a practitioner himself, and in order for this to be stimulated further which would lead to greater bicycle sales, the machines would need to be produced more cheaply. William had been asked by the owners of a local firm *Sansome, Teale and Company* to offer suggestions on how they could improve their production of bicycle fittings. The firm was based at the Premier Works, Salop Street in the Highgate area of Birmingham and had been making fittings for bicycles since 1884.[7] William saw an excellent business opportunity and advised that the firm should invest in American machine tools, but to do so the firm would have to raise money, and in 1888 they were floated as a limited company offering shares to raise capital with William becoming a director and subscriber.[8] As a director William brought his skill and knowledge to market the high quality cycle fittings. They obtained licenses to produce Starley's patent Balance gears, and Mr. Bowen's *Aeolus* ball bearings, and set up an agreement with a London agent, *Philipp & Company*. Full page advertisements were placed in the cycle press and the company exhibited at cycle exhibitions.[9]

William became well-known in the cycle business. His advice and investment paid off as in the 1890s cycling became a world-wide craze following the invention of the pneumatic tyre and the profits rolled in. Many firms in Birmingham which normally produced items such as bedsteads, sewing machines, and steel tubing had begun to diversify into the rapidly growing bicycle industry. Many businessmen saw an opportunity to jump onto the bandwagon, others to utilise their facilities when orders for their normal lines were slack. William had seen it coming.

William was not satisfied with his successes; he wanted more. He needed more. Striving for success was, to him what water is to fish.

Since the business had set up in Lombard Street, his activities had not gone unnoticed by other businessmen in the town. Many of these businessmen had been stunned by the work and energy of Joseph Chamberlain as he brought a new vigour to the town. Now a handful of new businessmen were to carry that torch and Hipkins was one of them, perhaps even the leading one. Old family businesses were finding it hard to compete with imports from the United States and Europe. High tariffs were preventing competitive exports to the U.S. and the costs of upgrading old equipment to the new machine tools was prohibitive to all but the largest concerns. Birmingham's industrial survival hung in the balance, and it was a simple choice; adapt or go under. Many family firms began to sell out to consortiums, groups of businessmen who took over old companies and restructured them as limited companies in order to meet the foreign challenge. One such firm was *John and Edwin Wright* of the Universe Works, Garrison Street, Birmingham.

CHAPTER 7

NEW MONEY FOR OLD ROPE

My power proceeds from my reputation and my reputation from the victories I have won.

—Napoleon 30ᵗʰ December 1802

Hipkins had made a name for himself as a modern forward thinking businessman, in many respects as forward thinking as the Chamberlains although without the political ambition. Joseph Chamberlain's generation had been critical of his (Joseph's) methods at Nettlefold and Chamberlain, but the generation that came after him were not; they were enthusiastic, highly motivated and were not afraid of change. Countless family firms of all sizes populated Birmingham and their success had made Birmingham prosperous. Birmingham itself had an international reputation for the efficiency of the town's management. In 1888 the town became a borough and a year later it had been granted *City* status. Hipkins saw the direction in which he was heading; it was etched on the City of Birmingham's Coat of Arms—*Forward*.

By 1890 the world economic situation had changed considerably; competition from other countries, especially the United States, was threatening the old established firms. Many fathers' sons seemed to be content to sit on the laurels of the firms they had inherited, and in many cases the sons were often unfit to run the firms that soon ran into financial trouble. There were others, like Hipkins who thought otherwise and had the skills and the foresight to move with the times. As early as 1860 many saw that the United States was going to eventually dominate world trade. In 1862 the government in an attempt to assist British industry introduced the *Companies Act* to offer limited liability to companies, and empower them to raise a great deal of capital through a share issue to pay for the new technologies in the manufacturing industry. There was a steady stream of old firms transferring from a private family business to a private company with limited liability. The result of these changes led to a break from the patriarchal style of management that had been the trademark of many firms such as Boulton and Watt and W. & T. Avery. Old family firms began to bring in outsiders whose experience was with accountancy, rather than engineering, and businesses began to be run more on informal systematic lines. It was a style that was not welcomed by many in the British workforce.

Hipkins' contacts within the business community of Birmingham was wide; he traded with many of them. Informal meetings often occurred, although William was not a great social animal. Only if the meeting was business-related would he attend. His accountant, Arthur Gibson, used his position as a lead writer for the Birmingham press to establish strong contacts within the business community, and bring like-minded men together. This led to a small group meeting regularly to discuss the future of manufacturing in Birmingham and what they could do to stay competitive.

The catalyst for this group appears to have been *George Howard Cartland,* a barrister with chambers in Waterloo Street, Birmingham. George Cartland was becoming a prominent figure in Birmingham having his fingers in many pies. Born in Kings Heath in 1853 he was educated at King Edward's School in Birmingham before moving on to Oxford University where he obtained his M.A. as a barrister and where he had shown that he wanted to discard the old traditional aspects of court procedures and take a modern professional business approach. The court officials did not always appreciate this approach as his first case demonstrated. Appearing at the Warwick Assizes he immediately called his first witness without the usual introductory speech to the jury. The presiding judge, *Lord Chief Justice Cockburn,* called the young Cartland to the bench to point out that he expected such a speech and he would be grateful if he would oblige.[1] It would be a number of years before the more businesslike approach to court procedures would be adopted.

Cartland was a man of many interests and in particular sport; while at Oxford University he gained a reputation in the high jump, hurdles and throwing the hammer. He became president of *the Oxford University Athletic Club* and secretary of the *Boating Club*. Cricket was his passion. Having played for Oxford he continued his playing in Birmingham, becoming Captain of the Kings Heath and Edgbaston teams and often being selected to play against select teams such as the *Elevens of All-England*, the *United North* and the *United South*. He was associated with the formation of the *Warwickshire County Cricket Club* in 1882, becoming the club's chairman in 1885, and helped in the securing of the cricket ground in Edgbaston playing in the inaugural match against the M.C.C. scoring the ground's first half-century.[2] He did not stop there; he had political interests being elected as a councillor representing Balsall Heath and was secretary of the *Birmingham Conservative Association* bringing him into contact with the town's leading political players, including the Chamberlains. His business interests had stemmed from his perception that business (as well as the judiciary) needed modernising. It needed a more professional approach, and he saw his skills in law as being useful to firms who were making the transition to limited company status. In this period he was chairman of three companies, *Birmingham Val de Travers Paving Company*, *Eadie Manufacturing* and the *Gorton Rubber Company*.[3] In terms of local commerce Cartland was a heavy-weight; his sharp intelligence, strong physical fitness and astute business acumen made him much sought after by a number of firms. William Hipkins and George Cartland shared the same views on business practice and where the future of industry lay. Indeed, Cartland saw Hipkins rise in Birmingham as an example of the new generation of Birmingham businessmen, an example that was to be followed.

It was through Cartland that another powerful businessman joined the group, Wilfred Williams. Wilfred was chairman and managing director of *D. F. Tayler and Company Limited* of Newhall Street, running it with the assistance of his brothers Francis and Clement. His father, John Alfred Williams, had been a pin maker in the partnership of *Edelstein and Williams* of Newhall Street, Birmingham. In 1843 they bought *D.F.Tayler and Company*, a pin and hairpin manufacturer then located at the Lightpill Mill, near Stroud.[4] The mill was maintained until 1848 when Williams and his partner, Peter Edelstein, moved the equipment to their Birmingham factory which they named *New Hall* for the large family home of the Colmore family which had stood nearby. The machinery was incorporated into the factory with the emphasis on automation, and by 1850 a single female worker could oversee a number of machines as they churned out pins. This machinery had a remarkable history, Tayler had acquired the patent of an American, *Lemuel W. Wright* for a fully automatic pin-making machine, a design that Tayler perfected. However, his great rival, Kirby Beard, (an American producing pins in Britain) had developed automatic pin-making machines based on the *Seth Hunt* patent (yet another American), and a trade war between them broke out culminating in reciprocal legal actions. The costs of these actions ended Tayler's interest in the original partnership and John Williams bought the concern.

By 1840 Birmingham had developed into one of the main centres of world pin making with around 20 million pins being produced each day. In 1851 Edelstein and Williams exhibited (along with other Birmingham pin makers) at the *Great Exhibition* held at the Crystal Palace in London. Williams brought his sons into the business and was an exponent of keeping the whole of the manufacturing process under one roof, and in the case of the pin making trade he had wire and rolling mills set up to receive copper and spelter in order to produce their own wire. Williams did not stop there, the printing costs of the firm became so high that he had built a printing works within the factory and turned out high quality colour printing enabling them to produce their own catalogues and high quality packaging.[5] In 1886 with Wilfred and his brothers in charge, the old family business of Edelstein and Williams was merged with D.F. Tayler and Company and formed into a private limited company. Under his guidance the firm grew larger by absorbing the concern of *Edridge, Merritt and Company,*[6] becoming one of the world's largest pin manufacturers with a large portion of their trade being with the United State;, trade that was very profitable even with the high U.S. tariffs. Wilfred had wide ranging connections with the local business community; his brother, Francis, had inadvertently formed an important connection when he married Edith Avery, the sister of William Bielby Avery, who ran the large weighing scale manufacturers *W. & T. Avery*. The Avery family were big players in the life of Birmingham, and the connection by marriage (even if fortuitous) was extremely helpful to Wilfred's own business ambitions. Hipkins had met Wilfred through the usual course of business, with Hipkins obtaining a variety of pins for his brassfoundry work. Unlike Cartland, Wilfred's disposition was much like that of Hipkins being quiet and reserved, although unlike Hipkins he had a very personable relationship with his workforce. Interestingly, whereas in many firms the patriarchal system was wholly replaced, at D.F. Tayler's a certain degree of patriarchal management remained.

The final member of the five-man group was John Redfern Deykin of Edgbaston; a harness furniture manufacturer with *Brown and Deykin* who had works in Park Street and Lionel Street. John Deykin came from a well-known local family which owned the gilt button and electro-plate manufactory, *Deykin and Harrison,* at 5-6 Jennens Row (not far from Hipkins' old Ashted works). He had connections in all aspects of social, political and industrial life of Birmingham. He was related to many who had played vital roles in the formation of Birmingham as a major town, such as William Schofield M.P. who was Birmingham's first Mayor in 1838; William Redford, Birmingham's first Town Clerk; and the Alderman James Deykin.

Thus in 1890, this small group gathered together in order to seek out business opportunities, and one such opportunity presented itself. The old established family firm of *John and Edwin Wright,* hemp and wire rope manufacturers of Garrison Street, was up for sale. The firm had been founded in 1770 by William Wright as a rope and twine making business in Dartmouth Street at the north-eastern end of Birmingham.[7] Rope making was an important industry in the 18th century and a new one for Birmingham. The greater part of the work was carried out in the open air by hand, with Wright only employing a few people, usually under a dozen full-time, with additional hands being called upon as and when necessary to meet orders. The rope making process was simple but laborious. Firstly, the raw material hemp was prepared for spinning and then spun into yarn. The yarn was then twisted into strands and stretched to great lengths along what was known as the *rope walk,* supported at various intervals by *stake heads.*[8] Once the various strands of yarn were stretched side by side they were then twisted together to form the rope. Lengths and thickness of rope made would depend on the purpose for which it was intended, with the rope in most cases being made to order. In general, Wright produced short lengths of rope with a maximum length of no more than five to seven hundred feet long. These lengths of rope were suitable for domestic, agricultural and industrial use with many of his customers being local. The cream of the work, however, was the production of rope for use in shipping where rope lengths in excess of a thousand feet would be produced. These ropes also had to be covered with protective material, such as tar, and the process of covering the rope meant that buildings had to be constructed to store and heat the coating. Many rope makers were not prepared to expend the cost and thus the *Woolwich Rope Yard* (part of the Royal Dockyard) produced most of the rope required for the Navy. Wright wanted a piece of this bigger trade and built suitable facilities at the Dartmouth Street site to make long lengths of rope, and house the necessary equipment to apply the coating.

The technological developments that had been affecting small engineering workshops also affected the rope makers. From 1792 machinery began to be employed which greatly sped up the rope making process and improved the quality of rope. In 1829 William Wright passed the business over to his invalid son, also called William. On his death his wife, Ann, took over the business and continued to trade under her own name until her retirement due to ill-health in 1846 at the age of eighty-five. Her two sons, John Turner Wright and Edwin Payton Wright, took control and changed the name of the business to *John and Edwin Wright*.[9] The brothers developed a reputation for making extraordinarily large ropes, culminating in 1854 when they made the largest rope in the world to launch Brunel's super ship the S.S. *Great Eastern*. This remarkable piece of work had a circumference of 47 inches and was composed of 3,780 separate yarns.[10] This rope became so famous that sections of it went on public display, including an appearance at the *British Empire Exhibition* of 1924. This rope marked the zenith for scale of the hemp ropes; soon thereafter wire rope was to dominate the high strength rope business. The works were transferred to Garrison Street in 1861, where they had improved facilities for making large hemp and wire ropes under cover. Five years later in 1866 Wright's opened up a factory in Millwall, London.

It was the Atlantic Cable that would thrust Wright's, and several other wire rope manufacturers, into the centre of world attention. The first Atlantic cable of 1857 had failed for a variety of technical reasons, and it was the cable of 1865-66 that was manufactured to *". . . sufficient strength to enable the great design to be successfully carried out."*[11] The cable was invented and patented by John and Edwin Wright and having passed examination of a scientific committee set up by the *Atlantic Telegraph Company,* the cable could be manufactured. The cable was a magnificent piece of work for its time with the conductor consisting of seven wires weighing 300lbs per nautical mile. These wires were surrounded by four layers of *Gutta Percha* laid on alternatively with four thin layers of *Chatterton's Compound*. For external protection ten solid wires of 0.095 gauge galvanised homogenous iron, each surrounded separately with five strands of Manila Yarn which had been saturated with a preservative compound, was laid spirally round the core which was padded with ordinary hemp and saturated with preservative. The cable had a breaking strain of 7 tons, 15cwts and weighed 14cwt in water. 2,300 nautical miles of cable was required.[12] Such a large quantity of cable necessitated a number of companies involved in its manufacture, including *Glass, Elliot and Company* of East Greenwich, and *Webster and Horsefall* of Birmingham. The 1865/66 Atlantic Cable brought together again Wright's and the steamship *Great Eastern*, Brunel's super vessel being used to lay the cable following her economic failure as a passenger liner. The success of Wright's cable led to a number of undersea cables being made to the same and improved patterns, which included the British Atlantic 1865, 1866; French Atlantic 1869; British India 1869; Toulon and Algiers 1870; Falmouth, Gibraltar and Malta 1870, Brazilian 1874, and the Australia and New Zealand Cable 1874.[13]

The success of the undersea telegraphic cables had brought in considerable money and Wright's used it to improve machinery. However, the company had found that American companies were catching up and wire rope production in the United States was rising at an alarming rate; naturally, the US tariffs were causing Wright's export problems. Edwin Wright had died in 1872 leaving his brother to run the firm alone. On his death in 1890 his two sons, John Turner Wright Junior and Edward Payton Wright, took over the business. Neither it seems wanted to run it, and John Wright Junior decided to sell the old family firm,[14] realising that like so many other family firms in Birmingham, the prospect of raising large sums of capital to develop the business further required a change in structure. Cartland, Hipkins, Gibson, Williams and Deykin formed the consortium that took over the rope company and in December 1890 the old family business was wound up and a new company formed—*John and Edwin Wright Limited,* with a capital of £35,000 divided into 350 shares of £100 each. Each member of the consortium invested £100 into the new company forming a board of directors with George H. Cartland becoming Chairman and William Edward Hipkins becoming Managing Director.[15] Additional subscribers were found from the business community these included: F.H. Cartland (George Cartland's brother) a brass manufacturer from Moseley; Francis Williams (Wilfred William's brother) of D.F. Tayler and Company Limited and William Hughes a manufacturer from Lionel Street in Birmingham.[16]

Together they set about modernising the company structure and improving the equipment for producing rope. William now referred in business circles simply as Hipkins, began to stamp his own mark on Wright's, asking Arthur Gibson to take a look at the company's accounting system and make any recommendations. Hipkins was keen to tighten control on spending and reduce any waste. Wright's were, however, already well organized; the nature of the rope manufacturing process coupled with only two sites (both of which operated almost as separate self-contained units) meant that waste was already reduced. He now had an excellent vehicle on which to test himself; to see for himself if he could live up to what everyone expected of him. He knew that he had a safe haven with his mother and sister in Edgbaston, and he needed it. He was in a game with high stakes and big players but so long as he was true to himself, his beliefs and his methods, he would be fine. None the less sleepless nights were common, and bouts of weakness came upon him. He still visited the Athletic Club in order to keep fit, and he read avidly, and most of all he kept his trusty copy of Napoleon's Maxims by his side. This above all else, gave him the inspiration to adhere to his task.

He had little to worry about; under his direction the company continued to produce large ropes of hemp, wire and a mixture of both. They also increased the range of products they made in order to stave off any short-falls if the demand for rope was reduced. These additional products included: boat covers, engine and railway lamps, fog signals, string canisters, tin boxes, sash cords, blind cords, brattice cloths, engine packing, cotton waste railway wagon covers and tarpaulins for all purposes.[17] By 1894 Wright's produced rope and wire for every conceivable purpose. Hipkins was a strong proponent of direct trading. He had had to deal with merchants, in many cases when he was at his family firm, and he felt that cost savings could be made both to himself and the customers by dealing directly, which was difficult in the rope industry. Ship builders often went through chandlers which sourced material; navies (merchant and military) often issued contracts to one firm which would then allocate parts of it out to other firms, with Wright's often being third or fourth in a chain of suppliers. Hipkins managed to circumnavigate some of these problems by promoting Wright's and its products directly at the embassies of various countries. It took time but it paid off, Wright's were able to sign contracts directly with a variety of governments, and when a ship needed to be built, Wright's were listed automatically as the prime supplier of ropes and cables. To many other rope firms Hipkins' manoeuvre seemed to be rather underhand. The level of co-operation in the industry had been high, although some firms did not exactly see eye-to-eye.[18] Hipkins, never one to do anything by half was determined to make the name *Wright* synonymous with wire rope. To this end he began writing a book entitled *The Wire Rope and its Applications*. The aim being to give a general history of rope and to describe in detail the uses of the material, with a complete catalogue of Wright's products appended to the volume. The book, therefore, not only acted as an excellent text book for the scholar but an ideal advertisement for the firm. Certainly, any engineering student would think first of Wright's when the time came to apply their hard learned knowledge. It was a very clever strategy and Hipkins had an advantage over other rope companies in order to put it in motion, he already had a publisher. His friend and fellow director, Wilfred Williams, had a printing department at his pin manufactory, and thus was able to print and publish Hipkins' book, right down to the beautiful colour illustrations. It was not the first treatise on wire rope but was the most practical and for several years it would be the only one on the market, and then it was American companies which decided to publish. Hipkins' book is a demonstration on just how detailed he learned the subject of his new company. He even went to the extreme detail of consulting Whitworth Wallis, the director of the *Birmingham Museum* and a noted archaeologist, as to the origins of rope. Wallis had worked on excavations at Pompeii where ancient roman rope had been found. The historical touches inspired by James Bevan lighten up what would otherwise be a rather technical book. Bevan's interest in archaeology was of great assistance, it was he who introduced Hipkins to Wallis, and Bevan helped him with his writing having penned several books himself.[19]

Although Hipkins had been handed control of a world-renowned company he remained in control of G.F. Hipkins & Son, but in name only, for the old family firm was up for sale. In 1892 an offer for the business came in from *Vaughan Brothers*, a firm that produced edge tools located in Dartmouth Street (not far from where Wright's original works had stood).[20] It was the end of an era for the Hipkins, although a condition of sale was that the name *G.F. Hipkins & Son* should remain. This suited Vaughan's who knew that products marked with *G.F. Hipkins & Son* would find customers readily. For Rebecca, it was the closing of a chapter that began way back in 1849, and she felt pride at how far she had come, but very sad that her late husband never saw just how successful the Hipkins' had become. Her Willie had become more successful than she had ever imagined. At most she had expected him to be successful with the family firm, but now he was in charge of one the country's most important companies, and what's more, he was associated with some of the city's most important men. She thought it couldn't get any better, but it would.

CHAPTER 8

WEIGHING THE WORLD

W. & T. AVERY LIMITED 1730-1895

In 1930 the Birmingham firm of W. & T. Avery Limited celebrated its 200th anniversary producing in commemoration a book celebrating the firm's achievements. The book's opening paragraph illustrates clearly the sense of history and tradition in the weighing scale business:

> *"Human error and human guile have always needed a counterpoise. Hence men, trading together 2,000 years B.C., had the goods weighed before their alert eyes. Hence Abraham had the 400 shekels for the burial place weighed in balance. And the Ark was made to measurement. And Moses ordered a set of weights and measures for the people. And from the ruins of Pompeii they unearthed a steelyard which worked on exactly the same principle then as it does now . . . And, since unspoken traditions influence the minds and deeds of all Englishmen, this would seem to be a fact of which an Avery man should be rather proud."*[1]

It was with a steelyard (or stilliard) maker named James Ford[2] that tradition states the Birmingham firm that would be known as *W. & T. Avery* was founded in 1730. The steelyard is a very old form of balance developed to enable heavy articles to be weighed, which would otherwise be too cumbersome using the even armed beam scale. It is comprised of a rod on top of which is a hook from which to suspend it; underneath at one end is a single or set of hooks on which to hang the item you wish to weigh. At the other end of the rod is another hook onto which you add a weight. Once the item you wish to weigh is suspended, you move the weight along the rod until you get a balance.

The system is very basic and very effective; the market traders of Pompeii used them in the same way as the market traders of Birmingham's Corn Market (later to become the famous Bull Ring Market). Located near St. Martin's Church at the top end of Digbeth the market was the centre of trade in the town and it was in Digbeth that James Ford had his shop. According to tradition it was located at 11 Well Street (also known as Cock Street and later to be 11 Digbeth).[3] However, later research casts reasonable doubt on this traditional view of the founding of the famous scale-making firm.[4] It is more likely that a man named Ford set up business at 109 Digbeth some distance down the road, where he may well have been producing steelyards. In 1730, 11 Well Street was occupied by Robert and Josiah Ellis who, as far as anyone can tell, had nothing to do with the steelyard business.

The Digbeth area was a hive of small businesses surrounded by numerous wells with the River Rea running under the bridge at the lower end linking Digbeth with Deritend. At the higher end was St. Martin's church and the Corn Market. The road itself was narrow and winding with half timbered buildings on either side. The various shops and smiths had signs that swung precariously above the ill defined and rather weather-beaten footpath. Rubbish was liberally scattered about and the pedestrian then, as now, had to beware of the road transport that constantly carried goods of all types to and from the town. The surrounding land was damp and prone to flooding which assisted in the erosion of the road, yet the area had been a major centre for smiths for decades. It was here that John Leyland and William Camden on travelling through Birmingham had seen the swarms of inhabitants hammering away. James Ford was just one of a number of metal workers specialising in steelyards, all of whom were located from Well Street along Digbeth to the bridge over the River Rea, near to the town's Weigh Yard. He worked from one small workroom selling his wares to the traders in the Corn Market, and to traders who came from other areas.

On his death in 1761 the business was taken over by John Barton and his son, William Bridgens Barton, who had been scale-makers in Digbeth since 1728. The Bartons *were* living at 11 Digbeth (11 Well Street) at this time and, in fact, John had been there since 1746 producing steelyards and other weighing devices. Thus the business of Ford was moved to number

11 where Barton was already in production. Barton's shop was typical of the area being a half-timbered house with the workshop itself situated in a shed at the back, with the front of the house being used to display the wares as was the tradition of the day. John Barton was an energetic man and had been keen to set up three public weighing machines in the centre of Birmingham. In 1744 he wrote to John Wyatt, who had invented a compound lever weighing machine, with an interest in producing machines of this new type. It appears, however, that nothing came of the idea. John died sometime in the mid 1760s and the business passed to his son William B. William continued with the reasonably successful business until his death in 1781. A year later the business passed to Thomas Beach, a scale beam maker who had a business in the Bull Ring having served his time as an apprentice to Robert French, another steelyard maker located at number 28 Digbeth. Beach closed his own shop and moved into number 11.

Beach's quality of work was superior to that of Barton's with all of his wrought iron beams being forged by hand, with the addition of ornamental details to the beams. All of the engravings were added using a process of fire welding. He was very successful selling a variety of weighing devices including steelyard, beam and spring balances, and he also produced the various types of weights used in different countries thus enabling a wider market for his products and developing a wide reputation for his craftsmanship. He retired in 1794 and the business was handed over to Joseph Balden who was the husband of Beach's niece, Mary Avery. In the 18th and 19th century it was very common that business' moved through family ties rather than open trading, and certainly the term 'Family Business' was valid in its most widest sense, Mary being the daughter of John Avery and Mary Beach (Thomas Beach's sister). Balden had produced steelyards in Moat Row near St. Martin's church having taken over his father's steelyard business.

Joseph died suddenly in 1813 and the business was taken over by his son-in-law, William Avery, a mercer and draper from 54, High Street, Birmingham. The exact details of the transaction are clouded in mystery, but he settled the debts and recovered the credits of the business. William also became the guardian of Joseph's two sons, Joseph Jr. and Samuel, (aged 18 and 9 respectively). When Joseph Jr. came of age it may have been expected that he would have taken control of the scale making business; however, he was quite ill and had been confined to the lunatic asylum in Henley-In-Arden. On New Year's Day 1817 he signed a deed of trust which resulted in the whole estate being handed over to his cousin and brother-in-law, William Avery, in exchange for a payment of five shillings with a provision being made to ensure that Joseph Jr. was cared for. The scale making business was not included or even mentioned in the deed, which seems to suggest that William may well have taken over the business just prior to Joseph senior's death. Whatever the technicalities, it was now William Avery's enterprise and he invited his brother, Thomas, to join as a partner in the business. They immediately set to work placing advertisements in local directories, and the firm became known as *W. & T. Avery, Late T. Beach.* This was not the end of the matter; the younger son Samuel, was somewhat aggrieved at the way the whole estate had been handled, and in 1836 he filed a lawsuit against William on the grounds that his brother Joseph Jr. was not in a fit state to sign the deed. Many years of bitter exchanges ensued with even a riot, resulting in gunshots being fired in a dispute over some land in Balsall Heath that once belonged to Joseph Senior! The issue was not completely settled until 1845 with Samuel losing the legal action. Samuel remained bitter over the affair, and died in 1879 still convinced that William Avery had cheated him out of the estate (although as far as one can tell from the deeds this did not include the scale business).

Thomas Avery died in 1824 leaving William to run the business with his two sons and the small firm continued to prosper. The name of 'Beach' was still useful as it helped secure repeat orders both from the UK and Europe. There was a lot of local competition with numerous little workshops producing scales, but in 1833 Avery's found themselves under threat from the United States as the firm of *Fairbanks and Company* of Vermont began exporting their patented platform weighing machine into England. The United States as a nation was still under a hundred years old, but was making very rapid progress in workshop technologies.

Fairbanks' scale business had been formed only three years earlier by Erastus and Thaddeus Fairbanks. Thaddeus was a remarkable man constantly inventing new machines, including iron ploughs and the diving flue stove. The brothers had been running a wagon works (which included the building of the ploughs and stoves), but they turned their attention to the manufacture of hemp dressing machines to meet a demand created in Vermont by a craze to raise hemp. It was while working in this area that Thaddeus became aware of the laborious way in which hemp was weighed using a steelyard. He and his brother built a platform scale using a compound lever system that made the weighing of hemp easier and far more accurate than the steelyard. He developed the scale further and in 1831 he rode to Washington D.C. to file his patent application.[5] These platform scales were a departure from the type in general use, and were soon finding a market in other parts of the world as well as the United States. Fairbanks began exporting them directly to the UK, and in 1833 was granted a patent in England.[6] They approached the British concern of *Henry Pooley and Son*, who were crate manufacturers, ironmongers and smiths located in Dale Street, Liverpool, with a view to granting them a licence to manufacture and sell the Fairbanks scale in the UK. Henry Pooley was reluctant to begin manufacture of the scale and had to be persuaded by his son, and thus Pooley's began to manufacture and sell the Fairbanks' design. Pooley's agreement with Fairbanks allowed them to grant sub-licenses at their discretion, which enabled them to meet any large demand. To say that Fairbanks' arrival on the market was a surprise would be putting it mildly. The platform scale they designed was ideal for use in railway goods warehouses, and with the railway system just beginning, Pooley's hit the market at just the right time. An order was received from the *Liverpool and Manchester Railway* in 1835, and other railway companies soon followed standardising on the Fairbanks machine. Avery's seemed unwilling to compete head to head with Pooley's and Fairbanks, partly because Avery's was more concerned with the lighter weigh scale business, and partly because at the time both Pooley's and Fairbanks were the new kids on the block, and were not perceived as a major threat. Avery's preferred co-operation, rather than confrontation, and entered into an agreement with Pooley's to sell the Fairbanks design, receiving platform scales from Pooley's with Avery's name embossed on them. Although one press report stated that in this period the Avery business began to fall into "misfortune and into serious decadence,"[7] Avery's were actually doing reasonably well with sales of scales up due mainly to the emerging railway industry.

William Avery died in 1843 and two of his three sons, William Henry and Thomas then took complete charge, and their first job was to remove the name of 'T. Beach' feeling that the name of Avery was good enough to stand by itself. The two brothers were very different characters, and over the years both developed their own unique eccentricities. Thomas Avery became a very well known figure in Birmingham, and a striking figure at that, with a thick mop of white hair and a large white beard. He could often be seen being driven around the town in a yellow coach pulled by a pair of Arabian horses with a cockaded footman in attendance! His two passions in life were chess and fishing, and he never missed an opportunity for either. On his travels around the country he would play chess matches against some of the country's leading players and supported a number of chess clubs in Birmingham. He also took a full and active part in the civic affairs of Birmingham, becoming involved in a number of local establishments such the Municipal Sewage Farm, and being a strong campaigner to provide a much needed water system for the town. He assisted with the Queen's Hospital and was a keen advocate of further education sitting on the council of the Midland Institute, and being Treasurer of the Mason and Spring Hill Colleges. Having a strong sense of justice he became a Justice of the Peace and gained a reputation for coming down hard on 'evil-doers,' desiring that Birmingham should become a decent town where men could work and women could bring up families in decent conditions. He entered the council in 1862 representing St. Martin's Ward, but his interest in civic duties meant that he spent less time at the company and in 1864 he retired from the business. Two years later he became Lord Mayor of Birmingham for the first of his three terms, and it was during his second term that he was made Alderman.

By contrast his brother, William Henry, was a much more reserved character. His first wife, Mary Ann Beach, was a distant cousin who died tragically after being hit by lightning in 1849. He remarried in 1854 to Maria Richmond Beilby. His personal interests were limited to religious and charitable work donating a great deal of money to such causes but shying away from any publicity. He was described as a thoughtful, modest and kindly man who was held in highest regard and esteem by his friends and workpeople. In all of his business relations he maintained a high standard of honour in conduct and of excellence in workmanship.[8] William Henry spent more time with the ever expanding business than his brother, with an approach of benign but strict paternalism towards the workforce.[9] Avery's tradition of paternalistic management was not unique although William Henry tightened the grip slightly. He had distinct Quakeresque views (not uncommon in Birmingham business of the period), and workmen would be fined for drinking alcohol at breakfast or being the worse for drink later in the day.

The two brothers had set about rebuilding the firm and enhancing the name of Avery. It was a name that had been damaged slightly from the,

99

at times, very public row with Samuel Balden. They hoped to maintain the co-operative ventures with other scale-making firms, but not all scale-making establishments were happy with the all too cosy agreements between Pooley, Fairbanks and Avery. Things came to a head when in 1844 Pooley's took a Warrington scale-maker named Kitchen to court for infringing the Fairbanks' patent. For Fairbanks and Pooley's this seemed like a straight forward action. However, other scale-makers supported Kitchen and evidence was presented demonstrating that for many years, scale-makers in Britain had been making compound lever weighing machines long before the Fairbanks patent of 1833. In fact, John Wyatt is believed to be the first inventor of the compound lever-weighing machine in 1744, and as Avery's history shows one of the firm's predecessors, John Barton, had approached Wyatt with a view of making such machines and setting them up in Birmingham. Pooley's lost the case and the 1833 patent was annulled. It was a blow to Fairbanks as scale-makers in Britain could now freely produce the same type of scale without having to pay a fee to Fairbanks and Company. Pooley's did not suffer too badly; Henry Pooley had not remained idle during the relationship with Fairbanks and had himself developed weighing machine designs and could produce their own machines.[10] In 1847 Pooley's began offering maintenance contracts to the railway companies starting with the *London and North Western Railway.* This bold move gave Pooley's virtual exclusivity to the railway companies, holding ninety-percent of all railway weighing machine contracts.

Avery's also stopped selling the Fairbanks' patented design and continued with their usual line in beam scales. Avery's renewed their link with Fairbanks in 1850 when they took up the offer to produce other Fairbanks' designs under licence. The 1850 deal with Fairbanks was only a temporary move; the Averys knew that if the business was to remain competitive in the market, they would have to develop their own, unique scales and weighing devices. The deal produced good results and production levels were constantly rising and became so high that the Digbeth premises were found to be too small to cope. By 1854 two hundred workmen were employed, and a new building had been erected on the existing site with additional property being obtained at numbers 5 to 7 Moat Lane. Three years later came the development Avery's desperately needed.

Patrick Henry Sharkey was a provision dealer in Liverpool, and one of the main tools of his trade was the counter scale. Over the years in the trade he noticed certain deficiencies in the construction of the scales, and began experimenting with methods to improve their reliability. This eventually led him to develop a new form of scale construction. His scale had the bearings and knife edges housed in box type shackles that would keep them dust free reducing wear, and most importantly, friction which might otherwise result in an erroneous measurement. In addition to this he made the bearings and knife edges out of agate. A hard mineral that was new to the manufacturing industry, this mineral naturally did not rust and, therefore, had a long life expectancy. He applied for a patent on January 24th 1857[11] and Avery's quickly acquired it. Thus was the beginning of the weighing device that is synonymous with the name Avery the *Avery Agate and Brass Beam*. It was not long before the Brass Agate Beam became the standard balance for weighing items such as tea and tobacco. These products were vital parts of the British economy and the trade in these commodities was essential for the prosperity of the nation and, therefore, the demand for accurate and reliable scales to weigh them was high. The quality of the balances was superb with decorative brass mouldings produced not simply as a piece of engineering, but in many cases a work of art equal to the fine pieces of artistry being produced in Birmingham's jewellery quarter. The development of the agate and brass beam scale raised the standard of scales both in accuracy and quality of construction.

The next twelve years were very prosperous. The agate beam scales were selling well, and in 1870 additional facilities were obtained when a settlement of debt involved the acquisition of the Atlas Foundry of Ephraim and Jacob Green located in West Bromwich. Up until this time ironfounding for Avery's had been carried out by subcontractors in the town. Now Avery's controlled their own ironfounding thus improving their product range, and it enabled them to operate a better quality control system. The foundry also enabled Avery's to produce heavier scales and they entered into an agreement with Pooley's to act as agents for their platform scales and weighbridges, producing the said items carrying the Pooley's name. Avery's and Pooley's also came to an understanding where it was understood that Pooley's would concentrate on the heavy scale business such as weighbridges and platform scales, and Avery's would concentrate on the light scale, business. This is a prime example of monopolistic competition where two or more suppliers of a product differentiate their production to the benefit of them all, although it did also result in a casual approach to competition.

William Henry was the driving force behind these developments and he never retired, he remained dedicated to the firm until his death in 1874. His brother, Thomas Avery, his widow Maria Richmond Avery, and brother-in-law Julius Henry Avery took control until William Henry's sons were deemed to be old and fit enough to run it on their own. The stop-gap management soon found itself faced with an ever-increasing demand for scales. In 1878 the *Weights and Measures Act* was passed by the British Parliament. This created a demand right across the country, although the types of scales now being produced were in demand all over the British Empire. Avery's international reputation was further enhanced when in 1879 they won a gold award at the Sydney International Exhibition. Their large display of platform scales, counter scales, dead-weight scales and, of course, the old and trusty steelyards created quite an impact. Avery's exhibits were generating a great deal of orders, and they were organised enthusiastically by Richard Robert Gibbs who was employed as an accountant clerk at the Digbeth works having started with the firm in 1867.

In 1881 when William Beilby and Henry Johnson Avery took over, nearly 700 were employed and over 17,000 square yards of floor space was given over to the production of weighing devices of all kinds. As with the previous Avery brothers the new owners were contrasting characters. Henry Johnstone was a quiet reserved man whose only hobby was fishing. He was in the main a dedicated businessman, the archetypal 24/7 man. He followed the whole manufacturing process through each step. Not only did he deal with the day to day administration of the business, but he also inspected each scale as it was completed. He would often be seen on the factory floor working at a lathe to make some parts or make corrections, and then at the end of the process he would help package and deliver the product! The workforce had a great sense of pride in their work and this was largely the result of Henry's leadership. He cared less for structured procedure and was more interested in the quality of the finished product; the length of time and method used to achieve the desired result was of less consequence to him. It was he, "Gaffer Henry" who paid out the wages at the end of the week, taking time to talk with the workers many of which he knew personally, exchanging a few comments about their families. His eyes always looked kindly on people and a smile was often seen under a magnificent moustache! He was wholly dedicated to the business and as a result never married; he looked upon the workforce as his family.

His brother William Beilby Avery was very different in character being loud and extrovert. He much preferred to spend his time enjoying country sports especially shooting. Very much in the mould of his Uncle Thomas he was a man who stood out from the crowd; well-built with alert eyes he enjoyed life and hated to be tied to a desk. He once flew over Birmingham in a hot air balloon, and was one of Birmingham's first motorists owning a Darracq driven by a French chauffeur who could not speak English! He organised a motor rally through Birmingham which resulted in a large number of police officers being in attendance to assist in stewarding the event. Apart from his magnificent collection of stamps and being President of the *Birmingham Philatelic Society,* he also indulged in the care of his pet, a Barbary Ape that stood over five feet tall. The ape was kept in a cage at the Mill Lane Depot, much to the amusement of the workforce who would throw the ape titbits, although the ape was served five shillings worth of fruit a day!

Yet, with all of these activities, William Beilby did spend some time improving the business. He was largely responsible for the 1889 Weights and Measures Act that led to the need for improved weighing machines, which as a result led to an increase in demand. He also expanded Avery's range of products by constantly seeking out new models and patterns. His own approach to business practice was as relaxed as that of his brother. He took a personal interest in the staff, and in the old ledger office it was the accepted practice that lunch was held in the middle of the morning, and tea in the middle of the afternoon; at either a beefsteak or bacon might be seen sizzling on the stove. With women appearing in the office for the first time much flirting was abound, and the light atmosphere was maintained so long as it remained within the realms of common decency. "Gaffer Bill" (or even "Buff") as he was affectionately known, would act as cashier with his assistant George Silver. George had a reputation for rarely squaring the cash, and Gaffer Bill would terrify the poor George about his failure to balance the books. George would count the money again and check the ledgers. Then when he felt that George had had enough, Gaffer Bill would put his hand in his pocket and pull out enough money to obtain a balance!

For the general workforce it was still very hard work although, as already stated, the emphasis at this time was in producing high quality products with no doctrine as to how orders were met, and little had changed for the average workman over the decades. Pay and conditions were usually a matter for individual negotiation, with working hours varying between trades within the firm as well as between various firms. Generally, people worked a ten-hour day or a sixty-hour week with some employees starting work on Tuesday morning or afternoon. 'St. Monday' was a common feature of Birmingham's industrial life with workers missing out Mondays and concentrating their efforts from Tuesday to Saturday. Other companies in the town, such as *Elkington* (electro-plate), had complained of the practice and had taken steps to stop it. Avery's, however, seemed unconcerned and although by the 1880s the majority of firms in Birmingham had regular hours, Avery's seemed to be content to stay with tradition. There were no paid holidays although in the main Fair Days and certain religious days were observed. However, more often than not scale workers had to work these days to keep up with demand.

Avery's had some interesting working practices; for example workmen signified their arrival by placing a brass check on a numbered board. There were many irregularities with this system as some of the boys working at the firm would place the checks for some of the workmen, who either were still in bed or had gone straight to the pub! Eventually, even Avery's relaxed management needed to tighten this up and a timekeeper was appointed to monitor the checking-in. Leading hands in the firm would often enter the factory, grab their aprons, and then leave to the nearest pub spending the better part of the day there. If they were needed an underhand or boy would leave the factory and fetch them! It was not uncommon for boys to collect beer for the workmen hidden in cans and described as 'tea'. This practice came to a shuddering halt when William Beilby Avery himself intercepted a consignment of this special 'tea'! In an attempt to reduce the level of drinking, and to discourage the St. Monday ethic, on December 10th, 1887 Avery's brought into being a set of *Workmen's Rules* which imposed fines on those who breached them. Being drunk would cost a workman over 2 shillings while being late cost a few pennies. Interestingly, the Mill Lane Works seems to have the highest number of fines with 27 shillings and 6 pence being collected during one week in 1888![12]

With no standardised pay system the Moat Lane and Mill Lane factories employed the 'Gang System' where a piece-master was employed on a piecework basis without time control. He engaged his own helpers paying them what he saw fit out of his payment from Avery's. A fine example of this system is that of Thomas Groom who was in charge of the Brass Department at the Moat Lane premises who was contracted to make brass counter and beam scales. His gang included four of his own sons with the youngest receiving only pocket money for his services. The working hours were generally 6am until 6pm although these could be extended to meet demand. The work was very tough, all the machinery was hand operated, and the workmen had to supply their own tools and make their own drills, taps etc, with all of the raw material and finished items being transported by hand cart to other areas of the works. The Mill Lane factory did have steam driven machinery for drilling, grinding and polishing but the piece-masters had to pay 6d a week for their use and this was in addition to a charge of 5d a week for lighting![13] These were the accepted working practices and little had changed for many decades.

The hard work was often softened by the close relationship between the Avery brothers and their workforce. It was not uncommon that senior workmen with their families would visit their masters at home where they would be made most welcome. If an employee became ill the brothers would arrange for eggs and fruit to be sent to the unfortunate workman's home. Birthdays and anniversaries were remembered, and when a workman announced that he had a new baby the Averys would send a present of a new blanket for the new-born. William Beilby was a keen student of industrial relations and had seen many other companies suffer from industrial disputes, something Avery's had few problems with. He commented on the causes of such disputes by stating:

> "... it is not plain work that is objected to, because some of the dreariest and hardest work is done within the family circle. It is work unrelieved by affection."

Trade union activity at Avery's had been sporadic. In 1861 a meeting of the *Scale Beam Makers' Union* was held at the pub *The Swan with Two Necks* in St. Martin's Lane but nothing appears to have come from the fledgling union. There was some disruption ten years later when a strike was called, but this only involved a few subcontracting masters and soon broke up. Some skilled workers joined the *Scale Beam, Steelyard, Weighing Machine and Mill Makers Trade Protection Association* that formed in Birmingham in 1873 to add some weight to a demand for a 15% wage increase. Avery's offered 2.5% and their skilled workers were happy. Not so the skilled workers at rival scale-makers *Day and Millward* where eighteen men went on strike. By 1882 the union had only 42 members and was eventually wound up in 1897. The workmen had a Sick Society which appears to have received the majority of its funds from the Avery brothers' pockets; this was supplemented from December 16th, 1889 when all workmen's fines were paid into the Sick Society account. There was also no pension scheme which led to workmen staying on for as long as possible and continuous service over 50 years was not uncommon. Certain valued and trusted workmen were paid a pension directly by the Avery family that varied between 8 and 16 shillings per month. Just like Matthew Boulton a hundred years previously, the Avery's looked upon their workmen and women as family and friends. The co-operation between the management and the workforce helped develop the firm; promotion was given as a reward to those who had worked hard or given special service to Avery's. In 1886 Richard R. Gibbs was rewarded for his hard work in the firm by being made a partner and appointed Manager of the South African Automatic Machine Company which owned the patent rights for the coin operated machines used for sweetmeats, pills, postcards etc and a personal strength testing machine. Gibbs had started as a clerk and his keenness and enthusiasm had brought him to the attention of the Averys who were always on the lookout for potential future managers.

Avery's began to expand and increased the rate in which they bought-out other scale making firms. In 1887 they started to offer a maintenance service, eventually catching up on Pooley's idea of 39 years earlier. The Avery—Pooley relationship had cooled by this time; in fact, as soon as Henry had taken control the cosy relationship with Pooley's was to end, although there had been cracks in the alliance from the late 1870s as Pooley's began to open branches across the country.[14] Avery's took Pooley's by surprise when in 1883 they secured orders to supply heavy scales and weighbridges in London. This was followed up by more orders in the Potteries, an area considered by Pooley's to be their territory. Henry did not relent; Pooley's home city of Liverpool found itself as a target for Avery's who supplied a weighbridge to the *Hide and Skin Market*. Pooley's had felt secure with the railway orders but Avery's even made in-roads here supplying platform machines which were straight copies of Pooley's own machines to the *Great Eastern Railway* and at a much cheaper cost than Pooley's! Pooley's responded by opening a branch in Birmingham located in Heath Lane in 1885 and two years later they began producing scales of the type normally associated with Avery's. It was open commercial warfare.

Avery's themselves had a large network of branches located in the key industrial cities; London was the first in 1876 followed by Manchester (1884), Leeds (1885), Cardiff (1885), Glasgow (1888), Sheffield (1890), and Liverpool (c.1892). In Birmingham and West Bromwich they had a number of sites including Mill Lane, Bradford Street, Rea Street, Greets Green and Moat Lane. These works were capable of producing anything in the way of weighing machines, whether it might be the delicately adjusted balance for assaying gold, or weighing chemicals for scientific purposes, or ponderous bridges for weighing locomotives and loaded railway trucks. They turned out patent automatic scales for the weighing of grain, automatic machines for filling and packing cereals, self-recording weighing machines, and other self-indicating and platform machines. The Atlas Works in West Bromwich produced the large castings that were required, and material was shipped across the Midlands by horse and wagon to the various sites. There was no real co-ordination, especially as the main castings came from West Bromwich, but the iron and steel warehouse was located in the basement of the Moat Lane factory. Every day a railway wagon brought iron and steel to the Moat Lane factory, workmen passed the material through a cellar grating to the warehouse man. The material, when requested, was then man-hauled from the basement to the Mill Lane factory for use by the blacksmith. Men and boys would form a line walking through Deritend carrying 28lbs of 3/8 inch round or hoop iron.[15] When large loads were required hand-carts were employed, some of these carts were extremely old and wheels often broke creating chaos on the busy thoroughfare. This practice had been in operation for many years and as business boomed it was clearly ridiculous to continue. A new set of buildings were constructed at Mill Lane and the old buildings were then used as the iron and steel stores. This made life a little easier.

As the rivalry with Pooley's heated up Avery's bought other scale-making firms, adding their expertise, patterns and models to the already crowded Avery catalogue. Pooley's were not the only major competitor and, perhaps, not even the most serious[16] as French and American scales were on the market with the French counter scales making inroads into the British market, and the Americans in the shape of the *Howe Scale Company* and the *Fairbanks Company* challenging for the platform and heavier weighing machine market. American industry was heavily mechanised, due in part, to the shortage of highly skilled labour which led to companies investing in the latest machine tool technologies.

Fairbanks had only begun making scales in 1830 and fifty years later had 900 workers and a catalogue of 400 patterns, making them much larger than Avery's who had been around for one hundred and fifty years.

Industry was facing major changes and the Americans were leading the way as they began to analyse industrial methods in a scientific manner. The greater use of machinery, the production of standardised components for ease of assembly, and a more sleek design reducing the density of material in the scales all helped to reduce the cost of the product. British firms were quickly trying to upgrade their factories including Pooley, Avery, Day and Millward and several other scale-making firms to meet the US challenge. The machinery and product quality was in the hands of the firms themselves. However there was an issue that was out of the hands of the manufacturers, and it was the issue which gave Avery's and other British firms the biggest cause for concern—the development of tariffs.

The tariff, or tax, was placed by a government on imported manufactured goods with the aim to give their home produced goods an advantage in the market place. The United States had introduced limited tariffs in 1873, but a new wave of aggressive tariffs started when Russia introduced high tariffs in 1879 and other countries followed suit.[17] These countries increased the level of tariff on a number of occasions raising the price of British goods sold abroad to a high level. In Britain there were no such tariffs against imported goods as successive governments supported the notion of 'Free Trade'. The issue of tariffs and the need for Britain to respond was forever in the news at the end of the 1880s, and it would become the dominant issue regarding trade for several decades with the famous Birmingham politician, Joseph Chamberlain, campaigning for *a Tariff Reform Policy* to counter the foreign competition.

With business doing well, in spite of the tariff problem, the Avery partnership was financially dissolved in 1890 as the first step in becoming a joint stock company with limited liability. Avery's had now joined the throng of firms making the change, usually in order to raise capital and protect their interests. Avery's had no need to raise additional capital and were operating successfully; there was, however, one slight problem. The Avery brothers still owed £42,388 to their relatives under the terms of their father's will, and when on March 25th, 1891 the new company was formed this, debt was removed from the accounts. The nominal capital for the new company was £200,000 in shares of £10 with the new business being described as:

*"Manufacturers and merchants and dealers anywhere in weights
and measures, scales, balances and machines and appliances of
every kind for or used in connection with weighing or measuring
or estimating any length . . . (including automatic machines and
appliances) . . . and also the trades or businesses of engineers,
machinists, brass founders, iron founders and shop fitters or
any other trade . . ."*

The description is very interesting as at this point Avery's were not involved in shop fitting or heavy engineering but have left themselves open to begin such work. The head office address is given as 12 Digbeth, (this was the old number 11 but was changed to 12 following a renumbering of the buildings in Digbeth). The patriarchal Averys were still in charge and to the workforce very little changed. In the boardroom there were quite distinct changes, new directors, Walter Chamberlain and Wilfred Williams, became the first complete outsiders to be brought into the family firm. They brought with them a broad experience of manufacturing and business finance, something Avery's needed to compete in the international arena.

Walter Chamberlain was one of the famous Chamberlain brothers that included Joseph, Arthur, Richard and Herbert. The famous Birmingham brothers had worked for *Nettlefold and Chamberlain* and were now spreading out on their own. Joseph, as previously mentioned, went into politics; Arthur who had been involved in a brassfounding business *Smith and Chamberlain* became Managing Director of *George Kynoch and Company* in Witton (later became *I.M.I.*). Arthur was also one of the founders of *Chamberlain and Hookham,* an electrical engineering firm that was getting in on the act of the new electric lighting industry. Walter had worked his way through the *Nettlefold and Chamberlain* business starting at age 18 in the workshops, progressing through the drawing office, and eventually becoming manager of the fitting shop. His move to Avery's would be a new challenge for him and an input of new blood and ideas to Avery's. His contacts in the brassfounding industry would prove very useful, not to mention his contacts through the Chamberlain family which included men of real power both locally and nationally.

Wilfred Williams as we have seen was a business heavy-weight in Birmingham; he was also a personal friend of the Avery family—following his brother Francis's marriage to William B. Avery's sister Edith. Wilfred's experience working with the United States regulations on trade was a big boost for Avery's who were keen to enter into the large North American trading market and, of course, he had connections with the brightest of Birmingham's business elite. Other share subscribers included two familiar names from J. and E. Wrights: Francis Williams (Wilfred's brother and William B. Avery's brother-in-law) who purchased 150 shares; and William Hughes a friend of Wilfred's who purchased 200 shares.

Things seemed to be moving well; W. & T. Avery Limited was moving forward and setting its sights firmly on the 20th century. Henry forever thinking about the company and the workforce, realised that with business doing so well should there be a need for more facilities it was going to be difficult obtaining them and it was growing ever more difficult to administer all the various sites efficiently. He was also becoming concerned with the costs of transporting material from one site to the other; as a solution he began drawing up plans to build one central site where all of the work could be carried out. The building of such a site would mean the closing of the other sites, and many of the workmen may find it difficult to travel to the new facility. He therefore proposed that apart from a new manufactory he would also build a village to accommodate the workers. Henry found a site that would suit them at Lifford in Stirchley.

In 1894 things took a down-turn. The Alderman Thomas Avery died; although not directly involved in the firm his spirit was present and his loss was felt deeply by all. A second blow came when a month later Henry Johnstone Avery died at the young age of 34. Perhaps his illness had been brought on by the vast amount of work and the long hours may have taken their toll. His brother, William Beilby, was greatly distraught and in his brother's memory made a gift of £1 to every employee for every year of service dating from the time the partners took over from the executors in 1881. The workforce was also grief stricken; it was like losing a father and grandfather. They presented William Beilby with an illuminated address of condolence. For the company as a whole the loss of Henry was a tragedy. It was his energy and drive that had moved the company ever forward and his plans for the future suggested that the 20th century would see a new greater Avery's. Fate appeared to have stolen, or at least postponed, that prosperous future.

William Beilby inherited his brother's stake in the company, and he now held a full 80% share and found himself in complete charge. He had relied heavily on his brother's dedication to the firm but he was more concerned with following his personal interests than running a major company. The weighing scale market also took a down-turn in 1894 and the workforce was placed on short time. In July he drew up a schedule of the firm's assets and found the firm was in a good financial condition with assets outstripping liabilities, yet an *Extraordinary General Meeting* was called on November 16th where a motion was passed to allow the firm to go into voluntary liquidation. Arthur John Williams, an accountant based in Colmore Row, acted as liquidator and the firm went formally into voluntary liquidation on December 4th, 1894 with the intention of forming a Public Company with Limited liability. From the point of view of the company it seems an odd decision, but from William Beilby's point of view it was the most logical course of action. He was certainly affected by the deaths of his two close family members, and he himself was keen to concentrate on his outside interests but another factor played a role in the decision to form a Public Company. The Stock Market had begun to pick up with share values slowly raising; by the Winter of 1894 it was the ideal opportunity to convert the firm, and thus on December 10th, 1894 *W. & T. Avery Limited* became a Public Company with a nominal capital of £200,000 divided into £5 shares. William Beilby Avery became Chairman and Managing Director *pro tem* with the other directors being Walter Chamberlain and Wilfred Williams, with Alfred Lloyd becoming the company Secretary. Other subscribers once again included Francis Williams and William Hughes, with Hughes also obtaining shares for members of his family. In January 1895 the goodwill, assets, patents etc were transferred to the new company with the uncollected debts being transferred in August. What the workforce made of all the changes can only be imagined. At first it seemed that it was simply a change of status of the firm, the same names in W.B. Avery, Wilfred Williams and Walter Chamberlain were all still there, but changes were afoot. It was clear from the board's point of view that if Avery's was to compete successfully it would need to modernise its structure. Although Williams and Chamberlain admired and respected the way Avery's had been managed, it was felt that overheads would have to be reduced and ways found to reduce the manufacturing costs of their products. Only through such measures could the cheap imports from the USA be countered. Williams knew the type of man he wanted to shake up Avery's, someone with the 24/7 mentality of Henry Avery but with the modern business ethic based on a scientific approach, someone not unlike his co-director at Wright's—*William Edward Hipkins.*

CHAPTER 9

THE NEW EMPORER

Nothing is more important in war as an undivided command . . .
there should be only one army, acting upon one base, and
conducted by one chief.
                                                    —*Napoleon Maxim number 54.*

Ever since Wilfred Williams joined the board at Avery's in 1890,
William Hipkins had had one foot in the door of the company. Williams had
asked him for advice regarding the restructuring of Avery's showing him
the general structure of the firm with its various sites scattered across the
midlands, and told of the plan that the late Henry Avery had of centralising
the company on one site. Hipkins agreed with Henry's plan pointing out that
the various satellite sites across the midlands were creating inefficiencies,
the cost of transporting material, site overheads, wasted time, and labour
all added costs to the finished product. It was clear to Hipkins, (and it
must be said to the other members of the board), that Avery's also needed
to get a tighter grip on the accounts of its branches which seemed, (to
him at least), to be operating in a rather cavalier way. These efficiencies
and reduction in costs would be achieved if the company centralised its
head office and midlands manufacturing facilities. A centralised company
meant that the satellite plants in Birmingham and West Bromwich would
be closed and their operations transferred to the new facility. Such a
radical, (for Avery's), change was necessary if the firm was to compete
with foreign competition. Williams agreed, and suggested that perhaps
Hipkins himself might be interested in taking Avery's into the modern
world. Hipkins knew that to change the firm into a very modern public
company would offer a challenge that to many, would seem daunting; but
to Hipkins it was an irresistible opportunity. There were problems. He
was still Managing Director of J. & E. Wright Limited, and he wouldn't

simply dump them; Williams was a fellow director and it did appear to be robbing Peter to pay Paul. Williams was however simply making the next move in a complicated game. George Cartland was already aware that Avery's would require a new managing director and had already agreed with Williams that if Hipkins was happy to take on the challenge then George Cartland would temporarily take over as managing director of Wright's until a suitable replacement could be found.

In early 1895, a series of private talks was held between Avery, Williams, Chamberlain and Hipkins at William Avery's home. Hipkins was formally introduced to Avery who had already known of him through his reputation as an excellent organiser and tough businessman. The two men hit it off well. Avery saw in Hipkins a reflection of his own late brother Henry. Hipkins appeared shy, quiet but when asked a direct question, he gave a direct answer, no bluster, no unnecessary verbiage just a straight answer. It was clear that Hipkins' knowledge of how a business should be run was extensive, and that his personal dedication to his firm was beyond reproach. To Avery it was like being reunited with Henry. As the ice was clearly broken William Avery began to talk openly about his plans for the future. He made it blindingly clear that he would only remain as managing director until the end of the year and that he wanted to leave the control of the company in the hands of a board that could satisfy him that Avery's had a prosperous future. Like the Averys before him, William Beilby was concerned for the workforce, any changes would be *". . . viewed with suspicion and this might damage the company"*. Chamberlain suggested that the changes to the company should be a gradual affair. The current board of directors, which included outsiders, was now well established, and a great degree of trust and acceptance had developed. Hipkins would be introduced as a director in August and the workforce allowed to become accustomed to the new face, at the same time Hipkins would get to know something of the firm with special responsibility for the centralisation of the company. When William B. Avery retired from the managing directorship in 1896, Hipkins would then slip into the role and it would appear to be more of an increase in duties rather than simply an outsider replacing an old friend. They all agreed this was a sensible measure, however, Hipkins pointed out that his style of managing a company was somewhat different to that of Avery; and in fact somewhat different to that of Williams and Chamberlain. It would remain to be seen how the workforce would react to such a change. Hipkins also wanted to ensure that his replacement at

Wright's was settled and that the change would not harm that company. It was agreed that Hipkins would be made a director for a period not exceeding twelve months, and if everything worked out he would be made managing director on William Avery's retirement. He would be allowed to remain as a director at Wright's and would be able to advise that firm as required. This satisfied Hipkins and the plan was set.[1]

Hipkins was still associated with Sansome, Teale and Company Limited; however they were now competing with a new big player in the field of bicycle fittings—The *Birmingham Small Arms Company*. BSA was an arms manufacturer that had diversified into cycle parts in 1893 due to a downturn in orders for rifles. Their high quality equipment and large production facilities gave them a distinct advantage over smaller producers. Sansome, Teale and Company Limited disappear from the trade in 1895, either taken over by another firm or ceased trading, perhaps due to BSA's strong position in the market, either way Hipkins was released from another commitment.

Thus William Hipkins was invited to join the Avery board. He accepted, and on August 1st 1895, he formally joined W. & T. Avery Limited.[2] In some respect for Avery's it was a gamble, never in the firm's long history had its future prosperity relied on an outsider, but as the 20th century dawned with mechanisation all around and foreign competition landing on the shores of the United Kingdom a gamble was what was needed.

His arrival at number 12 Digbeth went almost unnoticed by the general workforce; Hipkins was simply a new director. He was greeted by William Beilby Avery and given a brief tour of the offices introducing him to the staff. The figure of Hipkins cut a deep impression on everyone, immaculately dressed in a smart hand tailored suit with a fresh carnation in his buttonhole. He gave the impression of a six foot guardsman (although he was a little less than five feet nine), with his straight back and brilliant white president's collar, he could have easily been mistaken for an ex-army officer. He carried his trusty silver-topped cane, and on seeing a female office member he touched his hat politely. Most remarked (afterwards), how he had a boyish face yet it was set in a man's body, and that he seemed very serious—so much so that some were not sure whether to speak to him or not. He gave a distinct air of isolation, unlike that of William Beilby who bellowed hellos and waved his arms about, slapping people on their backs and making one or two jocular remarks. Hipkins' gray eyes starred intently at those he met, in the brief moment of a handshake he never broke eye contact and consciously noted every detail about the person he was greeting. It was a polite *"good morning"* and nothing in his voice offered anything deeper than a business-like courtesy. It was impossible for anyone to notice just how nervous Hipkins was at meeting them, he felt like he was on show and he wished he could move on quickly and start to discuss business. He didn't want to waste any time getting a feel of the firm.

He started by visiting all of the midlands' sites to see for himself how the firm operated down to the finest detail. He studied the firm's books, its history, the methods in which scales are constructed, the way customers, suppliers and rivals were handled. Beginning his study with the works in the Bull Ring, this was an excellent example of not just a local site but of the manner in which the branches operated. The retail and repair sides at Digbeth were separate departments within the company and operated independently from the manufacturing side. The scale of the work was such that in 1891 these departments were formed into distinct branches in their own right lead by Julius MacKenzie operating with their own accounts and separate trading account paying head office for goods supplied. They even paid the Head Office rent, rates and taxes for occupying the premises in the Bull Ring. Mackenzie had a number of staff to administer the branches including, George Herbert Allinson, who had joined the firm in May 1891 as a cashier and had developed a great interest in the development of business accountancy. He applied mathematics to his profession with great relish and his hobby was pure mathematics in which he excelled.[3] He loved the exactness of mathematics, of the way it could be used to explain the world around him, and he strived to find better ways of attaining accurate calculations. He had been forewarned of the impending arrival of the new director, and Hipkins' reputation had gone before him. Allinson and others in the office waited with some incredulity for his arrival. Hipkins greeted everyone with his usual detachment, and Allinson was surprised that he resembled a *". . . fashionable man about-town."* He noted that Hipkins appeared to be an *"oldish-young man with eyes keen yet tired looking"* and gave the distinct impression that his was *". . . not an intellect to be trifled with."* As is usual on such occasions the Branch Manager might try and generalize rather than give specific details, however, Hipkins would have none of this, he wanted to know everything. Every aspect of the accounting system was examined. During his examination of the way wages were allocated for repairs, he examined a fitter's wage book.

With his gold-framed pince-nez firmly on the bridge of his nose he ran his finger down the column of figures mentally calculating the totals. Allinson acting as the guide stood silently as Hipkins examined it in some detail, suddenly pointing at the book and asking *"And what becomes of this total wage figure?"* Allinson took out his pince-nez placed them on his nose and leaned over the book to see the figure, *"It goes in the Summary Wages Book."* Replied Allinson. *"Show me."* Responded Hipkins. So Allinson retrieved the Summary Wages Book and pointed out the week's entries; but Hipkins was not satisfied, he wanted to see the particular week where the entry in the fitter's wage book appeared. Hipkins repeated the process on several other entries to satisfy himself how the calculations were made. Hipkins was as meticulous as ever.[4] He saw in the faces of Allinson and Turner that they were not used to such scrutiny and he wanted no-one to be under any illusion that what he was doing was for the benefit of the company; this was not a personal issue. *"Gentleman a business like ours marches on its details, we should see that the details are correct, and then the broader issues will follow."* He told them.

Allinson was impressed, his passion for mathematics echoed Hipkins' desire for detailed accuracy.

Hipkins' dogged determination and acute searching abilities enabled him to learn quickly, and soon he had an excellent grasp of the business. His tour of the Birmingham sites left him in no doubt that they had to close as soon as was practicable. To him it seemed little had changed in a hundred years, and to a certain degree he was right! The workforce was busy, some people were chasing around and yet others seemed to be passing the time of day with the least amount of energy as possible. Records were scattered, with lots of little notes flying about. Boys would enter a site with wheelbarrows of material, drop it off and then race out with another wheelbarrow that was sometimes empty. At the Mill Lane Branch he observed keenly the arrival of castings from the West Bromwich site loaded onto a large wagon, pulled by a pair of horses. Its arrival sparked a rush of activity as people raced to do their unloading tasks, one to the horses, two to a crane, four on the back of the wagon, two more at the sides of the wagon. It seemed chaotic to the untrained eye, but each man (and boy) knew what they were doing. The castings were not delivered to any particular schedule, as they were produced they were loaded and sent to the relevant site that had ordered them, thus it could be quite a surprise when they arrived! It was a general rule that the wagon would arrive early in the morning, if possible, to enable the material to be used during the day. Small packages were included in the delivery, but also three or four large platform scale castings of around 60lbs. each were on the load requiring a crane to lift them from the wagon and place them on the ground. The small packages were placed on a trolley, and a boy wheeled it to the *goods-in* office. The workman in the office helped him unload the packages and they were placed in a corner with others that had arrived from other sites. The large castings had to be man-handled by a number of boys who were expected to raise them to shoulder height. These were then carried up a flight of stairs to the shop floor. William Allen who worked for Avery's for over 40 years referred to the system as "a joke."[5] Hipkins would have agreed with Allen that the system was chaotic, as he followed through a delivery process that had changed little if at all in 40 years. He witnessed one of the famous 'tea' runs and William Avery retold the story of the beer marked 'tea'. He knew from what he saw that most people were hard working and took a pride in their efforts but he also knew that there were many that felt the company owed them something and thus they took advantage of the relaxed environment.

So much for the local sites he needed to understand how the wider branch system worked and began an exhausting fact finding tour of the branches across the UK. He started with Liverpool and Manchester in late August accompanied by William Avery. To the branch managers it came as a shock to find that Hipkins did not simply stand and listen but asked questions too. Henry Marsh Jr. was the Manchester Branch Manager, and Marsh's father (also Henry) was the Branch Manager in Liverpool, and between them they essentially ruled a vast territory extending south-west over North Wales, and west and north-west over Lancashire to Berwick and Carlisle. Hipkins came as something of a shock as he wasn't simply making a courtesy call; he wanted to know how Marsh administered the area asking searching questions, especially relating to the travelling mechanics. These mechanics would tour the region repairing the light and counter weighing machines, these 'service tours' usually lasted three months at a time with the services of local blacksmiths being used as and when required. Some of the repair work was very haphazard and it was very much a case of improvisation to make scales work efficiently. The weigh-bridges in the region were maintained by sub-contractors *Hodgson and Stead* of Manchester, and *Thomas Steen* of Burnley. This work was far more professional, although, Hipkins was interested in how these sub-contractors charged for their work. Hipkins was not one who felt he had to explain himself but he would make comments in order that his managers understood the methodology. He would more often than not use a quote from Napoleon to underline his point; in the case of understanding the actual working of the branches he told Allinson:

> *"I will not rely on here say, I must see everything with my own eyes. I also want my managers to do the same. If they have to report on something they have not seen, then I want them to say that they have not actually seen it."*[6]

The word spread quickly to the other branches that the new director was "awake".

Hipkins arrived at Glasgow in September and had particular interest in this branch as it had been set up in order to win contracts to produce weigh-bridges to the shipping industry, with the first manager Finney believing that he could produce weigh-bridges cheaper in Glasgow than in Birmingham. E.J. Turner replaced him in 1892 after the envisioned sales never materialised. Turner was able to increase sales resulting in the need for a purpose built works. The *Partick Works* was the result, being constructed in 1893-94 and comprising of three large brick or stone buildings. One was a single storey building used as finishing and fitting shops which stood at the back of the site containing five smiths' hearths, three gas-heated japanning stoves, a portable tinsmiths' forge, a portable annealing forge, and three benches for the use of pattern-makers. A second building was of two storeys situated on the main road that served as the gate house, private house and metal store. The third building was also of two storeys situated across the gateway from the gatehouse and was used as a warehouse, showroom, offices and pattern stores.[7] Hipkins was interested in how the new works had been set up, and how new orders were being sought; and if indeed weigh-bridges were being produced more cheaply than in Birmingham. He knew from the accounts that the Partick site had been losing £1,000 per year since its construction, and he needed to know just how.

With the staff at Glasgow still reeling under the Hipkins onslaught, Hipkins headed to the London Branch. This was the largest branch, and had a small works attached. The showrooms at *Cow Cross Street* had just been extended to accommodate the 1,000 patterns that were on display. The London Branch was more than simply an outlet for the south; it was also an important publicity office. With many firms having London offices, it was seen as *the* major shop window. Hipkins, as director would hold monthly meetings at the London office, and use the showrooms as a meeting place for potential customers who happened to be in London. He used his time very efficiently, he had to. As Managing Director of J. &. E. Wright he had obligations for that firm as well, although, Wilfred Williams did help with some of the more routine matters; but the strain, although, not evident was there. The strain *was* evident on the faces of the branch managers and some foremen, who were rather taken aback by Hipkins' energy and knowledge. The board was deeply impressed, but not everyone was surprised at the energy and persistence of the new man. On several occasions Gibson and Williams had heard Hipkins say to managers and foreman *"Activity, activity, speed!"*[8] There was a feeling within the general workforce, that Hipkins would be active for a few weeks, if not a couple of months giving himself enough time to make his mark; and then things would settle down into their usual routine. Hipkins had no intentions of simply making his mark and then resting on the shoulders of the giants of Avery. He was going to complete the transformation of the firm into a modern company, fit to take on worldwide competition. He had just five months to prepare himself and demonstrate to the board that he was the right man for the job.

The workers returning to Avery's after the 1896 New Year celebrations found themselves commanded by a new man, and for the first time in the history of the company, the man was not called *Avery*. Their old beloved master, William Beilby Avery, had withdrawn from the active control of the business, and retired to his picturesque estate in the Thames Valley. He did, however, retain his place on the directorate. He was determined not to follow his brother into an early grave due to the pressures of work, and he believed he had set up the old firm with a strong board and a capable successor to the managing directorship. After being a director for only five months, William Edward Hipkins, was confirmed as Managing Director.

George Cartland at Wright's had found the man he wanted to replace Hipkins, George Turner. Turner had been born in Dudley and began his industrial experience at *Sandwell Park Colliery*, West Bromwich. Like Hipkins, he had developed a reputation as an organizer, and at the young age of twenty-eight had been sent to India by the *Assam Railway and*

Trading Company, to open coal mines for which the company had obtained concessions. His success in India was spectacular, and after 14 years his work there was complete. Cartland offered him the post at Wright's, which he readily accepted, and planned to take up his position in 1897.[9] Cartland was content to hold the fort until Turner's arrival. Wright's had a far more effective organizational structure than Avery's, and it was felt that Avery's had the greater need of Hipkins.[10] Hipkins did remain on Wright's board and would be able to assist if any issue became pressing.

In January 1896 Hipkins passed through the front gate at Avery's showing all the signs of a confident no nonsense managing director. He had passed through the gate many times since he had been appointed a director, but now it was different, *he* was in charge.[11] Unlike modern company structures, Avery's in 1896 had little in the way of middle management. At the top was Hipkins, the Managing Director, and with him was the board of directors. Below were the managers of the firm that equated to the works managers, branch managers, and the company secretary. Below these was the rest of the workforce. Hipkins would become involved in every aspect of the firm, and his personal influence would reach every corner of every site and branch. Large companies at the beginning of the 21st century have a number of directors to oversee parts of a company with a managing director responsible for these directors. Below these there is a team of managers, with possibly another level of managers below them before one ever gets to the workforce; who in turn maybe sub-divided into teams with team leaders. In fact, even the modern managing director finds him/herself answerable to a clutch of board members, various types of executives, a Chief Executive and even a President in the largest companies. The result of this structure is that the modern managing director has far less influence and direct control than his counterparts had at the beginning of the 20th century.[12] For this reason, whatever policy and work practice was enforced within Avery's, everyone knew that Hipkins had to either have thought it up, or given approval for it; and woe-be-tide anyone who instigated any new work practice or policy without Hipkins' approval. The workforce, and some managers may have been resentful of the dictatorial approach, but the rules of business had changed. When the Avery family ran the company they were answerable only to themselves. Hipkins and the board were answerable to share holders who wanted a return on their investment, and it was Hipkins who personally carried the responsibility for the success or failure of the company.

Becoming the first *outsider* to be appointed as managing director of W. & T. Avery Limited was not only a challenge with an incredible responsibility; it was also a financially lucrative position for Hipkins. He received a salary plus a commission on profits. The calculation for the commission was a remarkable piece of accounting, needing considerable and very secret calculations each year to arrive at a satisfactory figure for his salary and bonuses. These calculations included the purchases and sales of land and machinery that might affect the profit figure; for example the expenditure on building work at the Soho Foundry was excluded while the £1,000 obtained as compensation for the sale of a piece of land to the Corporation was included. In practice the figures speak for themselves. He first received £1,000 per year, with 10% of trading profits over £15,000 after depreciation. Two years later his salary was £1,250 with a limit of £2,500 being placed on the total of his share of profits at 10%; after this figure he received only 5%. A reservation was also made that the £15,000 figure might have to be altered following the purchase of the firm of *Parnall and Sons,* should their profits swell Avery's considerably. In 1900 William received a further advance of £1,500 a year in salary with the maximum commission being raised to £3,500, calculated at 10% of profits available to shareholders for dividend purposes, after a 5% dividend had been deducted. Nine years later more alterations were made![13] Compare this salary with the wages of those on the shop floor. Apprentices who had recently started might be on 5 shillings per week, and on average a skilled worker with several years' experience may get 35 shillings per week.

A number of workmen had turned out to see what the new man looked like. The smart tailor-made suit, the cane, the fresh flower in the buttonhole and the military style stride made a great impression upon those watching. He walked briskly into the offices, not glancing to the side. It was clear from the onset, a new broom was about to sweep Avery's. Hipkins entered his office, and sat down, he thought for brief moment that here he was in charge of a large company with all the power to mould it as he saw fit. As usual he wasted no time; he called his friend and accountant Arthur Gibson and asked him to investigate the branch accounting system with a view to reorganizing it into a departmental system centralised in Birmingham. Just as with his previous business interests, Hipkins used Gibson as his trusted financial advisor. A shrewd move as no-one at the lower levels of Avery's had even heard of Gibson, let alone knew of his methods and ideas on business accounts. It would be difficult enough for the staff to try and deal with Hipkins, now they had another new face, and a Hipkins appointed face at that to deal with. The board approved the move on February 18th.[14] Gibson would begin his tour of the branches in March. Gibson also investigated the Birmingham and West Bromwich sites, accompanied by George Herbert Allinson who had been appointed by Hipkins, as the Assistant Secretary. He discussed his views with Gibson who was impressed and recommended to Hipkins that Allinson would be the ideal man to take the newly created role of *Travelling Inspector* with the duty of supervising and auditing branch accounts. Hipkins accepted the recommendation[15] and Allinson found himself at the centre of the reorganisation of Avery's, and was dispatched to the various branches to prepare them for the visit of Hipkins and Gibson.

Manchester and Liverpool came first, the Marshes felt they were prepared for Hipkins on this visit, and then Gibson was introduced. Gibson had a face that suggested a very stern headmaster, his small beard and moustache added to the effect. The Marshes certainly felt as if they were in the headmaster's office as the work began. Record books were taken out and studied, new calculations made, figures cross-checked. Workmen's books examined, their figures checked. Hipkins and Gibson took copious notes working through lunch; it was a very detailed analysis. In the evening at dinner Hipkins and Gibson discussed the day's activities and then before retiring to bed, Hipkins went though some paperwork he had brought with him from Birmingham. The Marshes were rather shell-shocked by the level of detail Hipkins and Gibson were keen to see and the second day saw no let up in the pace and scope of the research. Two days later Hipkins and Gibson arrived in Glasgow and were greeted by the branch manager Turner. Turner and his staff found themselves under deep scrutiny with Hipkins and Gibson continuing the process they had started in Liverpool. Then it was straight off to London where Hipkins and Gibson discussed what they had discovered. Hipkins was keen to reorganise the branches as soon as possible with the branch managers taking on more responsibility for trading. They would be given guidelines and briefed on the *Avery Company Policy,* and they then should carry out that policy within their region using whatever methods suited the region best. Gibson would be auditing the branches for a full twelve months so that any progress could be monitored. Hipkins was not too happy with the system of agents that was being operated. Each branch would use various ironmongers and other shops as agents selling Avery scales. Hipkins much preferred direct trading from the branch, where discounts could be offered against local competition and a maintenance service could be placed in operation. His aim was to have an Avery Branch in range of every customer. At that time, ironmongers acting as agents for Avery's would carry out some routine maintenance and travelling fitters would carry out more substantive repairs. Avery's had no idea if their customers were ever getting the service they required, if the scale they were sold was the correct one, and even if the customer was satisfied. Hipkins felt that without a direct relationship with their customers it would be impossible to plan a sales and marketing strategy—something that many companies had never even thought of at this period. Even so, Hipkins saw a use for agencies where the population of an area was small a local retailer could be used as an agent, although, a workshop should not be too far away.

The Glasgow Branch was a particular problem; it was still losing around a £1,000 a year. Hipkins agreed that A.F. Nainby and W. Moseley would be sent from the Head Office to investigate ways to reduce the deficit by introducing economies at the branch. The two men were dispatched within a week and armed with Gibson's data they delved deeper into Glasgow's records, they had clear cut instructions from Hipkins to do whatever they felt necessary, and they had his full support. One of the branch's travellers called, Walton, was the first casualty; he was dismissed. Soon to follow was the cashier F.H. Miller, and several agency agreements were terminated. The branch manager Turner was outraged! After all *he* was the manager. Hipkins true to his word supported Nainby. Turner feeling that he was in an impossible position resigned, and thus Nainby took control as manager, as Hipkins would have preferred. All the Avery branches felt the effects of these moves, and any illusions that Hipkins would rest on the laurels of William Avery were finally dispelled. Managers and staff quickly focused their attention on the accounts and their relationships with other agencies. This is exactly the reaction Hipkins wanted, the pure thought that he was looking over their shoulder forced the branch managers to tighten their control.

His detachment from everyone but the board members (and even then only on a strictly professional basis), created an air of uneasiness throughout the firm. The foremen had been used to dealing directly with Henry Avery (and William Beilby), but Hipkins preferred to issue directives to the works managers who would then see that they were carried out. This disassociation was no accident. Hipkins' own experiences at the family business had taught him that business and friendship should be separated, and that he could ill afford to have close attachments to anyone in the workforce. The Avery workforce was not used to such a detachment and it made them nervous. Hipkins relationship with his workforce remains to this day a controversial issue.

When he joined the firm he was all too aware that the leaders of the firm were expected to present themselves, at least once a year, at a mass gathering of the workforce. This was usually during the annual picnic, and it was also thought wise to appear just before the Christmas break. William Beilby knew of Hipkins shyness and in August 1895 he accompanied Hipkins on one of the major workforce events—the *London Branch Outing*. Hipkins having just joined the firm as a director was nervous of the event, and it was a very family style gathering with the workforce dressed in their Sunday best clothes enjoying the sunshine. The day's events were a relaxed affair with William Beilby chartering a riverboat that gently took the London Branch workforce down the river to the *White Hart Hotel* at Windsor where everyone disembarked for dinner. The dinner was a semi-formal affair, with the head table featuring William Beilby and his wife, Hipkins, and Joseph Mcgrath (London Branch Manager) and his wife. Speeches were made, and all was positive with special congratulatory comments going to McGrath who had led the London Branch to great success. There was much jollity with William Beilby making a speech to thank the workforce for their efforts over the past year, making many references to members of the assembled. It was a speech that was interrupted many times as people laughed heartily at the quips and 'in' jokes that he loved to throw out at such an occasion. He led the exit out of the hotel at the end of the dinner, and the happy little crowd boarded the riverboat for an evening cruise up the river.[16]

Throughout the day and evening Hipkins was pleasant, but he had felt terribly uncomfortable. He was impressed at the way William Beilby could be so relaxed with everyone, and he saw that everyone truly loved this man, their boss. Hipkins was much relieved to return home the next day and he confided to his sister that it was going to be so difficult following in the footsteps of the Averys, and he wondered if he could actually do it. He did not doubt his ability from the business side, but the personal side; he certainly could not live up the Averys, and thus would not try to. He had been spared the annual picnic for the Birmingham workforce, which perhaps was unfortunate, as then he would have been prepared for his first picnic as managing director.

On a warm summer's day in June 1896 the Avery (Birmingham) picnic was set-up at Knightswick near Worcester. The preparations for the day had begun weeks before with the workforce eagerly looking forward to a day filled with excitement, good food and general fun. Six committees had been set up, each handling a particular element of the day's events: *Tobacco and Fruit* comprised of eight members who dealt with the distribution of all forms of tobacco and a wide variety of mixed fruit to those attending; The *Sports Committee* comprised of four members who organized the day's sporting events which included the men's 120 yards race, the boys' 120 yards race and the Tug of War. The *Entertainment* Committee comprised of five members who arranged for a variety of entertainment which included singers, a conjuring act, ventriloquist, Punch and Judy and a humorous recital act; the *Band* Committee comprised of three persons who arranged for a local band to be present to play music throughout the day; the *Dinner* Committee comprised of just two people who arranged the fabulous spread that promptly started at 12.30 and lasted two hours. This committee also arranged for the refreshments tent to be on site throughout the day that sold a variety of soft and not so soft drinks along with cold meats, sandwiches and salads. The last committee was *Transport* and the four members arranged the train times for those wishing to attend. All details of the event were itemised in a small programme proudly declaring the event as the *W. & T. Avery's Limited Workpeoples' Excursion*.

Hipkins saw the impending day as something he had to do rather than something he was openly looking forward to. For him, the Saturday in question would be a wasted work day, and it meant he would simply have to work all though the following Sunday to catch up. The workforce saw the 1896 picnic as a chance to see the new boss at play and this, they hoped, would give them an insight into the man, especially when the time came for him to give his speech to the assembled workforce.

The day duly arrived and Avery's workmen with their families gathered at various local railway stations across Birmingham to board the train to Worcester. On arrival at Worcester they were greeted by William Beilby and Hipkins, along with a brass band that played a welcome tune. After being mustered together they marched with the band at their head to the picnic site. Hipkins felt terribly self-conscious, he liked the sound of the children laughing but the atmosphere was something that he felt uncomfortable with. On reaching the site everyone let out a cheer and the festivities could begin. The site was a large field, the grass freshly cut with the large refreshments tent set up, and picnic style benches and tables had been placed all around.

Hipkins escorted William Beilby around the site and his nervousness was picked up subconsciously by those he came into contact with. A workman would see William Beilby and immediately light up "Good Morning Gaffer Bill," he would say holding out his hand. He would then turn to Hipkins, and in a much more submissive tone would bid "Good Morning Mr. Hipkins" nodding his head. Hipkins responded, but on every occasion it was an uncomfortable moment. Fortunately for all concerned, the day's activities meant that Hipkins and the workforce did not come into contact a great deal. The workmen enjoyed the sunshine with their wives and children, although, the men often hung around the refreshment tent; the women chatted together and the children played tirelessly. The brass band constantly played a mixture of classical and popular tunes, people danced, the wives at times receiving the attention that they deserved but rarely received. The dinner followed the sporting events, and everyone had worked up a big appetite. Roast beef with all the trimmings, more music playing, and life was wonderful—for a day at least.

In the late afternoon the singers took centre stage, with sentimental songs being the order of the day, followed by the light relief of Punch and Judy! Then it was time for the speeches, just a couple. Hipkins moment of truth had arrived, his first speech to the workforce. As he began he felt immediately that no matter how he tried his mood could not rise to the conviviality of the occasion, and this made him even more self conscious and a little embarrassed. He went on regardless determined to finish. He spoke of the question of right and duty, of master and workers. It was all abstract and not suited for the occasion at all. Allinson who was present said that it " . . . fell flat and chilly."[17] Hipkins was very relieved to finish and sit down, he must of felt like a London comedian at the Glasgow Empire! William Beilby stood up and immediately livened up the proceedings making references to those who had performed well in the sporting events, and complimenting all the ladies on their spectacular dresses. It was then time for the final activity—the dancing, the band struck. Polkas, waltzes and quadrilles were performed to loud shrills of joy.

As everyone departed to the train to take them home that evening, many remembered the fun and gaiety, but they also remarked on the new boss, how it seemed he didn't know how to enjoy himself. The wives felt that he needed a woman in his life, the men that he was a miserable b*****, either way he had made a poor impression on the workforce.

When Hipkins got home he was greeted by his sister who saw from his face how it went. She did not dwell on it, she chatted about her day, how the flowers in the garden were doing, how his mother was, and asked him to play the piano for her. Willie played Chopin, Beadie sat reading and his mother just sat and listened to the music. Willie's anxiety drifted away. The workforce and their families celebrated late into the night, their homes were filled with laughter, with plenty of food on the table, children happy and smiling, they were as content as they could get.

On the return to work the next Monday the air at the various Avery sites was filled with the chatter of the picnic. Jokes were abound as to the dancing performances of some, to the singing of others, but much talk was of Hipkins' presentation. Hipkins had made an impression, but it was not favourable. They had heard about his reputation as a great organiser and a ruthless businessman, but this did not quite equate to the man whose faltering speech held them with a grip of cotton wool. It was clear to everyone, Hipkins was no Avery, and it was felt by the more militant members of the workforce that Hipkins wanted to make a clear division between workmen and master.

Workmen in the late 19th and early 20th century saw themselves not only as a separate class to the management, but also as a wholly separate political movement, and radical elements within the workforce could create a very difficult environment for all concerned. Hipkins had been managing director for only a few months when he was learn just how radical things could get. His tightening of the grip on the management staff was being felt acutely, and his insistence that discipline be enforced without exception was causing some resentment. Several workmen had their contracts terminated immediately for poor time keeping, slack working, or aggressive behaviour. The shop floor culture was a tough one; it was not uncommon for minor disagreements to become fully blown scraps, even more so in the afternoons when many had been to the local pub for a drink or two. Hipkins wanted to curb such practices, but could only do so gradually.

Only a couple of weeks after the picnic on June 27th Hipkins entered his office as per normal at 6am and settled down for a day's work. He had many appointments and was due to see the Mill Lane manager at 10am.

Mill Lane was just waking up at 6am as some workmen arrived early. The day for them started with a fry-up of bacon and eggs, and the smell would waft throughout the site. The timekeeper set himself up by the gate to check those entering, and to list those who were late arrivals. These late comers had to supply a reason for their delay and more often than not the timekeeper would receive an abusive answer. The strict discipline that Hipkins was enforcing had reduced the number of latecomers, although a number of foremen would slip out later! The usual shouts of foremen to the boys to fetch and carry materials, of workmen loudly telling stories of their previous night's activities could be heard. Soon the sounds of hammering, tapping, cutting, stamping echoed throughout the site and it would have been recognisable to Leyland and Camden a couple of centuries previously. An ordinary summer's day had begun.

At 7am a group of boys and a foreman stood by the goods inwards entrance awaiting the two-horse wagon that would deliver materials from the West Bromwich Foundry. This wagon, the first delivery of the day, had been loaded the night before and had set off early with a couple of boys and a driver. It arrived a little after ten past seven and into the yard it drove. A boy placed a nose-bag on the horses which settled down for the well earned meal, the other boys directed by the foreman began to unload the goods, many of which were small packages, along with a couple of large 40lb. castings. As per the routine that had continued for decades, the larger castings were lifted by crane and placed on the ground ready for the boys to carry up the stairs to the workshop. The smaller packages were placed on a trolley and were wheeled into the office where they were unloaded and placed in a corner ready for sorting later. An hour later and another wagon arrived; this one was carrying packages mailed to Avery's from all parts of the country. They were unloaded by a group of boys who transported them to the office to be placed along side the packages that had arrived from West Bromwich. Quite a large selection of packages now littered the office floor. The goods inwards clerk began to sort them as he did every morning by dividing those addressed to specific persons or departments and those simply marked 'Mill Lane'. One package was 8 inches square and seemed quite heavy for its small size. This in itself was not unusual, heavy metal items were often packed into small boxes. The brown paper wrapping was removed, revealing a small wooden box, the lid had been fastened with two pins and these were easily removed. The lid was lifted and the clerk heard a small tap as something fell inside. He lifted the lid completely off and to his astonishment he saw a small hammer attached by its handle to the lid, the head of the hammer was attached to a nipple which itself was attached to a percussion cap. He stared at it for a moment and then realised that the main bulk of the box was packed with explosive! He had just opened a bomb! He carefully placed the lid back and ran to get the factory manager. The two of them returned to the office and locked the door.

Hipkins was sent for. He contacted Wilfred Williams and Walter Chamberlain, Chamberlain contacted the Chief Constable. Hipkins raced to the factory. He ordered that as few people as possible be told of what had been found. Hipkins, the works manager, and the clerk went into the works manager's office. Hipkins asked for tea to be brought to the clerk, and then he talked with him for a while. It was clear the young clerk was shaken by the experience, and only now was it dawning on him that for some reason or other the bomb had not exploded when he had opened the box. The police arrived and were ushered into the office where Hipkins explained that he wanted this whole incident to be kept as secret as possible, not a word was to be released to the press or anyone not connected with the investigation. The Chief Constable himself took control of the investigation and explosive experts took charge of the device. Parcel bombs had not been an uncommon occurrence in Birmingham during the 19th century, Irish extremists had sent small explosive devices to a number of people, and had thrown several during demonstrations; but by 1896 the incidents had stopped. Many hoax devices were constantly being sent to various firms, usually by disaffected workers and even sometimes by rival firms, but it was rare that a fully-fledged explosive device ever turned up. An examination of the device found that a metal box containing explosive had been placed inside a wooden box. It was to have been detonated by the falling of a hammer onto a percussion cap. The hammer would have fallen when the lid was lifted. The resulting explosion would have devastated the office and killed any persons in close proximity. The metal box would have shattered, spraying a large area with deadly shrapnel maiming people further away from the bomb. In order to prevent the cap falling off during transit the bomber had fastened the hammer to the nipple that was to come into contact with the percussion cap. It was this little provision that foiled the plot. When the cap was put on it was not pressed right on to the end of the nipple, and the result was that (owing to the method employed to prevent the cap from falling off) when the hammer fell the cap was prevented from being forced dead against the end of the nipple. The clerk heard the hammer fall, but fortunately it was not the last thing he heard.

The police kept the investigation low key and two days later arranged for a 'routine' check of all premises that were licensed to store explosives.[18] The police used this exercise to check out virtually all the premises in the city centre. Nothing seemed to be amiss. Hipkins offered a reward to be given to the person who could name the bomber that would lead to a conviction. The police put the word on the street, but still no one came forward. The police began working on the theory that the bomber was a disaffected employee or an ex-employee with a grudge. Men who had been recently dismissed were questioned, and so too were trade union activists, but still no information was forthcoming that would point to the bomber. At the July Board meeting Hipkins reported:

> ". . . the receipt on the 27th inst of a parcel addressed to the company, Mill Lane Works, containing an 'infernal machine', of an exceedingly dangerous character. The matter is being investigated by the police and explosives authorities, so far without result."[19]

Even with the level of secrecy that was thrown around the case, rumours soon spread. In the works it was suggested that it was a revenge attack by a sacked worker, and less credibly that it was an attempt to kill Hipkins! With so much gossip circulating it soon reached the ears of the press, although, by the level of detail in the Birmingham Daily Mail of August 6th it is clear that the story originated from someone who was close to the incident. The Mail reporter was particularly upset that the newspaper had not been officially informed, and suggested that had the Mail been involved then the culprit may have been caught.

> The members of the firm, it is said, enjoined the police to secrecy, but what useful purpose could be derived from this is difficult to see in view of the fact that over and over again the authors of such outrages have been brought to justice almost exclusively by the aide of publicity. A full description of the infernal machine and the box might—probably would—have led to some clue being obtained. Human life has been jeopardised by some miscreants who will in all likelihood escape detection

because of the apparent desire to hush the matter up. The bomb has been handed over to the police, and the Chief Constable has confirmed the news, but Messrs. Avery's manager, notwithstanding this, went to the length of stating that there was no truth in it. Up to the present time no clue has been obtained, but there is an impression that the author of the outrage was actuated by a feeling of revenge.[20]

The lack of publicity seems surprising in several respects. Hipkins would have been well aware of the assistance the local press would have given to the firm, especially as his friend Gibson was a regular contributor to the Mail. Hipkins was still establishing himself as Avery's managing director, and he wanted to avoid any adverse publicity or controversy that might hurt the firm and damage his position. The incident received no more attention from the press, and the culprit was never apprehended. All official written records of the incident no longer exist, but for Hipkins the delivery of a bomb to his firm was a wake-up call. He knew that any decision he made could have deadly results, and it would only be the first of a number of incidents at Avery's.

Hipkins needed to move on, he had no time for such distractions, with Gibson and Allinson taking care of the branches he could concentrate more on his main task which, was of course the centralising of the company. His visits to the branches and to the local sites had convinced him that he needed to get this project up and running as soon as possible. It was a project that had initially begun with Henry Avery and had passed to Walter Chamberlain on Henry's death. Chamberlain had even selected the ideal facility to house the Company—the famous *Soho Foundry* in Smethwick.

CHAPTER 10

THE SPIRIT OF SOHO

. . . the general alone can judge of certain arrangements. It depends on him alone to conquer difficulties by his own superior talents and resolution.

—Napoleon Maxim number 56.

Soho Foundry remains one of the most historic sites of the Industrial Revolution in Great Britain. Situated in Smethwick just outside Birmingham, it was constructed by Matthew Boulton and James Watt *in order to obtain the desired degree of perfection in their manufactory of steam engines.*[1] The famous firm of Boulton and Watt had revolutionised industry with the building of steam engines and Boulton's *Soho Manufactory* situated nearby had become the centre of excellence for the toy trade. The Foundry was required not only to continue the excellence but also to make great improvements in steam engine design and production. The Boulton and Watt Company had their cylinders produced by John Wilkinson, who had a patent on a boring machine which produced the cylinders to the exactness James Watt required. By 1795 other boring technology had arrived and with the famous steam engine patent soon to expire, it became a commercial necessity to construct their own foundry. Incredibly, the foundry was completed in just three months between September and December 1795, with the work being supervised by Boulton's son Matthew. Located in a position connecting it with the Birmingham canal with a wet dock able to handle four boats at a time enabling coals, pig iron, bricks, sand etc to be brought in, and their engines and other goods to be shipped out to all parts of the country. At the time of its construction the foundry was at the cutting edge of technology with steam powered machines for boring cylinders, machines for drilling, cutting, for blowing air into furnaces, large pumps and additional machines to assist human labour. The foundry was the source of great sense of pride in the region, and Stebbing Shaw writing of the curiosities and items of interest in Staffordshire wrote of the foundry soon after its completion:

> *. . . For by their superiority of all their tools, they are enabled to attain expedition and perfection in a higher degree than heretofore. In viewing this immense fabric, and its extensive premises, the spectator is most agreeably struck with the extraordinary regularity and neatness which pervades the whole, from common operations of the anvil to the working and fabricating the ponderous and massive parts of the steam-engine. The following facts shew the wonderful powers and superiority of the engines.*

> *One bushel of Newcastle or Swansey coals applied to one Boulton and Watt's engines will raise 30,000,000 of pounds weight of water one foot high; or 3,000,000 ten feet high; or the like proportion to any other height.*[2]

Some 200 people attended the opening ceremony of the Foundry in January 1796, where they heard Matthew Boulton give a rousing speech:

> *"I could not deny myself the satisfaction of wishing you a happy and joyous day, and expressing my regard for all good, honest, and faithful workmen, whom I have always considered as classed with my best friends.*

> *"I come now as The Father of Soho, to consecrate this place as one of its branches; I also come to give it a name and my benediction.*

> *"I will therefore proceed to purify the walls of it, by the sprinkling of wine, and in the name of Vulcan and all the gods and goddesses of fire and water, I pronounce the name of it Soho Foundry.—may that name endure for ever and ever and let all the people say Amen amen.*

"This temple now having a name, I will propose that every man shall fill his pitcher, and drink success to Soho Foundry.

"May this establishment be ever prosperous, may no misfortune ever happen to it, may it give birth to many arts and inventions, may it prove beneficial to mankind and yield comfort and happiness to all who may be employed in it.

"As the smith cannot do without his striker, so neither can the master do without his workmen. Let each perform his part well, and do their duty in that state which it hath pleased God to call them, and this they will find to be the true rational ground of equality.

"One serious word more, and then I have done:—I cannot let pass this day of festivity, without observing that these large piles of building have been erected in a short time, in the most inclement season of the year, without the loss of one life, or any material accident.

"Therefore let us offer up our grateful thanks to the Divine Protector of all things, without whose permission not a Sparrow falleth to the ground. Let us chaunt hallelujahs in our hearts for these blessings, and with our voices (like Royal Subjects) sing God save Great George our King".[3]

Following the cheers the 200 guests then feasted enjoying the beer and wine. The new foundry was well and truly christened!

Four years later in 1800 the original Boulton and Watt partnership ended after the termination of the 1775 steam engine patent, the father of Soho, Matthew Boulton, went into retirement; however, it did not end the collaboration of the families. A new company was formed—Boulton, Watt and Company with the leading partners being Boulton and Watt's sons Matthew Robinson Boulton and James Watt Jr. They had already been the main driving forces behind the foundry, developing a new industrial organisation by the application of a new scientific method of the management of labour and processes, eventually creating the world's first quality controlled production process. The foundry continued producing steam engines that were to work in all kinds of facilities from mines (where used to pump water), to mills where they were used to operate a whole variety of machinery. The foundry itself became one of the main powerhouses of Britain's industrial might, and in 1804 helped to usher in a new era of transportation when the company produced an engine for use by Robert Fulton in a steamboat. This was the first order in a long line of engines produced for use in boats and ships, with the firm famously producing in 1854 the screw engine for Isembard Kingdom Brunel's S.S. *Great Eastern*.

Matthew Robinson Boulton retired in 1840 and James Watt Jr. brought in three new partners, James Brown, Gilbert Hamilton and Henry Wollaston Blake. Boulton died two years later with Watt following him to the grave in 1848, and the company was reformed taking on the name of James Watt & Company with a re-organization resulting in the firm being run from London. A mint was opened in 1860 producing coins, although this venture ran into problems meeting delivery dates. The firm also developed new designs of marine engines, but by the 1880s the marine engine business was poor. Many countries in the world were producing quality engines, and ship-building firms such as Harland and Wolff were even producing their own engines. Henry Blake had become the sole owner and it was becoming more difficult for the old firm to remain competitive, which inevitably led in November 1894 to the firm being placed in the hands of a trustee. A month later the workforce was dismissed and the firm closed. In May 1895 the foundry with all of its equipment was put up for auction but withdrawn soon afterwards. It seemed an ignominious end to one of history's most important companies, and the 25 acres just sat quiet after nearly one hundred years of activity.

Walter Chamberlain saw the 25 acres of the foundry as being the ideal site for a centralised Avery's; it would suit as an alternative to the stalled plan proposed by the late Henry Avery. Chamberlain's plan was to purchase the land under Soho Foundry, clear the site and build a whole new complex there. Following the sudden withdrawal of the site from auction Chamberlain, on behalf of Avery's, entered into negotiations with F. Haydon, the trustee, making an initial offer of £23,000 for the freehold buildings, fixed plant and machinery, loose plant, stores and the goodwill *of James Watt and Company*.[4] Buying the goodwill of the *James Watt and Company* was being considered as an option, Avery's really wanted the land not the old engineering firm. They did however wish to use some of the engineering facilities of the firm until a full transfer from the other Avery sites could be made. The deal was sealed in late May. The freehold buildings, fixed plant, and machinery costing £19,500, plus an agreement to hire the works and plant until August 31st 1895 at a cost of £500;[5] by then Hipkins would be installed on the board and would take control of the re-organisation.

William Hipkins' past experience of transferring a firm and all of its materiel to new premises would be essential for his first main task at Avery's. As a director he was given special responsibility for the move, which included planning and advising the board on what action to be taken to ensure a smooth change over. The only difference between this move and the ones he had organised for his own family business was in scale. He was involved in the final negotiation with the trustees, that of the goodwill of the James Watt and Company. In September it was agreed to pay £2,000 for the loose plant, tools, fixtures, stock in trade and goodwill. Books and other items not included in the sale were duly removed by the trustees,[6] and thus a new chapter in the long history of Soho Foundry began. The news of purchasing James Watt and Company came as something of a surprise to many at Avery's. Following a discussion with Avery, Williams and Hipkins, Chamberlain agreed that there might be some mileage in a little divergence should the scale trade take a down turn. There was certainly plenty of equipment to be had, and as there appeared to be no other bids for the firm, it seemed logical to take the foundry lock, stock and boiler!

Hipkins now needed to prepare Soho Foundry for the transfer of the Avery's satellite sites, but unlike Chamberlain's original plan to immediately clear the site and build afresh, Hipkins had a different plan in mind. To him, it seemed wasteful to discard existing buildings immediately if they were serviceable especially as many had useful engineering equipment installed. His plan was to use available buildings and replace as required, which offered a logical strategy to achieve the transfer in the quickest time and most efficient manner without unduly disrupting production or wasting money. It was clear that Hipkins would stamp his own mark on the project; he knew that in a few months he would be in overall day-to-day charge of the company, and he could start building his empire in bricks and mortar. He ordered a general plan be drawn up so he could study the layout and plan a strategy, he clearly marked out the border of the 25 acres. Hipkins' first visit to the foundry was in September 1895 with Chamberlain, and Henry Blake. At his insistence they walked along Foundry Row, the private road that led into the works off Foundry Lane. On the right hand side were a number of cottages that dated from the late 18th or early 19th century, one of which the famous engineer, William Murdoch had occupied. Hipkins stopped to look at the outside of the cottage in question. All the cottages were let which brought in a little income for the James Watt Company, but Hipkins felt this was an encumbrance and wanted to free up the properties for other uses. They were sitting within the 25 acres and this acreage should be wholly dedicated to the Avery business. Notices would be sent to those occupying the cottages that they would have to leave. Chamberlain then talked of clearing all the cottages, but Hipkins disagreed. Given that the buildings were sound they could be put to some use, but as always the sense of history was not lost upon him. William Murdoch had lived in one of them, and although he could not show how he felt to his colleagues he did have a strong feeling that he was walking in the footsteps of one of the men who had set the country on the road to industrial greatness. He was humbled by the thought, but it did not overwhelm him, it just fuelled his desire to stamp his mark on the historical site and at the same time pay a little homage to what had gone before.

They left the cottages and moved further up the lane to the main entrance situated between a set of offices on the left and the smithy on the right. The end wall of the offices had a large clock fitted at the centre top that had been a famous landmark for many years. Through the gate and the whole works came into view, and it presented a desolate appearance, the buildings showing their age although hardly any dated back to 1796. The years of smoke and grime had darkened the brickwork, many windows had been bricked up, others had panes missing, and their appearance spoke volumes of the hard work that had taken place on the site for nearly a hundred years. To Hipkins it was so familiar; he thought of the old family premises at Ashted Row, all the departments of an engineering company in place, but this was 1895 and here he was in the famous Soho Foundry, and to all intents and purposes the owner. As he looked around taking in the rather disturbingly quiet site, he thought of Napoleon standing in Moscow, a major city had fallen to him totally at his command. For Hipkins, not a city but a major industrial site, and in terms of industry just as impressive a conquest as Moscow was for Napoleon.

Hipkins showed his plan to Chamberlain and Blake, and turning to face down Foundry Lane he pointed out that the entrance should be moved down to where the cottages meet Foundry Lane on the Eastern boundary of the site. The old offices could remain while building work in the production areas progressed. They moved into the old smithy opposite; the building gave the impression that it had not been in operation for some time, the boilers and pipe-work were in a poor state of repair and were long over due for replacement. Eighteen hearths were situated inside; these were blown by a blast engine that had three cylinders—a novel feature back in 1869 when it had been installed. In the centre there were a couple of steam hammers, the largest of which was a Thwaites and Carbutt design which had been an improvement on the famous Nasmyth design. The whole place was cluttered, thick dust, swarf, wood chippings, and a variety of flotsam was all over the floor. The smell was stale and although eerily silent, strange creaks and the sound of little things falling onto wood could be heard. It would have to go, it was unsuitable for Avery's needs, and a line was drawn across it on the plan.

The old mint was located on the south-west of the site next to the canal with its extensive range of shopping where copper and bronze coins had been manufactured. The building was in reasonable condition, the windows still had iron bars fitted for security, long wooden workbenches were bolted to the walls with hand presses bolted to the benches. It was a strange sight to see the large shops empty of people. To Hipkins the "Marie Celeste" sprang to mind and he wondered if the workforce had simply disappeared, and he joked that perhaps " . . . that since it is 10 o'clock they may have gone down to the pub!" He half expected to find a fire burning in the stove, but the stoves were cold and had been for some time. A large underground cellar that resembled a modern day nuclear bunker had been used as the mint's copper store. It was murky, dust blew about trapped in thermal currents, the entrance of the three men disturbing the air and sending the dust into frenzy. They didn't stay long. Hipkins pressed on, revelling in the experience, feeling not unlike Napoleon with his staff trailing several paces behind him as he inspected his new territory. On the left of the mint building was the canal and to the right was the canal basin complete with wharves. The canal was the responsibility of the *Birmingham Canal Company* and appeared to need some repair work; the basin which was the responsibility of Avery's was in a mess. The water was dirty, the brickwork crumbling and in its present state was of no use; Hipkins ordered a full survey to be carried out.

On the other side of the canal basin was the foundry itself. The foundry building was one of the oldest buildings on the site located on the western edge bordering the Smethwick Corporation Gas Works. Inside was all the equipment associated with a large foundry, with cupolas and air blowers with tuyeres and pipes with valves, a 4 foot 6 inch diameter by 4 foot tall Thwaites receiver and a large brick chimney rising high through the roof. Two large cranes fitted with iron jibs with blocks and chains produced by Tangye's stood in the middle bay. It was a self-contained facility and ideal for Avery's operation. Hipkins wanted this building up and running as soon as possible; the weighbridges could only be cast here and the contracts were vital. Even though the foundry was a functioning building up to the time of the sale of the site, it still required extensive work to bring it up to the standard needed for Avery's. On they moved into the erecting shop. This was a large building 250 feet long, 50 feet wide and 50 feet high which sat to the right of the foundry, and this was to be the home of the new Engineering Department (or the reconstituted James Watt and Company as it would be known to external firms). The roof was already under repair and the glaziers were busy fitting in the new skylights. The gas lighting was still in place and would have to remain so until the new fittings arrived in a few months time. Hipkins went inside. The incredible array of equipment was a history lesson in engineering with two thirty-ton travelling cranes, and on either side were arranged machines for planing, boring, facing and cutting. In 1869 the shop was considered to be unsurpassed, 25 years later it was now just one of many in the world. Hipkins, followed by Blake and Chamberlain who were desperately trying to keep up with his pace, headed for the far end of the shop where he turned right into the fitting shop which consisted of four large rooms and several smaller ones, all well fitted with machine tools. The same general appearance greeted them; the dust, the grime, the musty smell. He made copious notes in a little black book and marked some details onto his plan, then on to the next building. The stores buildings, the pattern shop, screwing shop, and the boilermakers' shop all came under the same scrutiny and most showed the same neglected appearance. A reporter from the magazine *The Engineer* had visited the site merely a week after the closure of James Watt and Company and reported that the foundry resembled a museum. Hipkins thought that the reporter was being kind, to him it resembled the neglected and weather-beaten remains of a lost empire.

The overall picture Hipkins had was that the buildings on the site needed either re-work or demolishing to be replaced with a more modern functional structure and on his return to the Digbeth office he laid out the plans of the site and prepared his strategy. The erecting shop needed to be up and running so that the new Engineering Department could be fully running within a couple of months with the rest of the site needing to be prepared for the transfer of equipment and material from the other Avery sites on a building by building basis. As a building was ready then equipment could be moved in, the existing Avery sites would be slowly evacuated in an orderly fashion. The schedule he set was for the design and planning of the first stage to take place during the latter quarter of 1895, and construction to begin in January 1896. B. Corser, an architect based at 59 Colmore Row, Birmingham was appointed to draw up plans for the buildings starting with the new smithy and foundry. These two buildings were critical for the Avery business with the smithy being used for counter scale production, and the foundry for the production of heavy weighbridges and platforms which required massive castings. The appointment of Corser was essential as Hipkins was now balancing two heavy weights. Firstly, he was still managing director at Wright's and he needed to keep focused on the issues there, and as a director of Avery's (and managing director in waiting), he found himself working incredibly long hours (even for him) and the strain was there. His sister, Bertha, was ever concerned, his sleepless nights were not all caused by insomnia. He would remain awake going through papers, checking the drawings of the new site, adding comments suggesting alterations. He would check to see if any unnecessary features were being added, if cheaper materials could be used, or where a new construction could be scrapped when an existing building would do just as well. He would present his recommendations to the board, and more often than not they were acted upon.

Corser himself was subject to tight control; he was hired for a little over two years and worked under supervision of a specially appointed supervisor—Walter L. Awdry who would take total control of the reconstruction after Corser left. Awdry had previously been working for D.F. Tayler and Company and had been personally recommended to Hipkins by Wilfred Williams—who was still a director at D.F. Tayler. Awdry had a wealth of experience having supervised the construction of new factories across the country and had been manager of the Karachi Ironworks in India for 4 years.[7] Hipkins gave him a salary of £4 10s a week and Awdry considered the task an important and historical one.[8] Hipkins was reluctant to pay for an outside consultant for longer than was absolutely necessary and to prevent Corser from making additional money by custom designing each building, he instructed Corser to use a basic design and repeat it across the site changing only scale and the general interiors to suit the function of the building. This general design was for a building to be of one storey with several levels of windows, some of which were filled in according to need. The walls were brick with a wood or galvanised iron roof (often referred to as an Irish or Belfast roof) resting on the outer walls and supported on iron girders across the bays and iron columns separating the shop bays. These pillars and girders would be able to support travelling cranes if required. The roof was filled with many skylights allowing illumination of the bays and electric or gas lights were also added. This basic design was ingenious as the building could be easily extended by adding additional rows of columns and extending the brickwork. The floors varied depending on the use of the building. The weighbridge shop floor was made of blue bricks set in cement or concrete, the machine shop floor was of wood and the counter machine shop and japanning shop had Yellow Deal Blocks set in 4 inches of concrete as a floor. On average the buildings were 200 to 300 feet long, however, one building was extended twice with its size increased to 500 feet long and 70 feet wide. Walter Awdry would ensure that Corser stayed within Hipkins' guidelines and followed through to the letter Hipkins' instructions.

When the design for a new or modified building had been approved Hipkins then offered the work to competitive tender where necessary splitting the construction of a building between a number of specialist firms thus ensuring the lowest cost to quality balance. In the case of the smithy, Corser located the new building on the south-eastern side of the site along the canal where the old mint stood, enabling raw materials and fuel to be easily delivered. It needed to be a considerable size housing between 30 and 40 hearths supporting 20 blacksmiths and their mates, 20 hot-stampers and their mates, 12 toolmakers and 18 press-workers. Corser planned a whole new building but Hipkins felt that the old mint building could be utilised in part to save money. Even so a large amount of building work was required including a new roof and a great deal of glazing with the cost of the construction being around £2,300. The contracts for the work went to a number of firms with *J. Harley & Son* of Smethwick winning the construction contract, *E. and C. Reay and Company* the roof, and *W.H. Heywood and Company* of Huddersfield providing roof glazing (as they already had for the erecting shop). Other smaller firms provided the drains, levelled the ground, carried out demolition work, laid paving, and fitted lighting and heating. All working to a tight schedule, Hipkins cleverly ensuring that each firm relied on the other to keep the schedule moving on time. As for the foundry, although the building was usable, it needed to be greatly extended at a total cost of £3,490. The foundry roof was of the same design as that of the smithy and the erecting shop but in this case was not contracted out, instead it was to be constructed in-house with Walter Awdry overseeing the work with help from a carpenter seconded to Avery's from *A. Kenrick and Sons* (by courtesy of Walter Chamberlain). With additional carpentry required as the site developed Avery's appointed their own carpenter, J. Baker, at a rate of 10 pence an hour.

The reconstruction of the old James Watt & Company's facilities moved at a frantic pace. Avery's had allowed the old firm to remain in operation (albeit with a much reduced staff) to clear any outstanding contracts since late May 1895. In August, when Avery's completely took over, Hipkins suspended operations during reconstruction, but it was clear that he intended to re-launch the firm in a new form. Ostensibly the James Watt & Company *was* the Engineering Department of Avery's and it was structured so that it could trade independently with outside bodies under its old name. This very shrewd move gave Avery's the opportunity of additional income during any lean spells. Even so, the old engineering firm operated as a separate entity in its own right paying to Avery's £250 per annum in rent for facilities, and charging Avery's for work carried out calculated at the cost of wages plus 33 and third percent. Although most definitely under the control of Hipkins, the James Watt and Company also had its own management structure that ensured smooth running even when the rest of the Soho site was a large construction site.

Over a period of 4 years Hipkins invested in new machinery and upgraded existing equipment which included new cupolas, muffles, milling and profiling machines, a steam hammer, a baker's blower, an Archdale notching machine, an Archdale machine for rolling markings on steelyards, American built radiators fitted to the japanning stoves as well as numerous small tools, and lathes. These new machines stood alongside those which Hipkins inherited including a wall-planer with a hand-cut screw, a face plate lathe built at the foundry prior to 1850 that was able to deal with work up to 26 feet in diameter, a radical drilling machine and a vertical boring machine. These historical machines remained in service for many years until eventually being donated to the Birmingham Museum of Science and Industry.

It was not just with equipment that Hipkins invested. A number of employees with James Watt and Company also formed part of the rejuvenation of the firm. For example, the vertical drilling machine operator, William Byfield was taken on to continue his work. Hipkins realising that here was the expert and no-one else was better suited for the position. Byfield had been born in one of the cottages in 1852 and his father worked for the James Watt and Company as a carter. He followed into his father's footsteps and although left for a period of time, he had returned to work with the drilling machine and notched up a staggering 66 years service! The firm's original representative, Mr. Frater, was also retained with his role to find new markets for the company. This investment in people as well as machinery meant the continued survival of one of the most important names in the history of industry into the 20th century.

In October 1895 Hipkins issued a circular intimating that the James Watt and Company was open for business. His draft letter to the secretary reads:

> *We should be glad to have a recurrence of your enquiries for steam engines, pumping engines, minting machines, lathes etc. as per margin. We have refitted our works and foundry with the most up to date appliances and are consequently in an exceptional position for turning out high class machining at the shortest notice.*[9]

New letterheads were printed that not only referred to W. & T. Avery Limited but also referred to the company being the *Proprietors of JAMES WATT & CO. LATE BOULTON & WATT, ENGINEERS.*[10] Hipkins also had printed letterheads for the James Watt & Co. which included images of steam engines, Soho Foundry, Boulton & Watt and the elephant trademark.[11]

The activities of the famous Soho Foundry drew much public and press attention, something Hipkins was always concerned about, none-the-less perhaps some good could come from it. The Birmingham Daily Post duly reported Avery's new purchase:

> *SOHO WORKS—We learn that Messrs. W. and T. Avery have taken possession of the Soho Works until recently occupied by Messrs. James Watt and Co. Since purchasing the freehold land*

and buildings they have acquired the goodwill and entire plant and machinery, also the patterns and drawings of the late firm. Such as the old workmen who as have not found employment will be glad to learn that Messrs. Avery are now making arrangements to continue the business lately carried on by James Watt and Co. in the reconstruction and repair of engines and machines. The extensive block of buildings now known as the erecting and fitting shops being in good condition, will be retained for that purpose; but we understand that the whole of the old buildings are to come down, as for their business (the manufacture of weighing machines &c.) Messrs. Avery intend to erect new foundries, workshops and warehouses.[12]

The report was partly true but was very positive regarding James Watt and Co. which was important. There had been some deep-rooted resentment in the town that the old firm had closed and that the foundry itself might totally disappear. There was more to this feeling than simply nostalgia. Industry had been swiftly changing over the last twenty years from a patriarchal to a cold professional business structure and age-old practices were being replaced. The loss of one of the country's most important firms was seen by many as another nail in the coffin of traditional working. It would be a recurring theme as the site was developed.

One of the key factors, which led to the purchase of the Soho Foundry, was that it offered superior transport arrangements to any of the existing Avery sites. The London North Western Railway ran along the southern edge of the site, with a railway siding running into the works ending next to the pattern shop and offices. Like the canal basin this would be very useful to transfer material from the other sites; however, the rails were in a poor state and would have to be replaced. Hipkins felt that such a large site should have more rail tracks (mainly narrow gauge) running through it so that horse hauled trucks could be used to move material between the various shops. Footpaths and general road surfaces were in poor condition and these needed to be paved. Work on these began in late October 1895 with the private roads and paths closed to the public on November 5 and 6 while the new tracks and paving were laid. With the completion of the roads and the laying of new tracks there was nothing to stop the redevelopment of Soho Foundry. To onlookers the speed of the changes was reminiscent of the incredible speed in which the foundry had been originally constructed, and as 1895 drew to a close the onlookers could scarcely have imagined just how quickly Soho would be transformed into a modern weighing scale production facility.

Hipkins appointment as managing director meant that he could now push through his plans for the site with little if any opposition. With the Engineering Department in full operation it was found that additional facilities were required and a galvanised shed was constructed. Opposite the cottages in Foundry Row were two fields which were let to a farmer who grew crops in them. He was paid £10 compensation with part of the land being cleared to build the timber shed, an incredibly long building with a rail link. The rest of the land was cleared to prepare for the construction of office buildings. These buildings would house the managing director and the administrative staff behind which would be a warehouse and japanning shop. Corser designed a spectacular building with a large clock tower acting as the main feature for the entrance. The problem for Hipkins of the design was the cost estimated at £12,000, which included £200 for ornamental work and £3,000 for the clock tower! Hipkins removed the clock tower idea altogether and instead opted for keeping the old clock tower in the James Watt & Company offices. He also insisted on modifications to the plans of the warehouse insisting that the interior walls be constructing using 120,000 reclaimed bricks from the demolished buildings, the damp courses could be built using old slates reducing the cost of the whole set of buildings to £7,200.[13]

To the right of the cottages the land was used for the erection of the machine, brassworkers' and counter machine shops. These were of the same basic design as the other buildings and comprised of eight parallel workshops. Awdry had the usual role of supervising the work with Corser drawing up plans. Following Avery's poor experience with the heating system in the smithy, Awdry considered a new system for the counter machine shop, and following a visit to *Nettlefolds, Rotherham and Company* and to the *Dunlop Company* where he examined their heating systems he opted for using a ducted air system. Behind the cottages stables were built with an entrance onto Foundry Lane, these would house the horses that were used to transport carts loaded with material to the railway stations and local firms, as well as the horses used on site to pull wagons on Soho's ever growing network of rail tracks linking all of the facilities with each other. More land was also purchased, three acres at a cost of £750 (following a dispute) was obtained in order to extend the site as and when necessary.

The survey of the canal basin and wharves arrived just before Christmas 1895 and it was not happy reading the basin needed to be completely excavated and relined. Hipkins, during his inspection, thought the canal might be useful for transporting material from the other Avery sites to Soho, and once the smithy and foundry were up and running it would be needed to bring in raw materials. Therefore it was a logistical necessity to get the basin up and working as quickly as possible and thus a contract was placed with *J. Harley and Son* to carry out the work scheduled to begin in early 1896. The survey also discovered that the canal itself was leaking and the tow paths were in poor condition. Hipkins politely requested to the *Birmingham Canal Company* that they make their canal watertight! The canal company agreed but complained that the water they supplied from the canal to the foundry for use in the works and for steam engines was being wasted, and unless Avery's rectified the matter they would cut the water supply in 14 days! Parts of the works had been silent since the closure and a lot of water was simply draining away, so Awdry arranged for a pump to be hastily installed to rectify the problem by pumping the water back into the canal. Hipkins was concerned that the canal company could prevent the foundry from operating properly, if at all, by simply cutting the water supply; he needed to remove a potential strangle hold. He ordered that additional water be found in case their supply was threatened in the future. Bore holes were drilled and water was found at a depth of fourteen feet. A well was dug on April 12th, 1896 producing 3,000 gallons per hour! He also brought in *J. Isler and Company* from London to advise on installing an artesian water supply, and a tender was accepted for a water main to be connected with *South Staffordshire Waterworks Company*. Nothing and no-one would be allowed to prevent Avery's from operating. Although water was plentiful now, problems still arose, the site had two ponds which, acted as reservoirs of water (one for boilers and one for cooling equipment), and one of these ponds had caused corrosion in some steam boilers which had to be replaced.

The original plan to make full use of the canal and rail links to transfer machinery from the other Avery sites to Soho did not come to fruition. The other sites had poor access to such links and the majority of equipment was transferred across the midlands by horse and cart. It was a slow laborious process that required detailed planning to ensure that Soho could receive the material as it arrived. This upheaval did cause some problems in weighing machine production, but that could not be helped, Hipkins could not stress too greatly upon his managers that round the clock working to install equipment was essential to reduce the impact of the move. Indeed to Hipkins it was like a military exercise with teams of men (and boys) working together on specific tasks. Carts that delivered machinery to Soho were sent back to the other sites not empty as he had before witnessed, but loaded with materials that the other sites needed, whether it be completed castings or tools or even people themselves! Never before since the building of the foundry had there been so much movement of people and equipment. Workers at the Tangye's factory virtually next door would watch in amazement as the never-ending trains of carts moved to and from Soho. Tangye was one of the most famous names in Birmingham; the engineering works producing hydraulic rams had made world headlines when their equipment was used to launch the S.S. *Great Eastern*. Being neighbours to Soho Foundry there had always been a close relationship with the historic site and Avery's take over of the plant had changed nothing. Hipkins himself was impressed by Tangye's business methods and knew that he could rely on his neighbours to help out in the event of a crisis. Normally, this might mean a couple of extra hands or a quick loan of some heavy engineering equipment while Hipkins' own machinery was being repaired. This business friendship was not uncommon in Birmingham and the Black Country and was often evident between dissimilar firms. Hipkins was soon to be very thankful for this relationship.

By 1898 the new Soho Foundry was virtually complete and world wide attention was upon the site, something that Hipkins cleverly played on for the rival scale-makers were not in the news as often as Avery's, and the press were courted in what appeared to be a reluctant manner. Journalists from various parts of the globe visited Soho in a manner reminiscent of the days when royalty and notaries from around the world would visit the old Soho Manufactory in the days of Boulton and Watt. *The Ironmonger* magazine constantly kept its readers (who were mostly trade) up to date as the site developed and visits from engineering societies and institutions kept the focus firmly on Avery's. One particular visit pleased Hipkins no end, although to those in Avery's who felt that Hipkins was becoming too powerful, it was a visit that would dash any hopes that Hipkins would only be a temporary appointment. It was a visit in Spring 1898 by a journalist of the *Canadian Trade Review*. His report published in May of the same year clearly illustrates how Soho Foundry had developed since 1895:

W. & T. AVERY, LIMITED

As an example of British Commercial expansion the business of W. & T. Avery, Limited of the Soho Foundry, Birmingham, England is especially striking. This colossal business was established 168 years ago in a small shop in Digbeth, Birmingham, where steelyards only were made. Today the works cover 25 acres of ground and every class of weighing apparatus from a 100-ton locomotive weighbridge down to the finest scientific balance to be operated "in vacuo" is made. The company have a special department for manufacturing their patent automatic machines, which accurately weigh all substances from 100 grains of powder up to 2000lbs. of coal at each discharge, and unerringly record their own weighings, and they have also constructed large machines which weigh 80 tons or 180,000 lbs. of coal per hour. Messrs. Avery buy only raw materials. Every part of the manufactures for which they are so celebrated all over the world is made and finished in works which embrace as many as sixteen different trades. In the Forge, 24 steam hammers dash out steel forgings of strange shapes at a single blow. In the Foundry, (where 500 men are employed), huge tubs of molten iron are carried about over one's head by mechanism of great power and speed. In the Machine Room, long ranges of the most recent automatic tools are turning out parts by the thousand on the interchangeable principle. The Weighbridge Department consists of 3 huge bays fitted up with every modern convenience for handling and manipulating heavy pieces. There are 80 weighbridges set out under construction in three rows including one locomotive engine weigher for testing the pressure on each pair of wheels. This huge machine has 10 distinct weighing tables with a capacity of 100 tons. It was accurately machined on every working and meeting part and so designed as to be capable of testing every known type of locomotive engine, a result hitherto unachieved. Other departments are devoted to platform machines, personal weighing machines, counter scales of endless variety, agate and other beams, wood working, Japanning, electro-plating etc., etc. Messrs. Avery make their own gas for manufacturing purposes, while the works are lighted by electricity, generated from a beautifully fitted up central station.They have their own telephone exchange, so that every manager, foreman, and clerk can inter-communicate without leaving their offices.Great bays of areas of 40,000 square feet are ventilated in summer and heated in winter by a special system of air currents. In fact, Messrs. Avery have spared nothing to bring these immense works into the foremost rank as regards labour saving machinery and system of working for the purpose of reducing the cost of production, while the health and convenience of their employees have been studied in ways which have not space to detail.We must not omit to mention that in 1895, Messrs. Avery acquired the world-renowned engineering business of Messrs. James Watt & Co., late Boulton & Watt, founded in 1757 by the great James Watt, which they carry on in conjunction with their own business, and at the moment, are busy on important contracts for pumping engines for a foreign government, and mining machinery for one of the dependencies.It is at the celebrated Soho Foundry, that Messrs. Avery have consolidated their different departments. But they have branches and repairing shops in all the principle towns in the United Kingdom and local factories in London and Glasgow. As they employ between 2,000 and 3,000 hands, they may claim to be the largest makers of weighing apparatus in the world.The enormous responsibility of this gigantic undertaking rests upon the shoulders of Mr. W.E. Hipkins, the Managing Director, to whose skill, interprise (sic), and experience, much of the company's success is due. It is not easy to imagine one man able to control and direct so vast an enterprise. But Mr. Hipkins apparently finds it an easy task, if we may judge from the success which has attended the company since it came under his direction.[14]

The report is glowing and the reporter was greatly impressed although it is clear he was fed much information. There were many within the company that would find the line: *while the health and convenience of their employees have been studied in ways which have not space to detail,* somewhat an exaggeration. Hipkins had installed better heating and ventilation equipment and had installed more efficient machinery, but this was not for the convenience of the employees, this was for the convenience of the company. Workmen who still paid for the privilege of using certain machines soon found that they had to pay more for this privilege. T. Payne used a Universal wood-working machine and found that he had to pay an increase of 5% for its use on the grounds that his piece rate earnings would increase with the greater productivity made possible by the new machine.[15] Hipkins had improved some of the facilities for the workforce such as the toilets converted to water having been the original sand closets. The proposed custom-built canteen never materialised on the grounds of cost, and this following an inspection of the canteen facilities at Cadbury's chocolate factory. Corser's final act was to consider designs submitted by local ironfounders for the factory gates to be placed in the newly built entrance on Foundry Lane. Hipkins reviewed Corser's final bill and declared to the board that Corser " . . . has incurred unnecessarily . . . heavy charges", and had the final settlement reduced by £16![16]

Unlike Matthew Boulton a hundred years previously, Hipkins made no great speeches to the workforce followed by a stupendous feast. It was simply a matter of continuation; in fact throughout the whole building programme Soho Foundry had at least one department operational so that the foundry had been stone cold for only a few weeks since it had opened in 1796. A new era had begun, and it began dramatically. In May 1898 a fire broke out in the pattern shop. The new sprinkler system was activated and three dozen buckets and two hand pumps were deployed to tackle the blaze. An old fire engine (inherited from James Watt and Company) was brought in to help fight the fire that was raging out of control and workmen played hoses onto the flames.[17] Hipkins saw that Soho itself could be in danger unless something was done quickly; he called on Tangye's assistance and their five fire brigades raced to the scene and saved the day. Over £3,500 worth of damage was caused to the pattern shop with twenty-two pattern makers losing their tools valued at £300.[18] As was the tradition of the day, workmen provided their own tools and in most cases were uninsured for the loss. The Board of Directors made a donation of £25 to a special fund set up to help the workmen replace their much needed tools.

Hipkins had achieved much in a short space of time. The Soho Foundry had been redeveloped, Avery's were now more commonly known than it had before, and he, William Edward Hipkins had by great determination, strength of purpose and unbelievable energy made it all happen. The Spirit of Soho lived on.

CHAPTER 11

THE HOME REVOLUTION

A good General, a well-organised system, good instruction, and severe discipline, aided by effective establishment, will always make good troops, independently of the cause for which they fight.

—Napoleon Maxim number 56.

Hipkins never expected to be liked by the workforce but he did hope to at least win their respect. The Reverend Bevan stated that the hard worker had nothing to fear of Hipkins, but those who were lazy had much to fear. His managers had felt the full weight of his intentions as soon as he had arrived. Although he had very firm ideas for the general workforce he had decided not to sweep all before him, which might lead to complete disaffection of the workforce, leading to strike action, or even worse, resignations with men moving to rival scale makers such as Pooley's, who would relish an opportunity to knock Avery's out of the market. Whether the bomb attack had an effect on his decision to only gradually change things on the shop floor can only be guessed at, but it must have had a deep impact on him.

Soon after he became a director he suggested to the board that the foremen should be given one week's paid holiday at Easter, plus the Easter, Christmas and Whitsun holidays. It was also agreed that at Hipkins' discretion foreman would be paid during their absence due to sickness at the rate of one week at full pay and then three weeks at half pay. This would encourage people to work harder for greater benefits and it would put the foremen on-side. Hipkins wanted to tackle the fundamental issues as to why Avery's had become very inefficient over the years. He wanted to reduce or eradicate the age old working practices that in themselves did not lead to poor workmanship but made the finished product more expensive than it should be. Time keeping was a major bug bear for Hipkins and was one of the major causes of inefficiency. Even though a timekeeper operated at Avery's it was clear that many workmen still came and went as they saw fit. The boys and apprentices were forced to cover for them, and indeed complete the work of leading hands who spent time in the pub. Hipkins wanted to introduce the newly available *time-clocking* machines that had started to become common place in the factories of the United States, and were now making an impact in the UK. The board was very unsure about the idea. Chamberlain felt that it made a clear statement that the workforce could not be trusted. Hipkins argued that they couldn't and that the pretence of trust had gone on long enough. He felt that it was plainly unfair that in some instances the under-hands and apprentices were actually doing far more than their fair share of the work for less money than the leading hands who preferred the pub. It was decided (after much debate) that the foremen would have their times recorded using a timesheet in the short term, with time recording apparatus being installed in a year's time.[1] Hipkins as per usual, wasted no time; within a year he purchased some time-clock machines from the *British Bundy Clock Company*. The company offered for sale a time-clock system based on the patented designs of Willard Bundy an American clock maker who had begun selling the machines to factory owners in the USA. The system required workers to 'clock-in' using a special key in much the same way night-watchmen clocked on during their rounds. Hipkins had the machines installed for a trial period. The key system was somewhat awkward, and following the trial Hipkins had them removed and replaced by *Rochester Card Recorders* produced by the *Willard & Frick Company* of Rochester New York.[2] This system is the one everyone has come to know as *the* clock-machine which was invented by Daniel Cooper in 1894. It used a card that was stamped indicating the time that the worker arrived; the card was then placed in a rack marked 'IN'. At the end of shift the worker would then clock out and place the card in another racked marked 'OUT'; thus, at a glance the manager could see who was in and who was absent. The first machine was placed in the Platform Machine Shop, followed a few weeks later by eight more machines being installed in the works.[3] The age of the time clock was well and truly here and Hipkins was keen to be seen as one of its champions.

The workforce was at first bemused then horrified. Many commented that the money could have been better spent by increasing wages![4] Hipkins, however, was determined to continue his reforms. He reduced the working week for the foundrymen from 54 to 53 hours with the cost of the loss of the hour being shared between workforce and Avery's. Hipkins then arranged for a ballot to be held to decide whether the working day should start at 6.30am or 7am. Hipkins agreed to abide by the ballot and duly the majority voted for a 6.30 start. Two foremen, Way and Birch, refused to abide by the new start times and came in at 7am. They were warned on several occasions with Hipkins sending word that he would give them a chance to get used to the new start time. They refused, leaving Hipkins with no room to manoeuvre; they were sacked. There was little that could be done for them as the rest of the workforce (save for the carpenters who had a separate time agreement) had abided by the ballot. The workforce, like the departmental managers a couple of years previously, had found Hipkins unblinking.

The departmental managers had come on board to Hipkins way of thinking either willingly as in the case of Allinson, or begrudgingly as in the case of several others. They were all, however, rewarded for their loyalty being granted an extra week's paid holiday. Hipkins had set up a structured system whereby improvement in position meant clearly defined improvements in conditions of service, something that had been lacking under the Averys. Although this may have appealed to those workmen that wished to improve themselves, to most (and generally these were the older workmen) the only issue that interested them was wages.

John & Edwin Wright's works at Garrison Street (*Author's collection*)

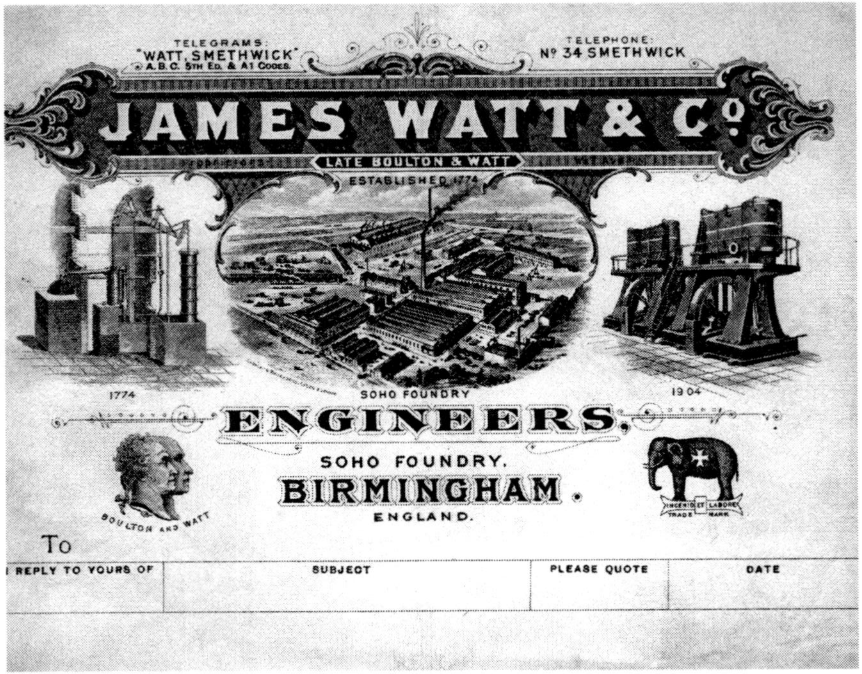

James Watt & Company letter-head (*Avery Historical Museum*)

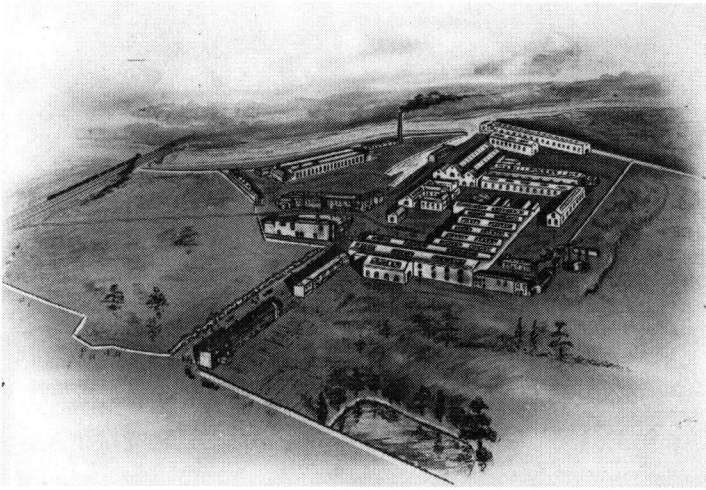

Soho Foundry 1894 *(Avery Historical Museum)*

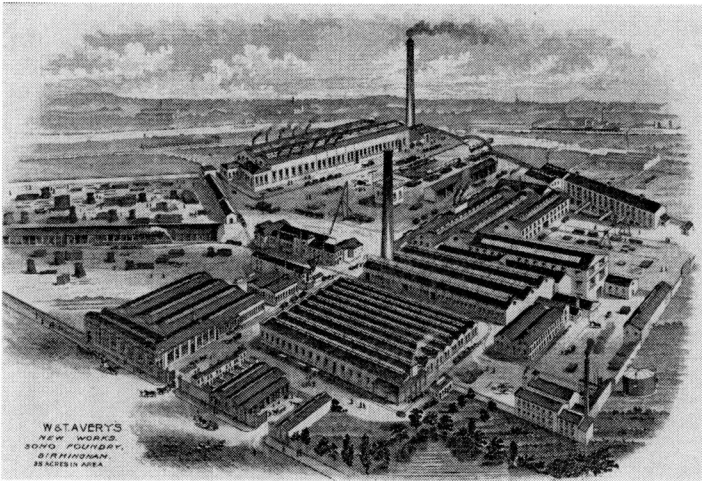

W&T.AVERY'S
NEW WORKS.
SOHO FOUNDRY.
BIRMINGHAM.
38 ACRES IN AREA

Soho Foundry 1899 *(Avery Historical Museum)*

Soho Foundry Entrance 1907 (*Avery Historical Museum*)

W. & T. Avery Fire Brigade

(Avery Historical Museum)

James Watt & Company, Soho Foundry
(Avery Historical Museum)

First intake of the Faculty of Commerce at Birmingham University (*Avery Historical Museum*)

Avery's controversial window advertisement

(Avery Historical Museum)

George Allinson, Avery's Glasgow Branch Manager
(Avery Historical Museum)

Henry Johnstone Avery
(Avery Historical Museum)

Hipkins was accused by J.T. Burford of failing to honour piecework agreements and of failing to pay the trade union/employers' federation agreed district rates.[5] Hipkins had cut piecework rates when earnings rose, and when new machine tools improved productivity the rates were cut again! This infuriated the workforce, especially the underhands. Hipkins had not altered the system where the leading hands employed their own helpers (often their own sons), and when these underhands complained about the loss of earnings Hipkins (or more likely the General Manager at Soho, Richard Gibbs) pointed out that the responsibility was with their leading hands who paid them and not Avery's. What was worse was that payment was not made for wasted work, even when it might not be the fault of the workman whose wages were being docked. The issue reached breaking point in the Summer of 1899 when Matthew Holmes had 7/3 deducted from his wage packet to replace 40 steels that he could not account for. This was the latest of many instances when money was deducted from wage packets, only this time Holmes decided to take Avery's to court. Holmes solicitor, Norris Foster, explained that his client had been employed at Avery's for ten years and that it came as a complete surprise when on July 8th 1899 he found his wage packet was 7/3 short. Mr. C.F. Vachell representing Avery's stated that Mr. Holmes had been given 240 steels in order to make twenty-four levers. Holmes made seventeen levers (using 200 steels) and found he needed more steels so he duly went to get some. The stores man refused to give him more, and thus he had to hunt around the workshop until he found some to complete his work. Vachell explained that this meant that 40 steels were still missing and Holmes was deducted the 7/3 to pay for them. In a scene that would not have been out of place in a TV court drama, another workman from Avery's admitted he had some of Holmes steels for use on another job! The case was immediately dismissed.[6] It was clear that the level of control on the shop floor was still below standard. Hipkins was not happy with the way the whole incident had been handled. New procedures were put into place to ensure that steels (and any other materials) were booked out and in correctly, and that any discrepancies should be highlighted immediately.

The level of distrust between the shop floor workforce and senior management cannot be over emphasised, it was a far cry from the days of the Avery brothers. One of the problems of the existing system was that it was based on time or piece rates without any formal written agreement, which led to both sides interpreting the rates as they saw fit. Hipkins actually preferred that there were written agreements with individuals that outlined the hours to be worked, wages to be paid, etc, much along the lines of a modern contract of employment. A typical example of such an agreement was that of Harry Barber. He began his contracted employment at Avery's in 1886 at age 18 having spent 5 years working with them under apprenticeship. The agreement was for three years employment with seven days written notice to be given by each side. His wages were set out at 3½d an hour in the first six months, rising at 6 monthly intervals to 6d an hour in his last months. Barber's conditions were laid out stating that he was:

> . . . *to serve the Company in their trade and in any and every branch thereof and in any other lawful way in which he may be directed by the Company or any other trade or business, but will devote his whole time and attention to his duties under this Agreement and he the said Harry Barber will also do and perform all work which he may be directed to do from time to time according to the best of his skill, attention and ability. The Company shall furnish the said Harry Barber with a shop in which and tools with which to discharge the work, which he may be required to do. The said Harry Barber shall do his best to preserve the prosperity of the Company from waste or injury and will promote its business and will keep its secrets.* [7]

With agreements being made with individuals there was no collective agreements and the practice of demarcation was not in evidence. Barber's wages were agreed up front and any changes would have to be negotiated after his three years employment. Barber successfully negotiated for further agreements eventually working for Avery's for over fifty years! Such arrangements did not prevent requests for wage increases. As the economy fluctuated, so too did the need for an income that could keep pace with the increase in the cost of living. Individuals could make a request in writing to the board or the Managing Director and there was no lack of requests! Foremen applied personally, such as J. T. Burford, who placed a request in 1898 only to be told that he was already receiving the maximum pay for a foreman—£4 per week. Burford's request had been prompted by his extra expenditure due to the move to Soho and Hipkins understood this, thus, he was granted an extra £25 to assist him. [8] The move to Soho had hit a number of workmen, and the Platform Machine Shop workers made a formal complaint about the increased travelling costs as they commuted to Soho instead of Digbeth. They were granted an extra one-shilling per week during July and August 1897 to assist in the cost of furniture removals. Hipkins was keen to encourage the workmen to move nearer the factory. This was a very common feature of working life in the Black Country over many generations, as mass transportation was not ideal at the latter part of the 19th century with some workmen having to leave their homes at 5am to be in work for 6.30. Hipkins had his own personal transport, but for most workers it was the omnibus, the train, walk, some combination of all three or by bicycle. It was because of the transport problems that the Late Henry Avery had considered building a number of workmen's houses close to a new factory. Walter Chamberlain was concerned over the transport problem, and with his brother Joseph was a keen advocate of better roads and transport systems across Birmingham. Hipkins, of course, wanted to be sure that the extra pay was used to assist in the move to Soho. As we recall it was in the Platform Machine Shop where the first clock machines were installed, so that he could see that everyone was on time and, of course, they could no longer use the excuse of having to travel farther having been reimbursed for their trouble. The Platform Machine Shop workers did fair better than the moulders who requested a one shilling a week increase in 1897 and didn't even receive any response.[9] Hipkins' and the board's view was to ignore requests and see what happened. In most cases the requests were not followed up by the workmen and the issue could then be forgotten.

Hipkins was happy to reward good work, and although he took a tough stance on wage demands it was also true that he would grant certain 'bonuses' for workmen who had done some conspicuous work.[10] Of course, Hipkins could not let it be known that it was he who had added some shillings to a pay packet, and thus many workmen (who probably credited Walter Chamberlain for the generosity) never realised that, in fact, it was the dreaded Managing Director Hipkins who had been generous. Hipkins liked the idea of being seen as the tough man in charge again freely quoting Napoleon:

> *"They think I am stern, even hardhearted. So much the better-this makes it unnecessary for me to justify my reputation. My firmness is taken for callousness. I shall not complain, since*

this notion is responsible for the good order that is prevailing,
so that there is nothing that needs to be repressed."

Hipkins' vision for the workforce was that they would be given gainful employment utilising their skills for the benefit of the company, which in turn would benefit themselves and their families through decent wages (although 'decent' is a subjective term). He did not subscribe to a paternal management, he believed that the workmen should be able to stand on their own two feet and not blame others for their own misfortunes; rather, they should find a way to work themselves out of any problems that life would throw at them. Loyalty was of great importance, "One loyal workman was worth five disloyal workmen" he told Allinson.

It is certain that his attitude to the workforce in his first two years as managing director was used to see who was loyal and who was not. One thing that he needed most of all was an ardent lieutenant on the shop floor, and this he had in Richard R. Gibbs the General Manager of the Soho Works. Gibbs extolled the type of loyalty and commitment to the company that Hipkins was looking for. Through thick and thin times, and with little personal consideration, Gibbs had served the Averys. Hipkins used him to instil discipline in the workforce, and to ensure that his policies were carried out throughout every department at Soho Foundry. Gibbs mere presence on the shop floor as he made his rounds was enough to snap workmen into shape. Gibbs was not the intellectual type, he was a tough workman who had dirtied his hands to reach his position, and he expected everyone to be just as dedicated as himself. Gibbs liked Hipkins, and on his arrival was delighted to see a strong force in the position that he knew would be of benefit to his own career. In the days of Henry Avery, Gibbs had often been held back from exercising what the Avery brothers thought was "excessive discipline", even so the reforms that had been made to bring the workforce into line prior to Hipkins' arrival had the feel of Gibbs' hand. Hipkins saw Gibbs as the ideal man to be the public face of his policies. Even after his term at Wright's he still felt uncomfortable in front of the workforce, or for that matter any large group of people, and the work's excursions had shown that he was not by his nature a man who could talk to the workforce. Gibbs had known many of the men at Avery's since they had been boys and was quite comfortable walking the shop floor and he certainly seemed to relish confrontation. Hipkins quoted Napoleon to Gibbs to make it clear how he felt on motivation of the workforce "There are two levers for moving men, interest and fear."

The parcel bomb may have been an isolated response to the stricter regime, but in October 1899 there was another 'isolated incident'. The Mill Lane Works had been transferred to Soho Works and the shell of the buildings were awaiting a buyer. The main four storey building a good seventy yards long by thirty wide, was standing quiet and empty (save for a few old machines). In the afternoon of October 5ᵗʰ a fire broke out which quickly swept through the building. The alarm was raised by Mr. T. Bolton, a local tradesman who saw smoke pouring out of windows on the Rea Street side of the block. The fire brigade raced to the scene from the Central Fire Station, chasing through the busy streets with bells ringing loudly scattering horses and carriages. On arrival at Avery's the firemen saw that the whole block was ablaze. The building was clearly lost but there was a fear that the fire could spread beyond the Avery complex to other establishments. Brigade Superintendent Alfred Tozer requested more fire appliances and the brigades from Harborne and Balsall Heath raced across the city to assist. The flames grew incredibly fierce, and one by one the floors of the main building collapsed throwing sparks and flaming debris around causing firemen to run for cover. No sooner had they got back into position when a large chimney began to topple, and again the firemen ran as tons of brickwork collapsed. Girders began to buckle in the intense heat and then collapsed bringing down the immense roof, debris was thrown in all directions and the firemen now had to tackle secondary ignitions from the flaming material. Neighbouring business began to be affected. *Richardson And Company,* a coach-wheel maker, took the brunt as their fitting shop burst into flames. Nearby, a storeroom owned by *A. Swingler* a cabinet maker took light and the *Fishwick Bakery* began to smoulder. Tradesmen of all kinds—ironworkers, chemists, carpenters and many others fled their premises as the heat grew more intense and the crackle of wooden beams filled the air. Some cottages in Mill Lane were now in danger of being overcome, the occupants began evacuating their possessions and carts arrived in front of the buildings as many hands began to pile on furniture in a desperate attempt to save something. An old man was asleep in bed when the fire started and neighbours burst into his room and rescued him. Still more firemen arrived, and local workmen and police joined-in pouring water on the roofs of buildings that were in close proximity to the fire. An escape ladder was hoisted high into the air, and a fireman smashed through some iron framed windows and directed a hose through the window hoping to quench the flames. Billows of smoke rose from the city centre blocking out the Sun, the area resembled a war zone. Traffic was completely stopped in Digbeth, and crowds of people gathered on the rise of the Bull Ring to observe the scene of destruction. Some distance away in Smethwick workman in the yard at the Soho Foundry saw thick black smoke high in the sky and some distance away. It was so distinct that many stopped what they were doing to look.

The frantic efforts of the many men involved were not in vain. The fire was brought under control although many commented that, had there been a wind that day, then the whole city would have gone up in smoke. Hipkins lamented that he had seen the results of great fires in Chicago and Boston; how ironic that Birmingham may have gone the same way starting at Avery's.

The fire caused £20,000 worth of damage and, incredibly, only minor injuries were received by firemen and no-one was killed. The cause of the fire was a mystery. Three men were employed to look after the buildings, but at the time the fire started they were at dinner. It is possible that the same miscreant who sent the parcel bomb started it; we will never know. If it was deliberate then it actually did Avery's more good than harm, as the firm was very well insured with seven companies and eight policies![11] Insurance companies on the whole were on guard for fires in Birmingham, as earlier in the year one of Avery's rivals *Day and Milward* of Suffolk Street, Birmingham had a fire that seriously damaged their foundry and machine shop. Unlike the Avery fire this one had started in the early hours of the morning, and one has to wonder just how aggressive the trade war had become.[12] Hipkins' must have wondered if there was a disgruntled employee just waiting his chance to strike again. One thing was for sure following two serious fires (Soho and Mill Lane) Hipkins decided that Avery's should have its own fire brigade.

Private fire brigades were the norm at this period run by manufactories or by fire insurance companies, although town brigades were just starting to be formed. Birmingham's Corporation brigade had been formed out of the old *Birmingham United Fire Brigade* and was under the control of the police. However following two major fires[13] the Brigade was separated from the police and re-organized by an ex-Royal Navy man, Alfred Robert Tozer, who ran the brigade under naval style regulations. Hipkins took advice on how to form his fire brigade from Superintendent Tozer and

Tangye's management who had five brigades of their own. These brigades were critical for the fire safety of the region. Although a public fire service operated they had only a very limited number of men and equipment, and in the case of a very serious emergency (such as the Soho and Mill Lane fires) Tozer could call upon the brigades of various manufactories and insurance companies to assist. Tozer's brigades were some distance from Soho, and anyway Soho came under the jurisdiction of Smethwick meaning that Hipkins had to rely on the small town's facility, plus help from other companies such as Tangye's. Hipkins never did like relying on other people thus he formed the Avery Fire Brigade. The works engineer, Goulding, was given the task of actually getting the brigade up and running with a Captain and seven men. The men selected lived within 500 yards of Soho and had ". . . sober and respectable habits."[14] The brigade had around 18 drills per year with the men being paid 1/6 an hour for each drill, the Captain 3/3, and 1/—and 3/1 respectively for attendance at a fire.[15] The brigade operated in a very professional manner with uniforms supplied by Avery's and special insignia purchased from *Hudson's Whistles*.[16] Patrols were made of the Soho works between 6pm and 6am. These patrols entered each of the workshops and ensured there was nothing wrong. Anything, no matter how slight that appeared out of the ordinary was recorded in a logbook and dealt with the next day. The japanning store received special attention with the temperature of the store being recorded on each visit. The brigade's equipment included a fire engine that was used to pump water from the canal; this engine was tested twice daily with every test being recorded. The brigade was drilled and given a variety of imaginative tests to ensure that they were ready to tackle any foreseeable incident within three minutes of the alarm being raised, and be available to assist with fires outside of Soho works if called upon by other brigades.[17]

The fire brigade, like all the changes Hipkins brought in, were for practical reasons and not just simply because he could change things, and yet these changes had caused some resentment in the workforce. Hipkins' view on the way that Avery's workforce should behave was not purely geared only to benefit the company. He believed that the benefits should be mutual and the workforce should be allowed to benefit from the changes taking place. He was all too aware that the changes were making some of the workforce feel very isolated, and he needed to make everyone feel apart of Avery's. He also felt that the British workman in general was unprogressive, due mainly to pressure applied by his peers or trade unions.

It was true that in many firms workmen were often prevented from doing better by union rules, or by leading hands who wished to control the level of output to suit their own ends. Avery's had no such restrictions and had always felt that their workmen could adopt whatever methods they saw fit that would improve production. Hipkins wanted to develop this further. As the firm was becoming more centralised he wanted to utilize the best practice of workmen across the company as a whole. To this end in 1900 he devised a form of suggestion scheme. Such schemes had been in operation in many firms, being run on informal lines with boxes situated on shop floors where a variety of suggestions (some impractical, some obscene) were forwarded to the management. Hipkins, however, devised something very different; a formal procedure for submitting ideas and suggestions with rewards for those whose suggestions were implemented. Hipkins had not dreamed the whole idea up himself, it was an idea he had seen in the United States. Chamberlain and Wilfred Williams had also seen such schemes in operation in U.S. factories and it offered a freer thinking attitude to work. Workmen on the shop floor were surprised to note that the managers, foremen and chief draughtsmen were exempt from the scheme. Hipkins felt that those who had reached managerial level were already being paid to make suggestions! Thus workmen were encouraged to submit ". . . new ideas, inventions and improvements in processes"[18] to a special Awards Committee which then scrutinized them and either implemented or rejected the ideas. Hipkins outlined the grounds on which a worker could submit his or her idea:

a. That he has introduced a new design or principle with advantage to the company.

b. That he has either invented or introduced a new machine or hand-tool into the works with advantage to the company.

c. That he has improved any existing machine or hand-tool with advantage to the company.

d. That he has applied any existing machine or hand-tool to a new class of work with advantage to the company.

e. That he has discovered or introduced any new method of carrying on or arranging work more economically or to better advantage of the company.

f. Or, generally, that he has made any change by which the work of the factory is improved in quality or rendered more economical in cost.

The idea was so novel that a reporter from the Sunday Telegraph took an interest and wrote an article about the scheme comparing British and American working methods. The article took a strong anti-trade union line, blaming trade unionism for the ever-growing lead of American manufacturers.[19]

The initial response to the scheme was disappointing and only 19 claims were made in two years with awards to the total value of £8 5/—being paid out. The workforce's mistrust of the company was deeper felt than at first thought. The whole board put their heads together to try and fathom out the lack of response. Hipkins re-launched the scheme in October 1904 with some modifications. The launch involved placing posters around the branches outlining the scheme's objectives, eligibility, the prizes that could be won and the procedure for taking part. The board, and Hipkins in particular were at pains to stress that *W. & T. Avery's Suggestions System* was open to everyone and that all suggestions no matter how small would be considered. The prizes were very impressive as described on the poster[20]:-

PRIZES. A prize of **5/**—will be given for Every
suggestion adopted, and will be paid on adoption.
In addition to above 5/—prizes,
TEN SPECIAL PRIZES will be given every Quarter
for the best Ten Suggestions Adopted, as follows:-

1 First Prize of £5.
2 Third Prizes of £2 each.
1 Second Prize of £3.
6 Fourth Prizes of £1 each.

The posters were clearly marked *W.E. Hipkins* so everyone knew that he supported the scheme personally. Within a few weeks 400 suggestions had arrived and 27 awards made with each person receiving a small presentation card with their monetary award.[21] It was a tremendous success and it was clear to Hipkins that the workforce needed clear and direct information if any such scheme was to be accepted. It was also a clear indication that many on the shop floor were, indeed, receptive to new ideas but it took time and effort to get them enthused. For Hipkins though, that moment of fulfilment when his suggestion scheme became a success was in the future. As the twentieth century began Hipkins' focus was on taking Avery's to heights never imagined by any Avery.

CHAPTER 12

INVASION

In forming the plan of a campaign it is requisite to forsee everything the enemy may do, and to be prepared with the necessary means to counteract it. Plans of campaign may be modified ad infinitum according to circumstances, the genius of the general the character of the troops and the features of the country.

—*Napoleon Maxim number 2*

It is not too difficult to imagine Hipkins sitting in his office, paperwork neatly laid out for his perusal, his writing pad always at hand. He was master of Avery's. He had surrounded himself with men of influence and power and he had brought the workforce more or less into line. The branches whether local or in far distant towns, had also been brought under control with his ardent lieutenants ensuring his orders were carried out, and sending to him monthly reports on sales, expenditure and other local intelligence. With a secure home base, and no fear of threats from within, he could now safely plan his next campaign on behalf of Avery's. Henry Avery had broken the cosy link between the various scale making firms which had gone against the traditions of business. Even now the Chamberlains, Wilfred Williams, George Cartland and many others were socialising with the directors of other companies, some of whom were rivals. At these social gatherings be they dinners, cricket matches or rounds of golf some business was discussed and gentlemen's agreements made. Hipkins was not a golfer, or a cricketer. He was a businessman.

In 1895 there were many scale making firms in the country, most of which were a lot smaller than Avery's, but these small firms were strong competitors in their respective towns and counties. Hipkins wanted Avery's to totally dominate the country, and with his insistence on direct trading this meant he would have to compete in every county with the local scale makers. To set up new manufacturing and repair plants in each area would be expensive and would take time, so Hipkins simply applied the strategy of buying-out Avery's competitors across the country. Scotland was a particular area where there were too many firms chasing too few orders. In 1897 Hipkins bought *Alexander Wood and Sons* of the Baltic Works Glasgow in order to support Avery's Glasgow Branch. This was an old scale making firm having been established in 1720 by James Liddell, an uncle of Alexander Wood's grandfather. The quality of their scales was at the lower end of the market, although they had supplied the British Admiralty with platform weighing machines for five years. The press certainly made much of the purchase, although Avery's and Wood referred to the deal as an amalgamation (as is usually the case). Avery's paid over £10,000 for the firm but it was considered to be worth a lot more. Alexander Wood was appointed General Manager of the Glasgow Branch of Avery's, replacing James Miller whose short reign had been a failure. Hipkins thought that Wood's expertise in engineering and of having run his own scale business for many years would make him well equipped to turn around Avery's fortunes north of the border. It had been the Glasgow branch that had caused Hipkins and Gibson so much concern after Hipkins arrival at Avery's, and if he thought that the appointment of Wood would help he was wrong. Wood caused a number of problems, much of it because he seems to have hidden some details of his firm's connections before the sale. Prior to the sale, Wood had opened negotiations with the German scale firm of *Steinfeldt and Hasburg* who wanted Wood to become an agent for the German firm's spring balances. The complication arose as Wood was already the agent for Salter's spring balances in Scotland. Salter's were a local rival of Avery's, although both companies were on good terms and Hipkins actually wrote to Salter's to gauge their attitude to the situation.[1]

Wood was unhappy on having to follow Hipkins' directives and he exaggerated the potential trade in his region, which resulted in the opening of a repair shop in Edinburgh. Wood, it seems, saw the Avery buy-out as an opportunity to improve his own position locally, taking advantage of the Avery name to ingratiate himself on local political and business figures. It worked. He had been appointed to the *Partick Commission Board* in 1891, and in 1897 he was raised to the magistracy on the death of Braillie Gardner. A year later he became Provost of Partick, and soon thereafter made a Justice of the Peace for the County of Lanark! Wood felt himself untouchable and his management of the branch suffered due to his 'official' duties. Hipkins was particularly frustrated by Wood's failure to cut the piece rate of workers at the branch in line with Soho. By October 1898 Hipkins had had enough and sent his very trusted colleague, George Allinson, to the branch in order to 'assist' Wood. Wood thought this was a good idea and never suspected that Allinson was auditing everything Wood did and monitored his every move, reporting back to Hipkins personally. Slowly, Allinson began to control Wood manoeuvring him into a position that left him with few options. By 1899 Wood had virtually retired from the scale making business eventually resigning. Allinson took total control of the branch and the fortunes of the out-post in the north changed for the better. Hipkins must have pondered why he hadn't sent Allinson up there in the first place!

Other purchases were not so fraught. *W. H. Marshall's* of Leicester was purchased and became Avery's Leicester branch followed by *Greenhough and Company* of Liverpool, *W.R. Hingett* and the *Midland Scale Company* of Nottingham. Avery's was taking out competitors in the major towns and replacing them with branches of their own.

The weighing machine manufacturers of Britain looked on in amazement as Hipkins marched into the big towns absorbing firms. Fearing a nationwide take-over by Avery's, the various weighing machine manufacturers arranged a meeting held in London to discuss co-operation essentially forming a cartel. It seems likely that Pooley's were the dominant force behind the cartel idea with the main aim of stopping Avery's domination. Avery's were invited and Hipkins went along. Hipkins was naturally not in favour of such an arrangement, but his agreement to attend the meeting gave the impression to other manufacturers that Avery's might agree to an arrangement that would forestall their branch development. They would be disappointed. It was clear to the scale making industry that Hipkins was not a man to play golf.

Pooley's felt particularly threatened by Avery's moves and decided to fight back. *William Bayliss and Company* was a medium sized weighing machine firm in Brook Street, Smethwick making bakers' cart scales and French counter scales with a turnover in 1897 of around £4,000. Bayliss, seeing an opportunity, offered the business to both Avery and Pooley. Avery's held back from making an offer, and when they did finally make an offer of £2,500 for plant and stock, it was too late—Pooley's had closed the deal! Hipkins appeared to be livid suspecting that Pooley's had done something underhand, probably on a golf course, but the move confirmed that a trade war between Pooley's and Avery's was in full swing with Pooley's landing a firm right on Avery's doorstep. Since Henry Avery had pulled the plug on co-operation, Pooley's had been very belligerent towards Avery's. They had watched as Avery's appointed Hipkins, to them an unknown quantity, and reeled in shock as Hipkins' aggressive approach to trading took shape. The Bayliss deal was not all it seemed. Hipkins had delayed making an offer for a reason, he wanted to see what Pooley's would do. Pooley's had moved quicker than he had expected, but Hipkins' tactic was reminiscent of Napoleon giving high ground to the Russians in order to launch a surprise counter-attack. Hipkins was happy to let Pooley's feel they had out manoeuvred him, for Pooley's had had to spend money they needed elsewhere. When Walter Chamberlain asked Hipkins why he was not acting against Pooley's on the Bayliss deal, Hipkins characteristically replied quoting Napoleon: *"Never interrupt your enemy when he is making a mistake."*

Pooley's had a shortage of funds and had become a private limited company in 1896 following the retirements of Henry Pooley III and Dr. James Wood, in what appears to be in part a reaction to the changes at Avery's. Avery's new Soho works had given the firm great access to transport in particular the railway, Pooley's wanted the same and hunted desperately to find a suitable facility. They settled for the *Albion Works* at Kidsgrove North Staffordshire, and just like Avery's at Soho, Pooley's expanded the Albion Works. This expansion was expensive and Pooley's were struggling to remain in competition with Avery's who always seemed to be one step ahead. To raise more money the firm became a public limited company in 1900 raising £130,000. The board of directors, like Avery's, was small consisting of John Chater (Chairman), James Hines, Lawrence Jacob, John S. Pooley (secretary) and Henry Pooley IV. Lawrence Jacob, who essentially acted as managing director disliked Hipkins intensely and resented his aggressive approach to trading when through co-operation they all could benefit. Jacob had been manager of Pooley's Birmingham Branch and had kept his tabs on Avery's development. It was as much as a fit of pique that he had purchased William Bayliss in order to enter the shop scale market to give Hipkins something to think about. In essence, Pooley's could hardly afford it. In 1901 he upped the ante by transferring the firm's headquarters from Liverpool to Birmingham, although this was partly due to Birmingham's superior transport connections and links to material suppliers. Even with these changes Pooley's were still struggling to keep pace with Avery's, with money being spent at a phenomenal rate to upgrade the Kidsgrove site and to develop branches and repair depots of their own.

Hipkins kept the Pooley's board on their toes as it was not only scale making firms in which Avery's took an interest. In 1899 they purchased *Parnall and Sons* of Bristol who made weighing machines, scales, grocer shop equipment and were shop-fitting specialists. Parnall's had been formed in 1820 and became a limited company 69 years later, after establishing themselves as one of the country's leading shop-fitters. This was a major purchase for Avery's costing £44,750 which included quite a lot of land and various works.[2] The Parnall acquisition would turn out to be one of the best moves made by Hipkins with the merger putting Hipkins on the Parnall board. Parnall's scale designs were eventually adopted as part of the Avery's catalogue, and thus the West Country was now an area well covered by Avery's travelling salesmen.

Right from the beginning of his reign at Avery's Hipkins had put into place his plan for direct trading. With branches now strategically placed across the country he began extending the repair depot network and even opened small shops. This act brought him into direct conflict with the local ironmongers across the country. Hipkins not only wanted to standardise the manufacturing process across the country, he also wanted to standardise the price of the products. As the 20th century was born the same set of Avery Scales would have a different selling price in different towns. This was due to ironmongers fixing their own prices, and the selling practice had been that local ironmongers bought scales from Avery and then sold them locally; the ironmongers would also handle repairs although Hipkins had put a stop to most of that activity. When Avery's began selling directly to the public through their branches and small shops the ironmongers complained bitterly. Hipkins, however, was not to be moved. He argued that the Ironmongers' mark-up was, in fact, making Avery's scales more expensive than they need be, and thus cheaper inferior scales—often imported from Germany, France and United States were being purchased instead. Members of the ironmongery fraternity suggested boycotting Avery's products, but with Avery's now involved in direct trading such action was pointless. Hipkins had placed his troops in position before he commenced the fight.

Another common practice that many ironmongers engaged in was in casting moulds from Avery scales and then making their own from these casts. The copies were grossly inferior and would reflect badly on Avery's. Hipkins wanted to eradicate such practices and to stamp down heavily on all traders that misrepresented Avery's products. As far back as 1895 the *Tobacconists Outfitting Association* of 186 Euston Road, London had to apologise to Avery's and pay £15 in damages after using Avery's scales in their catalogue with the Avery name removed![3] Three years later John Barritt of Burnley was convicted of selling non-Avery machines as Avery ones. If the branch managers had the feeling that Hipkins was looking over their shoulder then the ironmongers understood how they felt, and they didn't like it.

Hipkins was prepared for a long trade war, and also prepared for attacks from other firms and organisations such as the ironmongers and local authorities. In 1904 Derby Town Council was asked why it had purchased scales from Avery's rather than a local firm. The Council's response was simple; Avery's offered a cheaper price. A year later Avery's found themselves under attack from local traders in Yarmouth who complained about Avery's reduced price for a weighbridge. In 1906 *The Halifax Ironmongers' Association* passed a resolution informing Avery's that they should quote list prices and make no discounts when trading with local firms. Hipkins responded by telling the Association that if the ironmongers sold at the agreed price there would be no problems. The Halifax Ironmongers' Association passed the matter to the *National Ironmongers' Federation* which also wrote to Avery's pointing out that its members disliked Avery's methods of trading and their treatment of ironmongers in general, especially as (so the Federation claimed) it was the local ironmongers who had built up Avery's trade in the first place.

Hipkins response was predictable; he had opened branches essentially to deal with repairs, and if the local ironmongers stopped selling inferior products Avery's would not need to sell scales directly. He knew he couldn't lose he had, in fact put the ironmongers in such a position that he could make them an offer they just couldn't refuse and still be able to carry on direct trading and sell through ironmongers at the same time. He offered to sell scales to ironmongers with a special discount so that when they sold them at a price more akin to which Avery's preferred, they would still make a good profit. Avery's agreed to sell their scales to manufactories at a lower discount, thus the ironmongers may still get the trade. The price of the scales remained more or less the same. The magazine *The Ironmonger* even tested Avery's on the arrangement and found that Avery's offered a 33.3% discount to a local ironmonger and only a 17.5% discount to a local manufacturer. Avery's had kept to their deal. It took Hipkins 10 years to control the price of Avery scales nationwide, but it was a victory well worth winning. It was one that had unforeseen repercussions in the market place, for once the recommended retail price for one product had been accepted others were to follow, with many other firms following Hipkins' lead. It was the beginning of the end of local pricing in Great Britain.

Hipkins not only used the branches, repair depots and small shops to trade in Avery Scales, he used them as intelligence gathering centres. Hipkins chaired District Managers' Conferences at Soho at which local issues were discussed and strategies prepared based on local conditions. It was from the branches that workmen would be sent to various ironmongers posing as customers to buy scales and check on the types available and their prices. Catalogues were requested from rival companies around the world and designs and prices compared with Avery's.[4] Some of the requests were made in writing from supposed ironmongers, others from supposed manufactories enabling Hipkins to check on the discounts being offered by his rivals. This form of soft industrial espionage was backed-up by harder methods, which included placing workman inside rival firms to study methods and activities. Often this was carried out in dramatic fashion with an employee being dismissed from Avery's who, therefore, had a grudge to settle. He would then apply to a firm like Pooley's complaining bitterly of his mistreatment at the hands of Avery's, in particular Gibbs and Hipkins.[5] Once employed at Pooley's the employee would work as normal but would let Gibbs know of the activities within Pooley's. One can only guess at the scale of such actions (no pun intended) but Hipkins took a lesson from Napoleon words:

"To get information . . . you have to look for it. Intelligence never comes by itself."[6]

Hipkins also had some good fortune in ex-Pooley employees coming to work for Avery's and bringing with them inside knowledge of Pooley's trading practices. One such employee was J.A. White who in 1896 was a cashier at Pooley's, who told Hipkins the inside details of Avery's failed tender for 20 weighbridges for Barry Docks and Railways in 1896. Pooley's agent for Newport, Mr. Scott, drew £2 from the cashier to pay off one of the Barry Dock Officials who had supplied details of Avery's tender to Scott, and had recommended to his General Manager that the Pooley machines would be better. Pooley's, in fact, were able to charge a higher price than they expected and still won the tender! Hipkins would never forgive Pooley's actions, and Pooley's would live to regret their underhand dealing.

Hipkins was not, however, satisfied with the home market alone. As far as he was concerned the whole world was a market place, and Avery's were to be the world leaders in scale making. As soon as Hipkins became managing director he sent Kenneth Mackenzie on a nine-month tour to the Far East and the pacific visiting along the way Hong Kong, China, India, Australia and many other countries. Mackenzie reported back to Hipkins on the state of the scale trade and what actions he thought would be necessary for Avery's to take control of the markets there. India was an interesting example of the problems Avery's faced in the Far East. The Indians had a remarkable knack for making excellent copies of a wide range of western products. The Indian sub-continent was flooded with guns that appeared to have been made in Birmingham, only on closer inspection was it revealed that they were excellent pirate copies made in one of the many little workshops scattered across the many towns and cities. Madras was a particularly industrious city with Avery scales being duplicated to almost perfection! Avery's trade marks were being infringed as well, and Hipkins ordered that legal action be started to stop the practice. India was a market that looked profitable; the vast and ever growing Indian Railway had the potential to be far more lucrative than Britain's railway contracts. Just like in Britain, India had small traders and merchants that fixed their own prices. If direct trading was to be applied to India then it would have to be on a vast scale and, initially, it would have to be arranged through agents.

Australia was a market well known to Hipkins; his own brassfounding firm had a good trade in that country. Avery's also had a good trade with the country operating through merchant houses. Hipkins, knowing the nature of the Australian business community, decided to appoint agents for Avery's goods. Following a lengthy selection process Hipkins decided upon *Shirley, Clayton and Company* as Avery's agents in Australia. However, it was a short lived arrangement with the agreement being terminated after only twelve months. Kenneth MacKenzie's visit to Australia was used to try and find a replacement for Clayton's, with Hipkins eventually settling on *J. Barre Johnstone and Company* immediately producing results with an order from the Australian State Railways for four weighbridges. In South Africa, Avery's agent was James King. Hipkins decided to expand into the various republics of the country appointing Joseph Walton agent in the Transavaal, Orange River, Cape Colony and Natal. In South America Avery's shared an agent with Nettlefolds, and again the focus was on the railway industry especially that of Argentina.

Europe, although on Avery's doorstep was a difficult market to enter. German and French governments operated strong protectionist policies which kept out many UK firms. In 1897 an Avery's automatic weighing machine received a stamp of approval from the German and Austrian Weights and Measures Authorities. Hipkins as an ardent Francofile was keen to set up a Paris agent. He was successful at signing an agreement with *Amelin and Renaud* for the sale of automatic weighing machines. In 1898 Avery's had the distinction of having their automatic grain weigher passed by the French Weights and Measures Authority—the first such machine to do so. Between 1900 and 1904 Hipkins personally visited many European countries in order to set up trade agreements and agencies with particular emphasis on Norway, Sweden, Denmark, Finland, Italy, Holland, Belgium and Russia. European scale makers began to feel the presence of Avery's. However, unlike their British counterparts they could rely on their respective governments to use tariffs to put a halt to Avery's goods making much of a commercial impact. Even so, Avery's were doing well enough, Hipkins had been clever to ensure that Soho had been up and running before he began his expansion across the globe. Many firms in the past (and since) have found themselves over extending themselves and taking on orders that exceeded their build capacity. Avery's Engineering Department had been substantially upgraded and as already mentioned operated in two forms. Firstly, internally as the *Engineering Department*, and secondly, externally as *James Watt and Company*. Hipkins, by default, was the manager of probably the most famous name in engineering and although he was a hardened businessman, his own sense of history allowed him some flexibility in allowing the old firm to continue although it still had to pay its way. The old firm's problems did not disappear simply because Hipkins re-equipped it; the old problems remained and a succession of managers had tried to make James Watt and Company a success. Between 1895 and 1908 seven mangers had a crack at running the firm. The workforce of Watt's was treated, in general, different to those of Avery's. In 1899 James Watt & Company joined *the*

Birmingham, Wolverhampton and District Engineering Trade Employers Association (BWDETEA) which in turn joined *the National Engineering Trade Employers Association* (NETEA), and Hipkins agreed to abide by national wage rates for engineering workers at Watt's, making a distinction between them and his workers in other departments in Soho. This naturally caused some resentment, although to Hipkins the distinction between the two seemed logical. Hipkins saw the workers at Watt's as being far more flexible and able to transfer to a new product range very quickly—indeed, as the Engineering Department they were already turning out castings for an incredibly wide range of weighing machines. This flexibility was critical as the days when James Watt and Company could count on scores of orders for pumping engines were long gone, and Hipkins was all too eager to find alternative products and markets for the firm.

In 1899 an opportunity presented itself that nearly changed the history of manufacturing in the midlands. William B. Avery was a keen motorist; he had an interest in the French car makers Darracq, owning one himself and encouraged Hipkins to purchase a model. Avery was one of the great pioneers of motor transport, and his influence in Birmingham helped fuel a growing interest in the latest toy of the rich. Hipkins knew Alexandre Darracq when he was making quality bicycles, eventually moving on to motorcycles and then into cars. Avery had seen Darracq's display of vehicles at the Paris Salon in 1895, and discussed supporting the further development of cheap mass produced cars. In Digbeth an Anglo-French motor car company had been formed called *L'Hollier, Gascoigne and Company* importing cars from France for resale. They were interested in producing cars of their own using the latest Benz engine. Avery saw the car as an industry of the near future, and suggested to Hipkins that James Watt and Company might be able to manufacture engines of the Benz type and sell them to car body makers. Mr. Gascoigne was invited to give a presentation to the Avery's board, including a full description of how the Benz engine operated. Hipkins saw the historical significance of this presentation. In 1758 James Watt had discussed plans for a steam powered road vehicle with Dr. John Robison but the plan was shelved. Boulton and Watt's very able colleague William Murdoch also had plans for a steam powered road vehicle and in 1784 a prototype was tested in Redruth. Again the plans came to nothing. Here was Hipkins at the Soho Foundry 140 years later discussing horse-less road vehicle production!

Hipkins shared Avery's interest in the motor car but was not convinced that Benz engine production at the Soho Foundry would be profitable and the matter was dropped. It was not, however, the end of car engines and Soho Foundry. In 1908 Hipkins received an enquiry from the *Orleans Motor Company Limited*, which produced the *Owen* motor car, for the James Watt Company to supply them with engines. Again nothing came of the venture but one must wonder how different history would have been if the Soho Foundry had entered into motor car engine production; perhaps even now cars would be driving along our roads bearing the name *James Watt Motor Company* with perhaps a distinctive Elephant logo.

Hipkins saw a product line linked more closely to Avery's as being the way forward for the old firm. The weighbridge side of the business was expanding as Avery's opened up new markets in various parts of the world, and although Pooley's had virtually a world monopoly on railway weighbridges, they suffered from the development of petrol driven transport. Avery's Soho works were able to cut production costs of their heavy weighbridges and the Engineering Department and the Weighbridge Department worked closely together to reduce costs per item. Between 1895 and 1900 there was a sharp increase in weighbridge production especially in the 10-75 tons category.

The external work of James Watt and Company diverted widely from the weighing machine and scale making business, and tendered for contract for pumping engines and maintenance contracts for a variety of steam engines. They tendered for many jobs but most were unsuccessful. Cost seems to have been the major problem with Watt's being, in some cases, as much as £2,000 higher than competitors. Even when they did obtain orders they ran into problems, such as the pumping engine they supplied to the Crowborough District Waterworks in 1898. Following installation the engine suffered many problems eventually making a loss to the firm. There were, however, success stories. In a contract that must have owed as much to historical association as well as to price the firm supplied pumping engines to the Birmingham Canal Navigation in 1899. This large order valued at over £7,500 was to replace equipment that had originally been supplied by the Boulton and Watt Company a hundred years previously. The success stories were, however, few in number and on Hipkins' desk the monthly spreadsheets told him that James Watt and Company was losing money, yet he decided to keep it going. Perhaps he had allowed some sentiment to creep into his calculations or, more likely, he felt that the negative publicity of the closure of the name James Watt and Company would do far too much damage to Avery's.

The name *Avery* was being associated with scales and weighing machines throughout the Kingdom and its global reputation was growing. In November 1901 Avery's reached Royal status when they received a Royal Warrant. W. & T. Avery Limited was now manufacturers of weighing apparatus to His Majesty the King.

CHAPTER 13

THE TARIFF PROBLEM

*The secret of war lies in the secret lines of communication . . .
Strategy does not consist of making half hearted dashes at
the enemy's rear areas; it consists in really mastering his
communications, and then proceeding to give battle.*

—*Napoleon*

By 1904 Avery's were expanding everywhere and as the agents,
merchants and branches increased so too did Hipkins' intelligence gathering
network. Every week details of the activities of Pooley's, Fairbanks,
Salter's, Howe, Day and Millward, and a dozen other firms would appear
on Hipkins' desk from all parts of the world. This intelligence gathering
resulted in a number of legal actions against local ironmongers, traders
and merchants in a dozen countries. Hipkins' monthly meetings with the
branch managers were used to discuss tactics to fight off competition.
What surprised many of his branch managers was that Hipkins often had
intelligence about activities in their regions before they did! Hipkins made
it clear that now that he had "thrown a web" over the country they should
now attack all opposition as it arose. This web idea led many managers to
refer to Hipkins as 'The Spider' and this in-joke was illustrated in Avery's
book to mark the 200th anniversary of the company with a spider sitting in
his web!

By far the single most important issue that was affecting Avery's and
British industry, especially that of the Midlands, was *Free Trade*. Through
the latter half of the eighteenth and first half of the nineteenth century
Britain, with its empire, enjoyed unparalleled commercial control over
vast swathes of the planet. British goods were shipped everywhere and
raw materials were brought in. With such dominance successive British
governments operated a policy of *Laissez-faire* or Free Trade. Richard

Cobden was a highly outspoken supporter of Free Trade, arguing that with a world-wide market open to all it would lead to a reduction in military conflict. During the first half of the nineteenth century many trade agreements and treaties were signed between Britain and countries in Europe and the Far East, and it did seem that Cobden was right. In the 1870s with a depression affecting British (and European) industry, several countries felt that a modification of the trade agreements needed to be made. In particular, France was keen to abandon existing treaties to form new ones much to the dismay of the British government. None the less new treaties were drawn up with Britain following a strict Free Trade Policy and France following a more protectionist line. Many countries began to develop their own industries, in particular Germany and the United States of America. In the 1880s a reunified Germany was spending no time and vast sums of money in building its industrial power, and it was having great success in finding new markets for its products. Moreover, the structure of German industry allowed a great deal of flexibility in production. This development had been seen coming. Lord Harrowby in 1884 advised the government to negotiate trade agreements with new outlets for British goods; he feared that Germany would overtake British supply. Two years later a government report recommended state intervention to assist British trade, but this intervention would remain diplomatic and not economic, whereas other countries began to operate stricter protectionist policies by introducing tariffs on imported goods aimed at safeguarding their home grown industries from British imports. Although Britain's export levels were so high compared to her imports, the tariffs on British goods had a minimal effect in the short term. By 1903 the effect of tariffs on British industry had grown acute with the effect of these tariffs being felt no where as keenly as Birmingham and the Black Country—the workshop of the world. Manufactured goods produced in the midlands were sold abroad and at home which meant that local industries suffered a double blow—first the tariffs made their goods more expensive abroad, and secondly cheap imports reduced sales in the UK. British industry complained bitterly of unfair treatment in the world marketplace, but successive British governments refused to place high tariffs on imports to Britain citing the policy of Free Trade. Joseph Chamberlain, the well-known Birmingham based politician, campaigned strongly for British Tariff Reform and brought on board leaders of midlands' industries in support. Chamberlain's strong support for tariff reform brought him into conflict with his government colleagues, eventually leading to his resignation from the cabinet in September 1903. The resignation gave him time to campaign for tariff reform and the subsequent cabinet reshuffle placed his son, Austin, as Chancellor of the Exchequer meaning that he had a powerful ally deep in the heart of government; indeed, he felt (with some justification) that Prime Minister Balfour had leanings towards tariff reform, and instituting a protectionist policy giving preference to trade with countries of the British Empire. Touring the UK Chamberlain gave speeches emphasising that tariff reform was vital to improve the quality of life for the working classes, to create jobs and help cement the British Empire. Chamberlain faced many critics, in particular, members of the *Cobden Club* which constantly attacked any anti-free trade notions pointing out that the cost of bread would rise as most of the country's wheat was imported. The bread argument was a very attractive one to members of the public, so much so that at one major meeting at Bingley Hall in Birmingham Chamberlain stood on the platform holding two loaves of bread demonstrating there was no difference in size between a Protectionist and Free Trade one!

Although France and Germany had been the main concern the United States had steadily increased its tariff rates since the 1870s culminating in the Tariff Reform Acts of 1890, 1894 and 1897. The 1890 Act, known as the *McKinley Act* (after William McKinley who drafted it), took protectionism to new heights, coming down heavily on British goods especially in the iron trades. Britain had tried to negotiate a reciprocal agreement with the United States; however, the American attitude was a take it or leave it deal that left Britain heavily disadvantaged. Following the Act there was a strong movement in Britain to force the government to introduce tariffs on American imports, thus safeguarding British industry. The government refused, and as the years went by, more tariffs were raised against Britain and thus industry suffered. For Avery's, scales and other weighing machines from the USA, France and Germany were often very much cheaper than their own, although in many cases the imports were of inferior quality, surplus machines produced abroad were 'dumped' onto the UK market at a low price. Purchasers of scales were not necessarily aware of this fact and would buy the cheapest product regardless, although some grocers would fall foul of the Weights and Measures Inspector as the cheap scales often gave inaccurate measurements. American scale imports were causing Avery's the most concern, and in 1903 a new series of tariffs came into force. These tariffs hit hard on Avery's products with an import duty of 45% per scale ad valorem. American products coming into Britain were charged no duty at all![1]

Hipkins began to echo the concerns of Joseph Chamberlain on the lack of support given to British firms by the British government. He had remained publicly silent, partly due to his nervousness of public speaking, and partly because he didn't feel secure enough at Avery's. In 1903 he broke his silence following the new anti-free trade actions by the United States. On 10th December 1903 at J. & E. Wright's Annual Shareholders' meeting held at the Grand Hotel Birmingham, Hipkins outlined his concern:

" . . . the conviction of every businessman actively engaged in large manufacturing concerns must be that an alteration in the fiscal system is absolutely necessary if the trade of the country is to be maintained. In the particular business carried on by John and Edwin Wright a change is imperative. When the United States got possession of the Philippine Islands, where the manilla the company uses in such large quantities is grown, they immediately established a rebate of 30 shillings per ton on all manilla exported to the United States. That has given the manufacturers of ropes and twine in the United States an enormous advantage, and enabled them to send their manufactured products to this country at a price below that which could be met in competition by the manufacturers in this country. It is a gross injustice that that should be permitted, and manufacturers were looking forward to the proposed change in the fiscal system to enable them to compete on honest and fair grounds with any manufacturer in the world."[2]

The manilla problem had started in 1900. Following a variety of revolts the United States had taken total control of the Philippines with General Arthur MacArthur in charge. A further revolt in 1901 was crushed by the US Army, and William Howard Taft was installed as civil Governor of the Philippines. The United States controlled manilla supplies vital for the production of rope and they placed a rebate on manilla being exported to the USA from the Philippines, thus giving US rope makers an advantage over rope makers in the rest of the world, and in particular J. & E. Wright of which Hipkins was still a director. If that was not enough there was a US Tariff on imported rope at a rate of £3, 8 pence per hundredweight.[3]

Six months later at Avery's AGM, also held at the Grand Hotel, Hipkins made a devastating speech that was reprinted in many newspapers:

"The Chloroform of Free Trade has so tended to deaden the perceptions of those who did not toil, neither did they think, that they over looked the fact that every advantage held out to the foreigner as incense offered up to the fetish of the great Mahdi, who ran amok among English commerce half a century ago, is leading to the dumping of foreign goods into our ports, and placing a shackle on English trade. What has been the result in our line of business, of the country's present fiscal system—this trade-wrecking policy? Yankee made scales are dumped in England, which if made by an English manufacturer, would not be allowed in use for trade purposes on the grounds that they would facilitate the commission of fraud. Low-grade French balances are dumped in this country in enormous quantities at 4 shillings 9 pence; they are sold at a higher price in France, and cost 6 shillings 9 pence to produce. The Germans, who have a finger in every pie, dump a scale which is used for dispensing purposes at 1 shilling sold at 1 shilling 9 pence in Germany, and costs 1 shilling 5 pence to produce. The Americans are dumping in the colonies, South Africa, Australia, and India a certain well known scale at 7 shillings 3 pence, which costs 9 shillings 10 pence to produce, and which was sold in the States at about 4 dollars. They are dumping another scale into these colonies at 9 shillings 6 pence which costs 12 shillings 9 pence to produce. As regards to freight, from England to Durban there is a freightage of 40 shillings per ton on weighing apparatus, while from New York to Durban the amount is only 17 shillings and six pence. This is the kind of thing with which we have to contend, and while this was persisted in by our own Government, they themselves purchased in a cheap, and what I might term a protected market, scales on which they weigh our letters and parcels, and of which they were so much afraid that they refused to allow the inspectors of weights and measures to stamp them and test them. That is a bad case. I will not weary you with further instances; but could we be surprised that there is a falling off in profits under a fiscal system which I might term a system of protection for every other country but our own, since it allowed foreigners to dump their goods here under a preferential tariff, equal to the proportion of rates and taxes which our manufacturers have to pay on their cost of production. I have heard it objected that a tariff would mean higher prices. A tariff against the foreign dumper means more orders for the British manufacturer; more orders means running the works full time with a full compliment of operatives, and that means a larger percentage of common charges on production, or in other words lower costs. I might add for your information that if this one-sided fiscal farce is not changed after the next general election, I shall, in our interests bring forward before the directors a scheme which I have had long in mind, cut and dried for starting manufacturing in certain foreign countries. What is the great solution? As businessmen we should never lose an opportunity of doing what we can to assist Mr. Joseph Chamberlain in the enormous task which he has undertaken in the interests of the country. The question is one which is vital to the whole Empire. It will be solved by the working masses, the manufacturing and agricultural voters. On their shoulders the solution of a great Empire question rests. It was for them to decide whether they will be guided by the advice of living businessmen of experience or continue to act on the theories of the mouldy master of fifty years ago."[4]

Hipkins had poured gallons of fuel onto the flames of the tariff debate. Newspapers began to receive letters both in favour of Hipkins views but some against. A "Looker-on" from Walsall wrote to the Birmingham Gazette stating:

> *"Sir,—If Messrs. Avery would pay skilled labour at a reasonable price, thus enabling a man to do his work well; further, if they would reduce the number of non-producers, and also be satisfied with a reasonable profit, foreign competition in the scale trade would be practicably impossible."*[5]

One of his workforce sounding-off relating back to the pay arguments, but Mr. C.A. Johnson of Clapham was different, he criticised Hipkins for his argument that German scales firms appear to sell at a loss which in the end would cause the German manufacturers to go bankrupt. The Birmingham Gazette, which supported Chamberlain and therefore Hipkins, not only published Johnson's letter but also Hipkins' reply underneath it. Hipkins' reply showed just how killing he could be when it came to an argument:

> *"Your correspondent to a Gazette and Express representative yesterday, in common with many others does not understand how a protected foreign manufacturer can sell his productions in one-sided Free Trade England at below cost yet at an advantage to himself. To the theorist it is an apparent contradiction in terms, and Mr. Johnson endeavours to prove it to be so in fact by*

the gratuitous assumption that the foreigner sells only half his output to his own country, shipping the other half to England. As a matter of fact it is his surplus he dumps here . . . This is well understood and practised by foreign and is being slowly and sadly learnt by English manufacturers. It is the theorists who are ignorant of the facts. Unfortunately, they are stone blind to their own ignorance."[6]

Hipkins was a practical man and he respected those with practical experience, having little time for the theorists sitting in their armchairs and putting the world to rights. The Gazette finished off Mr. Johnson by adding 72 column lines thanking him for exposing the Free Trade ideology for the fallacy it was! Other workmen also entered the fray with one admitting he did not know which way to turn, and another criticising Hipkins. The debate raged on, but for Hipkins all the talking was wasting time, action was what was needed to combat cheap foreign imports. Hipkins had lost his patience with the Government over the issue, and if they wouldn't act, he would. In 1904 the *Computing Scale Company* of Dayton, Ohio U.S.A introduced into Britain their *Moneyweight Scale* selling it through a company set up in Britain for that sole purpose—the *British Moneyweight Scale Company* based in London. The scale was seen as a ground-breaking machine by not only indicating the weight of the item being bought, but also the price which was indicated on a scale. Aimed at the local shopkeeper it could, if marketed correctly, make a serious dent into Avery's, Pooley's, and Slater's market. By June 1904 over one thousand of the scales had been sold to shopkeepers across the country and were, therefore, becoming a serious threat to Avery's sales. Avery's had to fight back. Hipkins arranged for one of the Moneyweight scales to be purchased for examination, and found that there were many failings with the machine.

The Standards Department of the Board of Trade were responsible for approving all designs of scales granting each scale a certificate so that they could be legally used in shops for weighing goods. The Borough Council of Smethwick reported to the Board of Trade that they felt the new design of scale did not meet the required standards, and thus the Standards Department obtained a scale for testing. Smethwick is, of course, the borough in which the Soho Foundry and William Bayliss (Pooley's) were located, and it seems that both Avery's and Pooley's had some involvement in the Council making a report to the Board of Trade.

191

The Standards Department reported their findings on August 15th, 1904 refusing a certificate for the new scale citing that:

1. The mechanism was too accessible to the shopkeeper who could tamper with it producing a fraudulent reading.
2. The capacity range of the chart was too great.
3. The chart was not arithmetically correct when it priced small quantities, arbitrarily giving the benefit of halfpennies to either the shopkeeper or the customer.
4. The two dials (one facing the customer the other the shopkeeper) were not easily calibrated.
5. The eye level of the customer or shopkeeper affected the reading that could give an error of up to 2.5p.
6. The price ranges were too high for a spring balance.
7. The scales were affected by temperature.

The findings confirmed Hipkins' own examinations, and thus armed with good scientific data, he began a propaganda campaign against the Moneyweight Scale. His branch managers had found newspaper articles where the Moneyweight Scale Company had been brought before the courts over their new design, and these clippings were typed up, printed, and sent to each of the branches. Hipkins also had printed some cards that were to be placed in the windows of shops selling Avery scales, and in the windows of shops that used Avery's scales.

The small sign left no doubt as to what Hipkins thought of the Moneyweight Scale, and the following appeared in Avery's shop at Stockwell Street in Glasgow from September 5th 1904:

<u>*IMPORTANT*</u>
WE WEIGH OR GOODS ON AN
'AVERY AGATE <u>SCALE</u>.'
We do not use complicated <u>calculating</u> mechanisms
which are <u>calculated</u> to deceive.
BUY YOUR GOODS OVER SCALES THAT
GIVE HONEST WEIGHT.
The sign was supplemented by copies of newspaper
articles which were updated regularly:
IMPORTANT to

Users of Calculating Scales
And to the public who buy from
Shopkeepers using Computing Scales.

Evening Citizen, Friday, October 21, 1904.
Money-Weight Scale.—Owner has for disposal one
of these, almost new, cost £20; will accept £3 for
Cash.—3951 *Citizen* Office.
The Daily Record and Mail, Monday, October 10, 1904.
MONEY-COMPUTING SCALES.

To the Editor.
It will be of considerable interest to the trading community
to know that, as a result of numerous complaints through-out the
country to the effect that these devices may be used to facilitate
fraud, the Government have brought all calculating devices in
connection with weighing apparatus within the purview of the
new Weights and Measures Act.
This Act was recently passed as a Government measure,
and comes into force on 1ˢᵗ January next. Traders should
carefully consider its effect.
Hillhead. PROVISION MERCHANT.[7]

No one in Great Britain had ever seen such aggressive tactics deployed in full glare of the public. How would the British Moneyweight Scale Company respond? They sued Avery's, claiming damages of £10,000, suggesting that Avery's were trying to throw discredit on their scales, making false allegations, and supporting agitation among dealers in Glasgow against the Moneyweight Scales. It was a serious charge and brought into the public domain the trade-war between scale makers. There was more than simply money riding on the outcome of the action. Should Avery's lose then it could spell the end of Avery's as sales in their products would more than likely be affected. Pooley's would take advantage of the situation, and the British Moneyweight Scale Company would have an open field for its products. To many at Avery's, Hipkins had gambled. Chamberlain, Williams and others, like Hipkins thought otherwise. The card that had been placed in the window at the Stockwell Street Showroom did not (in Hipkins' opinion) in anyway state anything that could not be proven. The newspaper cuttings were a matter of public record. Hipkins was surprised that the BMS Company had sued for if they were to lose then it would totally destroy the market for their machine. The fight was on.

The British Moneyweight Calculating Scale Company also pursued an action against a merchant, James B. Campbell, as he had cancelled an order for scales following claims that the scales were inaccurate, and that contrary to what he had believed they were not approved by the Board of Trade.

Avery's defence was straightforward:

1. There was no title to sue.
2. The pursuers' statements were irrelevant and insufficient in law to maintain the conclusions of the summons.
3. Avery's not having slandered the pursuers or any goods manufactured or sold by the pursuers and thus Avery's should be acquitted with expenses.
4. The exhibits in Avery's windows complained of being so far as they were considered statements of fact, substantially true and otherwise being legitimate advertisement of their own goods, and fair comment on a matter of public interest, the defenders should be acquitted with expenses.

For Hipkins this period was one of great intensity; he was convinced that he was right and his faith in the justice of his defence made him feel secure that Avery's would be acquitted. Even so the sleepless nights were there; what if for some reason the Court found against him? Regardless of how good a case he thought he had. The stress was upon him.

The case was heard on January 17th and July 14th 1905 with Lord McLaren presiding. Every weighing machine company in the world watched with interest as the two companies argued their case. From the beginning it was clear that the two sides would not reach a gentlemen's agreement, it was a winner takes all situation. Lord Mclaren and his fellow judges had to decide whether W. & T. Avery was making false allegations and trying to discredit the moneyweight scales.

Lord McClaren delivered his judgement. The case against W. & T. Avery Limited was dismissed with expenses. In his adjudication Lord McClaren stated:

> *"It might be bad taste or bad manners to display placards disparaging the production of commercial rivals, and I am surprised that a firm like Messrs. Avery should allow their agents to exhibit such placards, but the law does not give an action for mere criticism of goods or machinery, and I am unable to say that according to any fair criticism the expressions on the placards could be interpreted as meaning an imputation of dishonesty on the pursuers."*[8]

Avery's could live with the criticism of the placards although they would not be placed in any shop window again.

Hipkins standing within the company and the world of weighing machines rose beyond belief. The BMS Company suffered catastrophically; sales of their machines in the UK crashed, and the machines they had sold already were returned. Worse was to come. In 1907 the Massachusetts Supreme Judicial Court ruled against the parent company, the *Moneyweight Scale Company,* under similar circumstances. Being beaten abroad was one thing; being beaten on home turf was another. Avery's took more from the decision than simply wiping-out a major cheap competitor, the general idea of the scale designed by the Moneyweight Scale Company was a good one, it was simply of poor quality. In 1909 Avery's co-operated with the *Toledo Scale Company* (USA), to market a similar scale. A year previously Pooley's, in collaboration with the *Dayton Scale Company* (USA), had begun marketing a money-weight scale. In many ways it seems sad for those who started the money-weight scale design for they were ahead of their time; had they paid more attention to quality they may well have taken a massive slice of the grocer's scale market.

It was another great success for Hipkins; it seemed he could never fail. The board at rivals Pooley's were dismayed. They thought that at least Avery's would have to pay some compensation to BMS Company; now they knew that Avery's had taken a moral lead in world scale making as well as a commercial one. Avery's was now courted by heavy political figures. Joseph Chamberlain was impressed at the way Hipkins had taken on the case it demonstrated that cheap imports had to be fought in the courts if necessary, and that the need for Tariff Reform was now in order to prevent further cases.

Chamberlain needed the support of prominent businessmen and he needed the support of the British workforce, but the workforce was mistrustful and many thought that the problems of imports could be solved by higher wages leading to better and higher production levels, thus reducing the price of British goods. Chamberlain was hopeful that at the next general election the Unionists would be defeated and the Liberals would form a government, which he believed would soon thereafter collapse leaving his tariff reform policy a vote winner.

Hipkins had an ingenious strategy to try and convince the workforce to vote for tariff reform. He hinted of it at Avery's 1904 AGM—the possibility of setting up a factory abroad. For at least two years the Avery directors had been in deep discussion regarding the possibility of setting up a manufactory in the United States. As early as 1900 Hipkins had considered setting up a joint agreement with one of the big American scale manufacturers in order to sell Avery scales within the United States, but he soon came round to the idea that only with an Avery owned facility would they be affective at combating the tariff problem.

Hipkins' idea became more urgent by the actions of the German firm of *I.G. Farben*—a conglomeration of the six big German chemical firms. I.G. Farben had been formed by Carl Duisberg, the Chief Executive of *Bayer,* following a trip to the United States in 1903. The principle aim of his trip was to set up a chemical plant in Renssaeler, New York in order to overcome American tariffs on German chemical products. Duisberg saw an opportunity of uniting German firms to reduce internal competition and to fight foreign competition.[9] Although I.G. Farben were not in competition with Avery's, it might be the beginning of a new German strategy in international commerce.

At Avery's 1905 AGM, Walter Chamberlain attacked those who supported Free Trade and stated that Avery's was prepared to manufacture anything from ". . . a pen-knife to a battleship" in order to succeed. Hipkins gave another of his powerful speeches in which he stated that ". . . there was the possibility of establishing a factory in a commercially happier-land, and steps have been taken by sending out a pioneer who was preparing the way in another quarter of the globe."[10]

This was a fearsome statement to many, and the local press ran headlines that sent shivers of discontent through workmen—

TO FIGHT TARIFFS,
FAMOUS BIRMINGHAM FIRM PROPOSE TO GO
ABROAD[11]

AVERYS MAY MOVE—
FREE TRADE'S EFFECT ON A FAMOUS FIRM[12]

Joseph Chamberlain was delighted; this was just what his campaign for tariff reform needed. Hipkins gained not only brownie points from one of the country's leading political figures, but it brought him to the attention of other national figures. Many local businessmen and some pro Free Trade politicians thought Hipkins' announcement was simply an idle threat, a scare-mongering tactic. It was not for the first time that Hipkins had been misjudged and likely it would not be the last.

Hipkins the man had changed. It had been ten years since the shy, self-conscious businessman had arrived at Avery's, and now he was beginning to shine bright enough to be seen by all. He felt a new energy surge through him, although not accustomed to over sentimentality or superstition, he had the inkling that destiny had something special in store for him. He knew how Napoleon must have felt standing in front of the Imperial Guard declaring his loyalty to France, and that if they wished they could kill him. Hipkins had offered the court in Edinburgh that opportunity, and he had triumphed.

CHAPTER 14

ARMING FOR THE FUTURE

Ambition is the main driving power of men. A man expends his
abilities as long as he hopes to rise.

—*Napoleon.*

Hipkins' success at Avery's made him many more friends in the
local business community and several in the national and international
community. His support for Joseph Chamberlain opened many doors,
making him a natural choice by many firms to become a member of their
boards of directors. Hipkins, however, was an Avery's man and he sat only
on two other boards, that of J. & E. Wright Limited and that of Parnall's
(owned by Avery's). He felt that he needed to dedicate himself as much as
possible to Avery's, thus it seems surprising that in 1905 he accepted an
invitation to become a director of the *Birmingham Small Arms Company
Limited*.[1]

BSA was a very well known firm founded in 1861 out of the
Birmingham Small Arms Trade Association, which had consisted of
fourteen local gun-making firms.[2] They had decided to form a public
limited company in order to produce rifles with interchangeable parts
along the lines of American manufacturers. Two years later a factory was
completed in Small Heath that was constantly developed, and by 1905 had
grown into a massive complex covering over 6 acres. Subsequently, they
acquired additional facilities making them a large international player in
the arms industry.

Since its founding the firm had gone through a variety of fortunes, and
to counteract the downturns BSA expanded into other areas such as bicycle
production, which fluctuated as the demand for rifles waxed and waned.
From 1893 BSA supplemented its gun production by making bicycle
components, an area that Hipkins had knowledge of from his days with

Sansome, Teale And Company. When the Boer War broke out in 1899, BSA became one of the main suppliers of rifles to the British Army producing 2,500 rifles per week in Small Heath. When the war ended in 1902 the slump in the arms trade returned with Government factories supplying most of the needs of the military, and even with the establishment of the *Territorials* which eased some of the pressure it was clear that unless a major war came along BSA would have to find a new market for its guns. The invitation to Hipkins to join the board was taken to bring to BSA his experience in finding new markets, and indeed it was not long before he developed a new strategy to help BSA.

As early as 1890 BSA had entered into the sporting rifle market eventually adding the miniature rifle in 1902 along with a variety of air guns. Here was BSA's opportunity. Hipkins had been quick to foresee the growth in the demand for bicycles, and he read something that sparked him into action. Field Marshall Earl Roberts V.C., K.G. had given a number of speeches urging the formation of miniature rifle clubs; such clubs (he thought) would train people in the use of weapons so that in a time of crises the army would have people who were accustomed to firearms. Hipkins saw this as an opportunity and thus decided to set up a rifle club at Avery's. In April 1906 he purchased 9 air rifles and a number of targets costing £20 19/6 from—BSA! Workmen could join the club, and during their lunch hour would practice or hold mini tournaments paying a penny for ten air pellets. The money from the sale of the pellets was paid into the employees' sick club, thus it was in their own interest to take part. Hipkins also saw an opportunity to promote Avery's and perhaps stimulate some interest in gun clubs thus increasing the demand for air guns, which would of course benefit BSA. He wrote to Field Marshall Earl Roberts who in turn had Hipkins' letter published in the magazine *The Rifleman.*

> *"My Lord, It may interest your Lordship, who is doing so much to encourage the formation of Miniature Rifle Clubs throughout the country, to know that your public speeches on this subject suggested to us the desirability of forming in our works an Air Gun Club as a possible means of recruiting for the Miniature Rifle Clubs above referred to.*

It occurred to us that the greater part of the dinner hour, which is usually spent in a less profitable manner, might be utilized for the purpose of inducing our younger employees to take an interest in a pastime, which might eventually lead to their becoming serviceable to their country, and at the same time serve to financially assist our Works Sick Club.

We accordingly provided the necessary Air Guns, etc, of the best English make, and the club was started under a necessary code of rules in April last. The idea gradually caught on, and to-day we have a club in each department, 10 in all, with a member roll which has increased to over 500 young men.

The pellets are obtained from the Secretary of the Sick Club, at the rate of 10 per penny, and the profit accruing to the Sick Club was £18 8s. for the three initial months.

Probably other manufacturers throughout the country would be glad to follow our lead if it were known that the scheme had your Lordship's approval.

> *I remain,*
> *Your Lordship's obedient servant,*
> *W. & T. AVERY, LTD.*
> *(W. E. Hipkins, Managing Director)"[3]*

This letter was also used by BSA in its own advertising, including adding a section to their catalogues emphasizing the fact that the guns were purchased from them. Naturally, the article fails to mention that the purchaser was actually a director of BSA![4]

The success of the Air Gun Club at Avery's was very satisfying to Hipkins and to BSA, which found that Hipkins' letter had helped drive the development of factory rifle clubs. The Avery teams did not, it seems, participate in any national competitions but the club remained part of Avery's social activities. Whether this was a decision by Hipkins or those running the club I cannot say, however, the gun club ran for several years.

From his own experiences Hipkins understood the need for good education, and how an educated man can not only help himself but also help the business he is in. James Oliver Bevan remained a strong advocate of good education for the masses and Hipkins was his ardent supporter. Bevan had done what he could within his position as a curate, aimed mainly at boys who had yet to serve an apprenticeship, although he was also a strong advocate for post school education. Hipkins was of the opinion that there was a distinct lack of technical education that would assist firms such as Avery's, and he found himself in a position where he could contribute to the education of boys and young men who were serving apprenticeships or had just completed them. In the November 1st 1904 edition of *The Educational Times*, a report appeared on a lecture given by James Bevan entitled "Study After School-Days". Hipkins wrote to the magazine adding his own point of view, which clearly illustrates his interest in after school education:

> *"Sir, . . . The subject is of national importance from an ethical point of view, and is vital in its bearing upon the prosperity of our manufactures and commerce generally.*
>
> *In an age when science is daily superseding the old methods of production it is imperative that the rank and file of the industrial army should have at least a fair technical knowledge of the arts, or the trade of the country will gradually drift to States where the units are better equipped.*
>
> *All large employers of labour can tell of the difficulty they experience in finding workmen of sufficient technical knowledge, when modern methods are perforce, introduced into their works, and how they are frequently obliged to import foreign operatives.*
>
> *Mr. Bevan makes some practical suggestions in the direction of creating an incentive to after-school study which are valuable; but, when faced with the problem of earning a living, the commercial conscript, surrounded by fresh associations, is apt to take too narrow a view of his position and prospects and to regard the continuance of study as a loss of time.*

201

Surely, then, it is to the interest of employers of labour to second the efforts of the school teacher by offering inducements to their employees to continue their studies on lines which in a few years time will render their services more valuable.

The perusal of Mr. Bevan's paper led me to recognize this, and I decided to offer a small monetary reward to every employee in the works which I control (where over two thousand are engaged) who shall secure an Elementary Certificate at the local technical schools.

If this meets with success, I propose offering larger rewards on securing certificates in the higher stages.

The experiment is at least worth a trial, and teachers throughout the country might make the suggestion to employers in their respective localities.—I am Sir &c

W.E. Hipkins "[5]

Hipkins' reward for obtaining a certificate was significant—5 shillings, which was nearly, a weeks' wages to the young men concerned.[6]

This was, however, just the beginning. Hipkins was also concerned that the quality of managerial material was lacking and something had to be done about that as well. In July 1906 Hipkins let forth in the press his views on education, and the need for modern education to meet the needs of business. It could have well been Charles Evans arguing his case for change at King Edward's School back in the 1860s. Hipkins went further. He gave a blistering speech at an Avery Shareholders' meeting criticising the modern youth for being "dull, un-ambitious and unashamed." He had come across many young men who instead of cutting a path for themselves were happy to:

". . . just walk in their predecessors' shoes, and for initiative, stick a patch on from time to time. Their only desire appeared to be to shuffle along the lines of least resistance. "[7]

His strong position on education formed part of his wider strategy on Tariff Reform, as he stated at the same board meeting that there were measures that he would like to employ to combat foreign competition, but due to the lack of quality managers it was impossible for him to do so. How was he to get quality managers? Since 1901 he had been watching with great interest the formation and development of the *Faculty of Commerce* at the University of Birmingham. The University itself was new having been opened in 1900 with Joseph Chamberlain as its Chancellor. Chamberlain had been the driving force in the formation of the University, although the seeds for the establishment had already been sewn in the shape of the (Josiah) *Mason Science College* which had opened in 1880. The university now occupied the college's building and with Chamberlain's influence the University was able to obtain support from the likes of Andrew Carnegie. Chamberlain also influenced the style of the establishment with it being run along a very modern line based more on the American style such as Cornell University with science taking pre-eminence over the classics.[8]

Chamberlain and the Chamber of Commerce had distinct ideas of how the university and business should co-operate. One idea was that the railway companies should sponsor a *School for Railway Engineering and Economics*, but the rail companies showed no interest.[9] Chamberlain, therefore, became a strong advocate for a unique *Faculty of Commerce*, which had been previously suggested by the *Birmingham Chamber of Commerce* in 1898.[10] Even though the Chamber and certain individual businesses expressed an interest in such a faculty, raising funds for it was a different matter. It was Chamberlain again who came to the rescue by somehow obtaining £50,000 from Lord Strathcona the Canadian High Commissioner.[11]

In May 1901 the University advertised for applications for the post of *Organising Chair* in connection with the future Faculty of Commerce, with the possibility of (in due course) appointing a Professor of the Faculty. The role of the professor was to set a curriculum to meet the needs of the business community. An *Advisory Committee on Commercial Education* chaired by Arthur Chamberlain had already laid down the basic criteria for a course in commercial studies which was:

1. *A knowledge of the theory and principles of trade.*
2. *A general knowledge of commercial law.*
3. *Knowledge of accountancy and costing.*

4.   *A knowledge of shipping and railway practice.*
5.   *French and one other modern language (Spanish, German or Italian).*
6.   *Shorthand.*
7.   *Theory of banking and exchange.*
8.   *In addition to lectures being provided by the faculty staff, specialists from business and industry should in the students' third year present lectures.*[12]

This was a ground-breaking exercise; there was no other university in the United Kingdom that offered a faculty of commerce and a course so dedicated to future businessmen. The person who was selected to head the faculty was William Ashley, a man who had boundless energy. Born in London in 1860, his parents were rather poor; however, he was a gifted student and managed to pay for virtually all of his education through scholarships. He obtained a first class honours degree in history at Balliol and then began studying economics. In 1885 he was elected to a Fellowship at Lincoln, and three years later became professor of Political Science at the University of Toronto. He made such a great impression at Toronto that he was invited to the Chair of Economic History at Harvard, a post essentially created for him. His own personal interest in the socio-economic situation in Great Britain led him to apply for the post in Birmingham. Ashley was married to Margaret Hill, the daughter of Birkbeck Hill and the granddaughter of Thomas Wright Hill who had founded the Hazelwood School in Birmingham. A very likeable man who had written a magnificent two-volume work entitled "Economic History" which remains to this day a standard work on the subject. His approach to the course was very modern, and after considering the views of Joseph Chamberlain and F.B. Goodman (Chairman of the Birmingham Chamber of Commerce), he realised he had a difficult political task ahead of him. The University wanted to be certain that the Faculty of Commerce met the strict standards of a university course, and that the course also met the needs of the business community without the Faculty simply becoming a training institution for industry.

The faculty was housed in two rooms above a shop in Edmund Street, and the first course began in October 1902 with just six students taking the three-year course. Ashley's general approach was, perhaps, slightly different to that expected by many businessmen. The third year of the course was vocational so that the students could experience the business environment. The language element of the course was taught not simply as a language as much as a cultural acclimatisation of the country concerned; thus the student learned something of French and German literature—much in the same way Achille Albites taught French many years earlier.

Support from local businesses and parents was extremely poor, and as the years moved on it was foreign students who were taking advantage of the Faculty. This is probably what prompted Hipkins to be so vocal about the need to train new men. Hipkins, always a man who practised what he preached, employed one of the graduates of 1905—Wilfred Bland who became confidential private secretary to Mr. Beakbane with a salary of £100. William Ashley was particularly pleased that one of Birmingham's most respected businessmen was throwing his weight behind the Faculty. Hipkins' views were shared by Joseph Chamberlain and J.S. Taylor of the Chamber of Commerce. Once again Hipkins found himself being singled out as the ideal man to do a job, that of getting more local businesses involved with the Faculty of Commerce. Hipkins himself was slightly reluctant as he didn't want any distractions from the normal course of his work. However, in 1906 Joseph Chamberlain suffered a stroke and withdrew from politics and was not able to become deeply involved in the new moves at the Faculty. Hipkins found himself in the driving seat.

As usual he pressed into service Arthur Gibson, and the two of them discussed with Ashley the forming of an advisory board to the Faculty consisting of local businessmen. Ashley had already considered strong links with the business community, and indeed Arthur Chamberlain had cited it in his report to the University. However, Ashley had had some problems getting local businesses interested. An approach to the business community by Hipkins and Gibson would carry greater weight to such an invitation, especially when they saw that Hipkins himself employed graduates. Hipkins and Gibson emphasised to Ashley that a more formal link with the local business community was required to increase awareness of the Faculty and attract students, especially if they felt that employment at one of Birmingham's leading firms was in the offing after graduation. It was Hipkins' and Gibson's business connections that were to be asked to join them on the first advisory board. On October 11th 1906 the Faculty of Commerce agreed to constitute an Advisory Board along the lines specified by Hipkins and Gibson.

The board's make-up was a who's who of Hipkins' business connections in Birmingham, and is testimony to his standing in the local community that these men accepted to join. Firstly, there was a member of the Chamberlain family; certainly if anything was to succeed in Birmingham the Chamberlain's had to at least give tacit approval. Arthur Chamberlain was too preoccupied with other interests and Joseph was already Chancellor of the University; he wasn't a big supporter of Advisory Boards stating that they tended to be bland and that their use was mainly for publicity, and anyway his ill health precluded any in depth involvement. Thus, his son Neville was seen as the obvious choice. Neville Chamberlain was a director of *Elliott's Metal Company* with connections with *BSA* and *Hoskins and Son* (bed makers). He was beginning to rise in the world of business following his return from Barbados where he had managed his father's plantations. Neville's approach to business was gentler, and he lacked the ruthlessness of his father preferring to discuss differences and negotiate. His powers of persuasion would seem ideal on such an advisory board where representatives of possibly rival firms would meet.

The railway carriage industry was well represented on the board. This industry employed large numbers of skilled workers in Birmingham; with foreign competition from Germany and the United States putting pressure on their exports, anything that might boost their competiveness was welcomed. Following the failure of Joseph Chamberlain's idea for a special school for the rail industry, it was important to have the industry represented on the board. Edward Hickman, who was on the board of the *Midland Railway Carriage and Wagon Company Limited*, accepted with little hesitation along with F. Dudley Docker the Chairman of *the Metropolitan Railway Carriage and Wagon Company*. F. Dudley Docker was also Managing Director of *Docker Brothers Limited* (paint) and a Director at *Birmingham Small Arms*. The arms trade was another major employer in the city and had additional representation on the board by T. Sidney Walker the Managing Director of *Thomas Walker and Son Limited* (ship's log manufacturers), and director of *the Birmingham Metal and Munitions Company Limited*.

Dudley Docker was very well known to Hipkins. The two had dealings when Hipkins purchased paints and varnishes from Docker Brothers. Docker had been slowly clawing his way up the industrial ladder making important connections through his business, and through his social activities. The Dockers had cricketing ties with Edgbaston and thus with

George Cartland—Dudley was the 'Man of the Match' in the inaugural game played at Edgbaston Cricket Ground. He used his connections well and, although seen by some as something of a wide-boy, made good essentially by amalgamating firms together, with the deal that made his name being the merger of five rolling stock companies in 1902.[13]

Docker was unhappy with inefficiency in business and government, and was naturally a supporter of tariff reform. Although he lacked many of Hipkins' talents at business practice, he was more adept at manipulating the political situation. Although no record survives of Hipkins-Docker communications it is likely the two clashed in many ways, with Hipkins being the far more competent business professional. Docker had criticised those businessmen that adjusted piece rates for workmen once they had adapted to new machinery—something Hipkins had done at Avery's! It may be likely that as Docker used Hipkins' friend Gibson as a business lawyer (by being associated with the same law firm of Pinsent), the two became acquainted. Hipkins had been one of the directors at BSA to approve of Docker's appointment to the BSA board in 1906.[14] Indeed, Hipkins and Docker worked together on behalf of BSA when they inspected the works of the *Eadie Manufacturing Company Limited*; they prepared a report for the BSA board which recommended the purchasing of the firm, which they did in 1907.[15] Docker gleaned more from Hipkins' expertise than vice versa. Certainly it seems that some of Docker's business ideas originated elsewhere, with some of them having already been applied by Hipkins at Avery's!

The Agent of the Earl of Dudley—G.H. Claughton, was also invited to join the advisory board, he held directorships at the *London and North Western Railway Company*, the *Birmingham District and Counties Banking Company Limited, Birmingham Canal Navigation, South Staffordshire Waterworks Company Limited, South Staffordshire Gas Company Limited*, as well as several others! Hipkins knew Claughton through his dealings with the waterworks, the canal company and the L&NWR.

The final member of the first board was another friend of Hipkins, Joseph S. Taylor, who was Chairman of the council of the Birmingham Chamber of Commerce as well as a director of a number of companies, and Chairman of *Taylor and Challen Limited* (mechanical engineers).[16] Taylor represented the interests of the Chamber of Commerce and could act as a liaison between the Chamber's Education Committee and others in the business community.

It is interesting to see who isn't on the board. Avery's are the only scale manufacturers represented, and it is highly unlikely that Pooley's would have sent a representative even if they had been asked. Although Hipkins and the other board members share a genuine interest in education, it is motivated by the need to keep their respective businesses competitive. The board members were not appointed for life. They would serve a three-year term and be replaced in order to introduce new blood and new ideas, thus the Faculty's curriculum could be updated to meet the changes in the business world.

In January 1907 the board was finally established and announced to the press. It represented an excellent cross section of industry in Birmingham, and what is more, it bound together an elite group of businessmen who didn't meet on the golf course but met in formal sessions of the Faculty of Commerce Advisory Board. From here they could direct the course of those who might become the future elite of Birmingham business. Even so the board was more than simply a club for the business elite. The members actively took part in some of the curricular activities by sending speakers to the faculty, or by arranging for Faculty students to visit and take a tour of factories in the region (irrespective as to whether or not the business was represented on the board).[17] A 'Commercial Society' was formed at the University where students could discuss various topics and take tea with leading businessmen. At the end of the year a dinner was held with a specially invited guest who would give a presentation, and the students would offer a vote of thanks to their Dean Professor Ashley. Hipkins and Gibson were both involved in these activities, both of whom gave presentations and offered advice to the students. Certainly, the Advisory Board was far from the bland committee that Joseph Chamberlain had feared.

Hipkins' education initiatives were welcomed by many in the business community and within Avery's it was the younger men; those joining in the clubs and obtaining certificates; those who had benefited from Hipkins tightening of the discipline on the shop floor who could see opportunities being offered to them. These were the men who welcomed Hipkins' ideas and approved of them. The older hands were more sceptical, more resistant to change, they were at times scathing in their comments about the managing director's initiatives, and the usual complaints of 'The good old days have gone' echoed through the factory. Hipkins was clearly moulding the younger generation to meet the needs of Avery's.

Outside of Avery's Hipkins was now seen as a great Captain of Industry, so much so that the Birmingham Gazette ran a feature on him under the heading:

Midland Captains of Industry
XXXVII—Mr. W. E. Hipkins M.I.Mech.E. [18]

The article, complete with photograph, gave a brief history of W. & T. Avery Limited, followed by a brief biography of Hipkins himself. It was probably written by his friend Gibson who was the only writer he would have allowed to pen such an article. It speaks of Hipkins in terms of restrained praise.

Hipkins was now more known than ever before, and if he believed in destiny, he must have felt that he could never fail.

CHAPTER 15

SANCTUARY

Love for one's children, and one's wife are those sweet affections which subdue the soul by the heart, and the feelings by tenderness.

—Napoleon.

William E. Hipkins' life was dominated by his business interests; this quiet devotion to duty was recognised and respected by other business men in Birmingham. William Beilby Avery, like George Cartland, had taken William to his heart and wanted to help this self-made man. In 1898 they convinced him to become a member of the *Institute of Mechanical Engineers,* an esteemed organisation, the membership of which would improve William's standing in the wider engineering community—not that he was not already well connected. His application form included the names of prominent engineers. He was proposed by J. Barbard Hall, seconded by Samuel W. Johnson (of Avery's) and supported by William Beilby Avery, J.S. Taylor, and Henry Lea.[1] Henry Lea was a very big name in Birmingham having been a pioneer of electrical lighting, becoming the man who lit Birmingham Town Hall in 1891, and was a consulting engineer on many projects; a powerful ally in the world of engineering.

William was, therefore, surrounded day in day out by people associated with business. His every waking moment was focused on Avery's or Wright's; for a man of such temperament he needed a sanctuary in which to shut out the world. In 1899, following the completion of the move of the Avery sites to Soho, William Hipkins himself moved house. His personal status and salary was now of a level he could afford to rent one of the best houses in Edgbaston. A fabulous set of houses had been built in the mid 1870s at the far western side of the exclusive district in the leafy *Augustus Road*. These houses numbered 16 to 19 were owned by James

Wilson, and each were of similar design, yet each had their own distinct identity.[2] William rented number 16 known as 'Westmead'; set in beautiful grounds, the three-storey house was the height of middle class luxury. Lavish decoration around each of the windows, a highly elaborate porch, and even a balcony announced to anyone riding past that the occupant was a person who had achieved a degree of success.

Edgbaston though was *the* area where Birmingham's successful and professional elite made their sanctuary from the smoke of the city. William not only wanted the house as a symbol of his success, he wanted a comfortable home for his mother and sister and a refuge for himself. Yet, even so, the house contained a study where he could work, and a small library where he could read undisturbed.

The tree-lined drive up to the house from Augustus Road was long and led to the stables and coach house. By 1901 he had a motor car parked in the coach house, a Darracq thanks to the assistance of William Avery! William also stored his bicycles here. He had begun cycling following his interest in the emerging sport in the 1880s, and had continued cycling as a means of keeping fit. Fitness was important to him, although appearances to the contrary, he still suffered from ill health. Bouts of fatigue and restlessness had plagued him throughout his adult life. His regular attendance at the Birmingham Athletic Club had to some extent made him feel better physically, but mentally he had a tendency to ponder over matters. His sister Beadie was forever concerned over his health. During the planning of the move to Soho he had been under great strain, and now with that behind him he was under new stress from the reorganisation of Avery's and the battle he was waging with rival firms. He worked hard at holding back his emotions during the working day, but in the evenings at home they could flood out and he would sit alone reading and writing poetry to vent his feelings. The workforce at Avery's would have been surprised to see him grieve openly over chastising a workman, with Beadie comforting him.

Night-time brought no relief to him; he suffered terribly from insomnia and would often remain up reading, writing and planning into the early hours of the morning. Beadie would lie half awake in her bed ensuring he was well. The house servants were also aware of William's restlessness and were very understanding, helpful, and more importantly, discreet. William's obsession with privacy bordered on paranoia having its roots in his childhood. For all the security of his home life he was personally very insecure, with his mother acting as his anchor. Rebecca had had a hard time running the family business, and following the death of her husband she had realised just who her true friends were. William had learned from her that it was far better to have a few trusty friends than many acquaintances. William (and Rebecca and Beadie) were very loyal to those they considered friends. William's cousins, Annie Mary and Emily, had been very supportive over the years and William ensured that his success would be to their benefit as well. When Avery's had become a public company, debentures were issued and William obtained some for Annie Mary, Emily and Beadie allowing them some financial security and a certain degree of freedom.[3]

Beadie, his devoted sister, had given up much in support of her brother. Her life had revolved around him, and although, in William's formative years this would seem to make some sense, the fact she remained by his side as they both grew older sacrificing any personal life of her own seems is, perhaps, a little more surprising, although it must be said that William was the senior male in the household and Beadie's future depended greatly on him. William was a very proud man, and although he needed much comfort at times he would never actively seek it. Beadie was always there to give such comfort, and she knew exactly when to approach him and when to leave him alone; when to encourage him and when to sit outside his room late at night just in case he needed something, or someone. The Reverend Bevan and his wife often visited and were always in contact and, indeed, concerned that perhaps Beadie was a little too self-sacrificing, yet Beadie herself commented about her devotion to her brother:

> *"What are women for, but to comfort and strengthen and minister to such men?"*[4]

Why such devotion? Her mother had always instilled in her the need to tend to William's needs for he was their future, and as their mother had grown older, more and more did Beadie become responsible for the health of William. Her personal interests revolved around the home, gardening, reading and playing the piano. What social entertainment she became involved with centred on William and the old family friends.

The devotion was not all one-way however; William was as devoted to his mother and sister as he could be and ensured that both were well catered for. House servants attended to the daily chores, and financial arrangements had been made to ensure that any needs were met. The bond between the three of them was exceptionally strong and it was a bond of intellect as well as heart. It seems quite amazing that with his vast amount of work he found any time to dedicate to his family, but he did. His cousins, Annie Mary and Emily, had a special place in his heart. It was Annie Mary who had helped his mother through her most difficult period, such help was not forgotten. When Annie Mary met John Boothroyd, a draper from Holfirth, the Hipkins supported her decision to marry with William and his mother, Rebecca, acting as witnesses at their wedding.[5] A few years after the wedding William secured a job for John Boothroyd as a traveller for Avery's in the Bristol area.[6] William always shared his success with the family. He paid for a family tomb to be built at Warstone Lane cemetery having the bodies of his father, brother, and his uncle William Edward reinterred in the new plot. This plot would also serve as the resting place for his grandmother. It was his attention that in death the whole family would be together.

William had his own interests to take his mind off work—although that was rare, even on Sundays he would be working at home. His interest in Napoleon had grown in intensity, and he visited Paris on many occasions retracing his steps as a boy, spending time at the tomb of Napoleon. He amassed a great collection of medals, coins and books relating to Napoleon Bonaparte and Napoleon III, becoming a well-known collector among the Napoleonic fraternity regularly corresponding with other collectors. His collections didn't just focus on Napoleon though; he became an expert on items of vertu[7] possibly recalling the times at the old family business, obtaining select pieces and displaying them in a wood and glass cabinet. The house, in keeping with period, contained many pictures and paintings. In his study paintings and engravings of Napoleon Bonaparte and Napoleon III hung, positioned so that he could look up from his writing desk and contemplate the images and perhaps seek inspiration.

The family sanctum was the drawing room, beautifully set out with photographs and paintings of his family hung on walls or in silver frames on a shelf. One painting stood out as not being a family piece, it was a large oil painting of a woman and cupid; it was a serene picture and one that appeared out of place. To the eye of anyone visiting the home who didn't know William, they would see a warm and comfortable family environment so far removed from William's austere office in Soho Foundry. Sunday afternoons were special and even William found time to relax with his mother and sister, usually sitting in the conservatory taking tea or joining Bertha in the large greenhouse inspecting her plants.

William was not a great socialite yet due to his position and connections within the business community he found himself mixing with some important people at important events. In 1902, William formed part of the procession at William B. Avery's wedding to Suzanne Crets, a beautiful Belgium Society Lady. This was one of the big social events of the year in Paris. William being an ardent Francophile and fluent French speaker, his services to the Averys on this occasion would have been invaluable. The ceremony took place on September 2nd at St. Pierre de Chaillot, and was performed by the Abbé Ledein. By all accounts the wedding was a brilliant affair, with William escorting Mme. Beernaert the wife of the Belgian Minister of State (who accompanied Princess Zurlo). Members of the Avery family were present, but no other members of the Avery board attended. William Avery now had a new young wife, and was clearly spending more time with his social activities; which left William Hipkins to take care of the business. Three years later, William Avery was made a baronet, and as Sir William he now had more social and charitable activities, and left the company to Walter Chamberlain and William Hipkins; with Hipkins taking on most of the pressure of the business. Could he ever afford time to relax?

A man of William's standing made an ideal catch, as a very eligible bachelor of the sort that society women would naturally be interested in courting. William did little socialising save for that connected with Avery's, and even then he saw it as a duty rather than a social event, thus he made no efforts to be matched. His views on women were naturally coloured by his mother and sister, he railed at the irreligion of women who paraded themselves at church, but he also admitted (to Beadie) that he liked to see the well dressed ladies walk to church on a Sunday. With his private life being kept very private little has survived that can give a deep insight into William Hipkins the man at home, thus to even consider his more intimate relationships would be purely guesswork. He would see it as a disgraceful intrusion, and he would be right.

What is known is that sometime in or a little earlier than 1904 he met Lavinia Ellen Green. Very little can be found about this woman, her marriage certificate states she is a widow whose father, Samuel Phillips, had served as an officer in the Royal Irish Regiment serving in Australia, New Zealand and Afghanistan before returning to Ireland.[8] Lavinia, however, never really knew her father. It appears from the scant records that her parents came from Tipperary in Ireland. Her mother became pregnant out of wedlock with the then young Samuel Phillips as the father. The result of this liaison was that he was sent to join the army and Lavinia's mother was duly paid maintenance. Nothing is known of her childhood. Although her marriage certificate suggests she is a widow, it makes no mention of her maiden name and it is possible that she was not a widow at all. How she came to meet William remains a mystery, but the meeting led to a romance that would change William (as most romances do) for the rest of his life. His sister Beadie, cousins Annie Mary and Emily were pleased that William had finally met someone. Lavinia Ellen was a strong healthy woman ideal for the shy and unhealthy William. Family members commented on how pleased they were that Lavinia would be able to look after William (perhaps in a similar manner to how his mother and Beadie had). Although I know that his cousins and Beadie were aware of Lavinia, his mother was probably not. According to James Oliver Bevan, William kept his relationship with Lavinia secret due to his devotion to his mother. Bevan thought this was unnecessary. However, to William, he felt his devotion to his mother should be absolute following her devotion to him. Lavinia entered William's life at an opportune moment. For a number of years his mother had begun to grow ill and dementia had taken a hold. For William and his sister it was a distressing time, their mother had been so strong, so active, and now old age was dimming the light. William more than ever needed emotional support.

Yet this romance, although approved of by some of his family, was something William wished to remain secret from the workforce at Avery's. He wished the image of the managing director being wholly devoted to the firm to remain intact. His closest friends were aware, Gibson, Cartland, Avery and Bevan, but his managers such as Allinson were unaware that William had succumbed to the attentions of a woman. If no-one actually knew by being told that there was a woman in William's life, they should have at least realised by the behaviour of the man. William had shied away from public speaking for much of his career, with the only speeches he felt confident in making being those brief ones made during annual general meetings and shareholders' meetings. He made no attributable comments to the press, instead he made his feelings felt through the company secretary or through 'an informed source,' or even through his friend Gibson. His success at Avery's had the effect of improving his self-confidence at public speaking and commenting to the press, but also his private life was exceptionally secure and this had an extraordinary beneficial effect on him. Following the arrival of Lavinia, William's confidence had grown further. His performance as a speaker in public somewhat improved, and where once he was nervous and self conscious, now he showed great control and was more forceful in his delivery.

This newly found confidence enabled him to set even higher targets for himself and his devotion to Avery's seemed to have no bounds. There was nothing that was too much trouble for him when it came to the firm, and that meant long periods away from the cosy home. Trips to Scandanavia, South America and Europe he considered a vital part of the job as well as his regular visits to London, Manchester, Liverpool and Glasgow. William seemed to have more energy although still physically delicate; his willpower drove him on and where once it was his mother and sister who fuelled him now he had Lavinia as well.

The romance grew, and in 1905 William bought a leasehold luxury apartment at 50 Albert Hall Mansions Kensington and Lavinia Ellen moved in. This was one of the most fashionable apartment blocks in which to reside. The apartment comprised two bedrooms (one with a dressing room), a dining room and a large drawing room. This was no sordid love nest, William had proposed to Lavinia and she had accepted. It was usual for the marriage to take place in the town of the bride, and thus the plan was for Lavinia to qualify for London residency so that they could marry in London away from the business community of Birmingham; it seemed very few were to be told of the marriage. Thus, on July 15th 1905 William Edward Hipkins married Lavinia Ellen Green at St. Georges Registry Office, Hanover Square, London under an ordinary licence. It seems a remarkable time to get married. The court case in Edinburgh was still going on with a judgement due in just a couple of days. Was he so confident of victory? Apparently so.

The wedding ceremony was a small scale event, nothing too elaborate. William wouldn't wish too much fuss to be made; only feeling confident to show how he felt to a select few. Those attending[9] watched the civil ceremony, and William and Lavinia returned to Albert Hall Mansions. The whole marriage appears almost like a business arrangement. His friend Arthur Gibson was one of the witnesses, but the other witness says much about the whole arrangement; this was Reginald Robinson, a solicitor, located at 20 Budge Row London. This solicitor seems to have been used as his office was next door to the London office of Gibson & Ashford Accountants; so a friend or at least a business acquaintance of Arthur Gibson. Even given William wanted the marriage kept secret for his filial devotion to his mother, why the extreme detail of the secrecy? We may never know.

For William, marriage was a new enterprise, but for him a wife could not merely be a woman who tended house she had to be intelligent, caring, and most of all be his best friend, someone who he could whole heartedly rely upon. He considered such a relationship as something very sacred; this was how his mother had viewed her marriage. Lavinia would remain in London; William would commute weekly spending time with his wife at the weekends. For most at Avery's, Hipkins jaunts to London were normal and thus his 'secret' was safe. There was another reason why his weeknights were spent in Birmingham, he was concerned for his mother who remained ill, and he wanted to ensure that he spent as much time as he could with her. For a man who felt things deeply, yet being the typical Englishman of the age, holding the emotions back, the strains must have been great. His sister Beadie was, of course, always at the family home to look after their mother (aided by the servants) and one must wonder what she felt at this time. Her life (by consent) had been dedicated to her brother, now he was married and would need to commit more time to his wife. From all accounts she seems to have been content with her lot and, perhaps, in an age when family values have declined, such devotion is hard to understand. William did hope to start a family and pass onto his children all that he had learned in much the same way his father had hoped to pass on his knowledge to William. He would instil the same ideals that his mother had instilled in him, and he would make the family home a sanctuary from the business world, free from the prying eyes of managers and workforce.[10]

The future never looked better. William was now rising ever higher. William Avery was now looking upon Hipkins as a future Chairman of the Board, Chamberlain saw him as a useful political ally, and with his new wife William saw himself gain the confidence that he needed to push forward his most ambitious ideas. He could now see the summit of his career just a few years ahead of him. Sadly, his mother would not see it. In 1906 her health became increasingly a cause for concern and Beadie spent all her time at her mother's bedside. On November 10th Rebecca lapsed into unconsciousness, William and Beadie remained on vigil. James Bevan arrived on the 12th. Rebecca passed away quietly on the 13th aged 80.

The path that runs from the main entrance of Warstone Lane Cemetery to the Hipkins' plot had been well worn by the footsteps of William, Beadie and Rebecca as they visited the plot where George Frederick had been laid to rest in 1863. Now, the day that every son dreads had arrived, the day when a beloved mother has to be laid to rest. It was a chilly Saturday in November when William was joined by Lavinia, Beadie, James Bevan, Emily, Annie Mary, John Boothroyd and a very few close friends in Saint Michael's Church, Warstone Lane to hear the service. The Hipkins were strong, typically Edwardian, and there was no outward sign of emotion, not in public at least. There was a marked difference in this death to the others experienced by William; this one had been expected, the deaths of his father and uncle were sudden, he had been spared that at least. Even so, part of William died that day, and he needed all the support of his wife to carry him through.

CHAPTER 16

OVER THE TARIFF WALL

. . . to advance or not to advance is a matter for grave consideration, but when once the offensive has been assumed, it must be sustained to the last extremity.

-Napoleon maxim number 6.

In July 1905 Hipkins made a statement at Avery's Annual general meeting that was widely reported in the press:

". . . there was the possibility of establishing a factory in a commercially happier-land and steps have been taken by sending out a pioneer who was preparing the way in another quarter of the globe."[1]

To many it seemed an idle threat, a way of rousing the rebels for tariff reform. They were wrong.

Hipkins' venture into the United States began with Henry Richardson, the head of Avery's Automatic Grain Scale Department. Richardson had invented a grain scale that was produced at Avery's, whO in turn paid him royalties for the privilege. He wanted to promote these scales in the United States as the market there was far larger than the UK, and it offered a way into the United States home market for Avery's. In 1902 Richardson's assistant, Charles Frankland Beakbane, was given leave of absence and sent to the United States in order to try and form a syndicate to sell Richardson's grain scales, with the understanding that Avery's (at Soho) would manufacture them. Richardson and Beakbane had help from a clerk at Soho. Herbert E. Godfrey's uncle, Edwin Schofield, lived in Passive, New York and Herbert visited him annually.[2] Richardson (along with his family) sailed out to Passive in 1903 and moved into a house arranged by

219

Edwin Schofield.[3] Godfrey joined him a few months later,[4] and they met with Beakbane to draw up plans for a syndicate to sell scales in the United States. The *Richardson Scale Company* was the result, formed with a capital of $125,000 with Richardson himself receiving $45,000 worth of shares. Richardson, now established in the United States saw his opportunity to overcome US tariffs. He was still employed (albeit part-time) by Avery's. Godfrey was still in full-time employment at Avery's, and on his return he tried to entice some of Avery's best scale makers and managers to go back with him to work with Richardson. Richardson was especially keen to obtain the services of Charles Beakbane, but Godfrey couldn't convince Beakbane to return with him. Not all of Avery's employees were so loyal; two workmen Murray and Green defected to the USA. Godfrey returned to the States and became the firm's (Richardson Scale) secretary.[5] Beakbane who had now taken over Richardson's old job at Avery's, reported to Hipkins what Richardson was doing and tensions began to grow. Hipkins felt that Richardson was wholly untrustworthy and that sooner or later he would make further moves against Avery's with the intent of sewing up a USA-UK market for scales.

In 1904 Hipkins' plans for the USA moved on when Wilfred Williams visited the United States as a 'tourist' taking in the key industrial areas to see what opportunities lay in setting up a subsidiary factory across the Atlantic.[6] He made many contacts and in a manner not too dissimilar to Hipkins' own tour of the USA in 1873. Wilfred gathered information about various cities. Information about types of manufacturing companies, access to raw materials, workforce availability, land prices, access to rail links, commercial facilities, dynamic activity of the cities' administration, and a dozen other statistical notes were gathered. Hipkins knew from his own experience in the USA that records were avidly maintained and the local authorities were more than happy to supply the information. When Wilfred returned to Avery's he was loaded down with data that Hipkins analysed in extreme detail.

Several cities showed themselves to be dynamic and growing industrially, however, there were some problems. East coast cities, such as Boston, were already well established, and although the whole New England area had excellent transport facilities and access to raw materials, many industries were already set up and Avery's would have to compete with them for labour and material. Avery's wanted to sell scales to the American market and it would be better if a city was located more inland on the continent (not unlike Birmingham in the UK), so that goods could be easily distributed to all the major industrial cities.

The city that seemed to meet Hipkin's criteria was *Milwaukee* in the state of Wisconsin. The city is located on the western shore of Lake Michigan 740 miles west of New York and about 1,800 miles east of San Francisco, being in the northern half of the United States about 400 miles south of the Canadian border. This location placed the city half-way between the commercial east and the agricultural west. The city had begun life as a fur-trading station and slowly developed with its port on Lake Michigan becoming a major link with Canada to the north and Chicago (84 miles) to the south. Settlers heading out westwards would stop at Milwaukee and supplies of food and raw materials needed in the west were also transported though the city, and to meet an ever growing demand the port facilities had been extended. The city fathers had been keen to develop Milwaukee as a focal point for rail connections to the United States vast hinterland. On April 15, 1857 rail connections were established with *Prairie Du Chien,* and within just a few years 1,200 miles of track had been laid linking the city with many towns and cities in the state and beyond. Immigrants from the Old World (mainly German and Irish) poured into the city bringing with them their skills. The German immigrants were responsible for developing the brewing industry for which Milwaukee would become famous.[7]

It was the railway that brought great prosperity to Milwaukee, linking east and west, with Milwaukee acting as the major staging post. The railway was transporting everything from grain and wheat to metals and finished goods from the east, and the commercial strength of the City was strong. Like other cities in the USA and the UK the economy began to change to an industrial one with industrial output rising rapidly from $18,798,122 in 1869 to $123,786,449 in 1899, and by the time of Wilfred William's arrival in 1904 industrial output exceeded $200,000,000. The city's Chamber Of Commerce was actively encouraging business to set up in the city where the transport links were superior to any other city on the continent, and access to a keen workforce would enable any new business to flourish. It was this kind of hard sell, enthusiasm and energy that impressed Hipkins.

Hipkins liked to plan a strategy carefully; however, events were moving rapidly. The British Government under the premiership of Arthur Balfour, was ever more divided over the issue of tariff reform and it was highly unlikely that a change to policy was going to take place, regardless of the efforts of Joseph Chamberlain in the meeting halls and his son, Austin, in the government. To add to the pressure Richardson made the move that Hipkins had been expecting. Richardson's grain scale patent expired and he decided to play both ends of the Atlantic against each other by selling US made scales in the UK. Little did he know that Hipkins had a surprise for him.

Hipkins unlike many other businessmen, was not prepared to wait and see whether or not the Government would introduce a Tariff Reform Bill. He sped up his plans for a foreign-based factory and thus set into motion a plan to build or buy a facility in Milwaukee. As a reward for his loyalty Charles Beakbane was given the post as manager of the 'American Factory,' with the responsibility of setting up the new facility. This 'promotion' of sorts came as a surprise to many at Avery's. Thirty-two year old Beakbane was the brother-in-law of T. St. J.B. Parnell, and was taken on at Avery's following the purchase of Parnell. Parnell's had kept him, it seems, purely on the grounds that they had purchased some of Beakbane's patents. In 1896 he became a traveller for Avery's under Richardson, moving to Acocks Green in Birmingham. On Richardson's departure to the United States he had taken over the Automatic Grain Scale Department; his performance though was less than satisfactory. His assistant S.H. Johnson was perceived by many as the man who really did run the department as Beakbane, having no engineering or scale making experience, was wholly impractical and was often jealous of those who had superior skills.[8] He was loyal, it seems, and Hipkins knew he could trust him in that respect. He also knew that while in the United States the Automatic Grain Scale Department would not be adversely affected—even so Beakbane's stay in the United States was to be brief.

In November 1905 Beakbane was dispatched to Milwaukee to hire land, buildings and plant with a spending limit of £4,000.[9] He found that the United States was in a boom period and everything for hire was at a premium if available at all. Thus, it was necessary to purchase all that was required. Beakbane set about scouring Milwaukee to find the land at the right price. There was none in the heart of the city near the railway yards and shipping port, thus he had to look further afield eventually settling on some land on *Hopkins Street* in North Milwaukee. The building of the new factory began. Some members of the Avery Board wondered at the boldness of the move. Walter Chamberlain was a big supporter of Hipkins' plan—but then, as a Chamberlain, he would be. Hipkins told the board that after two years of operation he could see the American Factory employing 500 men! With this facility he could attack foreign and home competition at the same time. Scales made in Milwaukee could enter the British market cheaper than the same scales made in Soho, removing the low price disparity with American and German imports. Milwaukee-made scales could also be distributed across the United States at prices more akin to their home grown products. To Hipkins it appeared to be a win-win situation.

Events at home were still moving at a pace. Prime Minister Balfour resigned due to the continuing divisions within the Conservative Party, and the Liberal Campbell-Bannerman became Prime Minister. Joseph Chamberlain and the other tariff reformers saw that, at last, the opportunity had arisen to force through protectionist policies. As expected a general election was called and Chamberlain worked hard to get the reform message out to the public. Hipkins personally urged his workforce to support the protectionist candidates at the general election, emphasising that it was a vote for their own livelihoods. In January 1906 the Conservatives were resoundly beaten, although Chamberlain and his supporters did well in Birmingham. The new government maintained a policy of Free Trade, resulting in the United States (as well as other nations) maintaining an advantage over Avery's (and other British manufacturing companies). Many firms, who had waited to see what would happen realised too late that they would receive no support from the government. Avery's on the other hand were already several steps ahead.

Beakbane, with lightening speed, had got the Milwaukee Factory constructed and ready to begin production by October 1st 1906. The factory was constructed in much the same manner as the new buildings at Soho; a double story though single floor building of brick with large windows running down the side on two levels. The inside of the building was steel-framed with a large overhead crane running down two thirds of the factory that could be used to lift large castings. Various lathes and workbenches were very neatly set-out, and the wooden floor was surprisingly clear of the usual clutter as often seen at Soho. The building was lit with electric lighting and a boiler house supplied heating which was especially needed, as the winters in Milwaukee are very cold indeed. The factory lacked heavy forging facilities being set-up mainly as an assembly plant with only smaller castings being produced. Bigger items could be cast by contract or speciality items could be shipped from the

UK, although this was not intended to be the norm. Transport wasn't a problem, the factory was on the main road which led right into Milwaukee and its ports.

Beakbane had a more difficult task than expected in hiring skilled workmen, with many of the American factories utilising machine tools, skills needed by Avery's were not forthcoming, although assemblers were readily available. It meant that a period of training was required for new workmen and as a result factory fell behind schedule. Even so, October 1906 would see Hipkins' dream come true. The first board was made up of three Americans and one Englishmen. The President was Louis G. Bohmrich; Vice President—James K. Ilsley, a Milwaukee banker; Secretary-Treasurer—Charles J. Simeon;[10] and the Assistant Secretary—N.C. Webster. Beakbane stayed on as Works Manager.

Hipkins read the Wall Street Journal with a sense of satisfaction as the *Avery Scale Company* was floated on the US market. The new firm was launched by issuing 1,250 $100 shares (around £25,000), with 10 shares being issued to Beakbane for his hard work. The main task now was to obtain orders from US companies for scales, a task now easier as the American factory could trade at the same if not lower prices than other American firms. A team of salesmen had been recruited and branches were set up in New York, Chicago, Minneapolis, St. Louis and Dallas.

All was not rosy, however; the factory itself having to be built from scratch was constantly in need of additional elements. By 1907 £22,000 had been spent on the factory—more than three times the original allowance. Sales were slow, a slump in the US economy was adding to the problems, plus Hipkins treated the American firm as if it was a branch and tried to maintain a tight control that was not as easily achieved as with other branches. The managers at the factory, being so far from Birmingham, acted independently knowing that Hipkins' web did not cross the Atlantic. They assumed that as the factory had been Hipkins' baby he would never let it fail and would, therefore, always subsidise its activities. This led to some rather slack control and over spending.

Having achieved his main goals reasonably well, Beakbane returned to the UK with Charles J. Simeon to discuss progress. Hipkins was disappointed but understood that it would take time to crack the American market. Wilfred Bland (a graduate of the School of Commerce) was sent out in 1907 in order to use his skills and knowledge to help the fledgling firm.[11] Charles Simeon returned to the USA to take over as works manager—a role better suited to him; his six foot 2 inch frame was an imposing presence on the shop floor! He had been one of the highly successful managers at Avery's London Branch and was very keen to make a name for himself in the USA.

Hipkins had re-lit the tariff reform debate in Britain, and many politicians were concerned that work may be taken abroad as in the manner of Avery's. The British General Election had placed Herbert Asquith in the hot seat, and it seemed that once again, it would only be a matter of time before Britain introduced tariffs on imported goods. The United States Government certainly thought so and by 1908 President Theodore Roosevelt was concerned for the upcoming election in 1909 and wanted to come to an arrangement with Britain. Such a suggestion was jumped upon by Hipkins as justification for his actions in regard the American factory. In an article from an 'informant' published in the Birmingham Mail dated August 25, 1908 the approach from Roosevelt is attacked as being a trick to help him to re-election and stave off British tariffs on US goods, while at the same time keeping British goods out of American markets.[12]

Hipkins could feel very pleased with himself, his achievements had been great and now with the USA plant he was making a name for himself across the Atlantic. Avery's, with its strong board, was on the brink of dominating world scale manufacturing. Hipkins thought it would take a few years, but it would happen.

Yet, as Hipkins had seen before, tragedy can strike when it was least expected. With Avery's now on the verge of their greatest conquest, on 27th February 1908 Wilfred Williams suddenly died at his home in Newhall Street, Birmingham aged 65. Wilfred had been a great inspiration and help to Hipkins, and now he had gone. A few months later on October 28th, Sir William Beilby Avery passed away following a serious illness that he had kept secret from all but his closest friends; he was only 54. In the final few months Sir William had provided Hipkins with additional information and advice, and let it be known that he hoped that Hipkins would become Chairman of Avery's sometime in the future.

The loss of Sir William Beilby Avery was not only felt by the business community, all of Birmingham felt the loss. It was not only the loss of a great character and businessman but it was the end of an era. One of the last great family business dynasties was coming to a close—the Averys.

Sir William was cremated at Perry Barr Crematorium on November 2nd with the funeral service being held the next day at Witton Cemetery.

It was attended by the great and the good of the city led by the principal mourners: Sir William Eric Avery Bart, Mr. J.F. Wright, Messrs Clive and Claud Wright (nephews), Misses Gladys, Hilda, and Gwendolin Wright (nieces), and the Reverend G. Beilby. At the crematorium waited over 300 Avery employees with friends and colleagues, many of whom had travelled from London by special train. The employees formed a double line on the pathway, and as the family mourners filed past they were joined by Walter Chamberlain, Arthur Gibson, William Hipkins, Lieutenant Colonel Mayhew, H.H. Avery, Dr. and Mrs. Athill, Messrs. L. Brierley, R.S. Jackson, J.H. Beilby, J.H. Mackenzie, F. Athill, R.A. Pinsent, H.K. Bather, G.J. Johnson, F. Williams, J. Macgrath, B. Corser, T. Burford, J.W. Ryland, A.J. Williams, T. Grimley, D.E. Alves, F. Mackenzie, Julius Mackenzie, Edward Bather, Herbert Bather, H. Hawkes, Miss Williamson and Sir William's Nurse. Behind these came those representing various organizations of which Sir William had been associated. The small chapel was over-crowded and many had to stand outside. The list read like a who's who of local commerce. The Reverend W.H. Bather, vicar of Meole-Brace, Shrewsbury and the Reverend H.S. Pelham, curate of the cathedral church officiated. A magnificent choir sang as the urn containing Sir William's ashes was carried on a small bier covered with a violet pall, the urn itself being encircled by Lady Avery's wreath—a heart composed of Parma violets. The remains were placed in the Avery family vault. Floral tributes had been received from some of the country's most well known and respected people—Lord and Lady Newborough, Lord and Lady Edward Spencer Churchill, Captain and Mrs. Pretyman, Baroness Emile d'Erlanger and the famous motor car entrepreneur A. Darraq.[13]

It was a solemn occasion, and that evening the Avery workforce drank many a toast to the memory of Sir William, and the older hands lamented that from now on there would be no counter to Hipkins' management style.

Overall 1908 had been a difficult year. A world depression was beginning to bite yet Avery's was in profit, expenditure was down, and at the Annual General Meeting in March 1909 Walter Chamberlain announced how impressed he had been with the progress of the company and the attitude of managers and workers. He then spoke of the *American Factory*, stating that he expected a hopeful future, that the aim to secure Avery's position in the USA had been achieved although with hindsight he would have set up the plant two years later, thus avoiding the sudden slump in the American market—although at the time this could not have been predicted. Hipkins' decisions were supported publicly, and when a question from a shareholder was asked regarding the status of the bonus, Walter Chamberlain replied:

> "... *As regard the bonus, the directors are anxious to make sure of continuing the 10 per cent. dividend and not to be under the necessity of reducing it. In business as in nations, the good old rule obtained, the simple plan of "Let him take who had the power and let him keep who can". I trust our Managing Director will take all he can and will keep all he has got!"* [14]

Chamberlain then launched the annual attack on the policy of Free Trade.

CHAPTER 17

LOST LOVE

Oh, my adorable wife! I don't know what fate has in store for me, but if it keeps me apart from you any longer, it will be unbearable! My courage is not enough for that.
              -Napoleon Bonaparte to Josephine April 3rd, 1796

For William Edward Hipkins, life was on the up. He was successful, respected; his business moves had made Avery's a household name, he was Vice Chairman and being groomed for the Chairmanship, something to take him into his old age and retirement; and what's more his personal life was settled. His wife, Lavinia, had proved to be as much as a comfort to him as his mother, and he also ensured that his sister and cousins were looked after and happy. James Bevan often called and wrote. It was a safe comfortable world. Hipkins exuded confidence, many commented on his performance during the AGMs and how he now commanded the stage. There is little doubt that Lavinia was responsible for this self assured image, she could bolster him when he had self doubts or when he felt he had been too hard on an employee. Married life had brought to him a level of personal comfort he had needed, he was even looking forward to having children, perhaps a son that would follow in his footsteps, a son with whom he could teach and develop in much the same way his mother and James Bevan had taught him.

It must, therefore, have been a heavy blow when this happy lifestyle was shattered by bad news. Lavinia had been seen as a good strong woman to take care of William, no one could have imagined that Lavinia would become ill. In May 1909 she became bloated and lost her appetite, and she was losing weight.[1] The family doctor, Richard Arthur Newton of 92 Newhall Street, was consulted. After a series of tests he diagnosed that Lavinia was suffering from cancer of the bile ducts, which had more than likely spread to her liver. This rare illness has no symptoms until it is too late, even in the 21st century the outlook is bleak. Yet William insisted on trying anything and everything. He checked her weight on his personal weighing machine, monitoring Lavinia's weight as various treatments were tried.[2]

William was distraught but he was not about to let it show. With the assistance of Dr Newton he visited local doctors and surgeons such as Mary Sturge, Frederick Edge and the somewhat eccentric Jordan Lloyd. Lloyd was an extraordinary man educated, like William, at King Edward's School sweeping the board of prizes and exhibitions during his study years. He had vast experience working at Queen's College Paradise Street, then in London, and later in Newcastle Upon Tyne. He obtained his MS and MB at Durham being first in each examination. In 1881 he was appointed casualty Surgeon at the Queen's Hospital, and two years later he was elected to the honorary staff.[3] His colleagues saw him as a surgical genius—if anybody could advise it would be Jordan Lloyd. But even the best of people can be defeated, and in the case of Lavinia Jordan Lloyd's prognosis was not good. This didn't stop William, he travelled the country speaking to surgeons and doctors hoping to find something that might help. On his regular business trips to London he took time to consult with medical experts, find books on liver disease such as *Burnett's Diseases of the Liver*; but no one and nothing seemed to offer any hope at all. William read so much about conditions of the liver he was soon able to converse with senior medical men, asking the right questions and offering suggestions. His sister, Beadie, looked after Lavinia while he was at work and the house servants were a constant source of support.

Lavinia grew weaker, losing weight, and after a few weeks began to suffer pain. William was a business man dedicated to his work, but above all else he was dedicated to those closest to him and his closest business associates were aware of Lavinia's illness and they took some of the pressure from him at work. Arthur Gibson was of particular help looking after some of the more routine financial material, and visiting William at his home in Edgbaston to simply discuss matters with him, thus leaving William to be with his ailing wife.

Lavinia celebrated her 41st birthday on February 5th 1910 from her bed. She was now very ill, William, Beadie and William's cousins were there to make the best of the day; for most it was just William and Lavinia together.

As the week went on Lavinia grew weaker and was mostly sedated with drugs to ease the pain. With William beside her holding her hand she passed away on February 24th. William broke down and his sister comforted him, it was a devastating blow even though it had become inevitable. William had lost two of the three women closest two him within five years and it cut through him. The funeral was held at the family plot in Warstone Lane cemetery on Saturday February 26th with a brief mention in the press.[4]

William now buried himself in his work, he became slightly more irritable at times; however, according to James Bevan he did not become bitter, if anything he became even kinder and more generous to those he considered close friends and family. Indeed, Bevan commented on how loving William could be. Yet, even so, William must have been deeply shaken by the loss of his wife, his soul mate and lover. William was never the same again as part of him died with Lavinia.

Already a driven man, William now drove himself harder. Beadie was his main support at home and at work . . . he never asked for support and thus his stern expression and cold appearance hid his inner most feelings. The American factory was an enterprise in which he had staked a great deal, but developments in other markets were still moving on. His attempt to challenge Pooley's in the weighbridge market had gone well. Avery's built the largest weighbridges in the world, something that had rankled Pooley's management. Ever since Hipkins had arrived at Avery's he had made it clear that the only position for the company was number one, and with the installation of a 100 ton weighbridge at the North Eastern Marine Engineering Company of Newcastle Upon Tyne set a new standard. This machine was operated by five levers and was used to weigh the new generation of marine engines being fitted to the new large ocean liners. Pooley's had built their reputation on supplying weighbridges to railway companies, but now Avery's had broken that monopoly with combined weighbridges (a multiple weighbridge) being supplied to the North Eastern Railway Company, and one to the *Central Colliery* at Vereeniging in the Transvaal. China was a new market and Hipkins had Avery's represented there supplying five weighbridges to the *Shanghai-Nanking Railway*, each embodying two 18 foot platforms with a capacity of 66 tons which came complete with a duplex printer! The USA was the territory that Hipkins was targeting, and here inroads were being made with tenders for railway weighbridges being submitted to the big US railroad companies such as Grand Trunk, and Pennsylvania. US weighing machine manufacturers were competing hard with Avery's in all corners of the globe with Fairbanks desperately trying to enter into the Australian market, with Hipkins countering Fairbanks generous discounting.

The Avery Scale Company Inc. of Milwaukee had yet to establish itself as a company capable of taking on the likes of Toledo, Fairbanks etc. and Hipkins was concerned that his great adventure across the pond might be a step too far, and that concern was in his mind; he loved success and the thought of a major failure would be disastrous especially for him now personally. Certainly Walter Chamberlain and Arthur Gibson were aware of the strain that Hipkins was placing himself under, Beadie noted how his sleeping patterns were more erratic than usual, but with the love and care of his friends and family Hipkins would be protected.

Life though always has its surprises and as the second anniversary of the death of Lavinia approached Hipkins received a letter on February 21st 1912, a letter from C.F. Beakbane of the Avery Scale Company:

Gentlemen:-

You will be interested to hear that after six months severe trial by the U.S. Government of various makes of Automatic Weighing Machines, including that made by the Richardson Scale Company and ourselves, it has been decided by the U.S. Government to equip the boiler house at the U.S. Navy Yard, Washington with scales of our make to the exclusion of all others, and they have placed with us a contract to supply a large number of these machines.

The scales of other makes have been shipped to their respective owners.

Yours very truly,
The Avery Scale Company [5]

Hipkins would have been forgiven if he gave a yell of delight; he probably just smiled to himself. It was a stunning victory which bucked the trend of US firms capturing UK markets. The Board of Directors couldn't hide their pleasure at the news; Hipkins' bold move to the United States had paid off. He was naturally pleased and Beadie noticed for the first time in two years the pressure seemed to lift from him a little. For William he wished his beloved Lavinia could have shared in the moment.

The contract with the U.S. Government could open up the entire North American market to Avery's which included the postal service, Army, merchant marine, dockyards etc. Hipkins now went into full attack mode, it was important to demonstrate to the new customer the level of importance the order was to Avery's. He as Managing Director would travel to the U.S. to ensure that the contract was started on a sure footing that nothing was left to chance. From his first visit in 1873 he knew the Americans were impressed by the biggest, the best, and were always expecting people to go the extra mile. Hipkins would ensure that the Americans would be under no illusion that they were dealing with the top man from the world's largest and best weighing machine company. To this end he realized by a happy coincidence that within a few weeks the pride of Britain's merchant marine, the largest ocean liner in the world was to depart Southampton for New York on its maiden voyage; he knew he should travel on this vessel and make an entrance into New York that would impress. The ship was the White Star Liner *Titanic*.

CHAPTER 18

ATLANTIC ODYSSEY 1912

Perhaps I should not insist on this bold manoeuvre, but it is my style, my way of doing things.
                    -Napoleon 1813, letter to Prince Eugene.

Hipkins had taken the train from New Street Station to London many times, and on four occasions the trips had been the first leg of a journey across the Atlantic.[1] His first such journey had been thirty-eight years previously when, as a wide eyed youth, he had set off with Thomas Guest to learn something about the New World. So much water had flowed under the bridge since then, and as he sat in the carriage reading through his paperwork, he would have spared little time to reminisce. He was more concerned with the *American Factory,* and the newly won order for weighing machines for the United States Navy. This order, he hoped, would transform the subsidiary company, and begin to deliver his promise of capturing some of the American home market.

On Monday April 8th, the 8.20am train from New Street Station left on time pulling out and beginning its two hour high-speed race to London Broad Street calling only at Coventry on the way. It was the 'City to City Express' a special train that carried a breakfast car and typists for use by businessmen.[2] Like all of Hipkins' activities he used his time efficiently spending two days in London meeting with the managers at the London Branch and discussing general business matters. He made copious notes outlining what he wanted to discuss and since the death of his wife he had been sharper with his managers, and they did not relish his arrival. As always prior to a trip abroad, Hipkins wanted to ensure that everything was in order and that everyone knew what was expected of them.

Avery Advertisment *(Avery Historical Museum)*

Avery Branches (*Avery Historical Museum*)

Rochester Time-Clock machine in the Engineering Department

(*Avery Historical Museum*)

August 20th 1912

To the Branch Managers of
W. & T. Avery

Gentlemen. Some of you have been good
enough to offer me your sympathy in my
severe bereavement. others of you I have not
the pleasure of knowing. but I have seen a
copy of your joint letter of regret addressed
to your Directors in which you very feelingly
refer to the high esteem in which you held
my dearly beloved brother, & these expressions
although not addressed to me. have been
a comfort to me in my deep sorrow.

I take this opportunity of thanking you
for the loyal manner in which you
assisted my brother in his conduct of the
firm's business, and I know that he very
much appreciated it.

I who know the character and the
beauty of the map of life which he marked
out for himself, hope that you esteem his
example highly enough to let it be still
a help to you although he has passed away.

Yours faithfully
Bertha N. Perkins.

Bertha's letter to the Avery managers
(Avery Historical Museum)

Avery Scale Co. Milwaukee factory
(Avery Historical Museum)

Milwaukee factory interior
(Avery Historical Museum)

PRESIDENT, C. F. BEAKBANE
SEC. AND TREAS. H. C. WEBSTER

DIRECTOR AND CON. ENG. H. D. GRAY
CON. ENG. (POWER STA.), WILL J. SANDO
CHIEF ENGINEER, H. W. WELSH

BRANCHES
NEW YORK
CHICAGO
MINNEAPOLIS
ST. LOUIS
DALLAS
AND FOREIGN

The **Avery** SCALE CO.

ADDRESS ALL COMMUNICATIONS
TO THE COMPANY.

NORTH MILWAUKEE, WIS.

In Reply Refer to No. 1825-E
Your reference H. 2143

Jan-29th-1912

W. & T. Avery, Ltd.,
    Soho Foundry,
        Birmingham, England.

Gentlemen:-

You will be interested to hear that after six months severe trial by the U. S. Government of various makes of Automatic Weighing Machines, including that made by the Richardson Scale Company and ourselves, it has been decided by the U.S. Government to equip the boiler house at the U.S. Navy Yard, Washington with scales of our make to the exclusion of all others, and they have placed with us a contract to supply a large number of these machines.

The scales of other makes have been shipped to their respective owners.

Yours very truly,

The Avery Scale Company

C. F. Beakbane
President.

CFB.GHS.

**Avery Scale Company letter confirming
US Naval contract** *(Avery Historical Museum)*

In Memoriam.

WILLIAM EDWARD HIPKINS.

Vice-Chairman and Managing Director of W. & T. Avery, Ltd.

A Life Governor of the Birmingham University.

Sometime a Director of The Birmingham Small Arms Co., Ltd., and Managing Director of J. & E. Wright, Ltd.

Member of The Institute of Mechanical Engineers.

BORN 1st JANUARY, 1857,

AND

PASSED AWAY IN THE WRECK OF THE "TITANIC," 15th APRIL, 1912.

W.E. Hipkins' Memorial Booklet
(Avery Historical Museum)

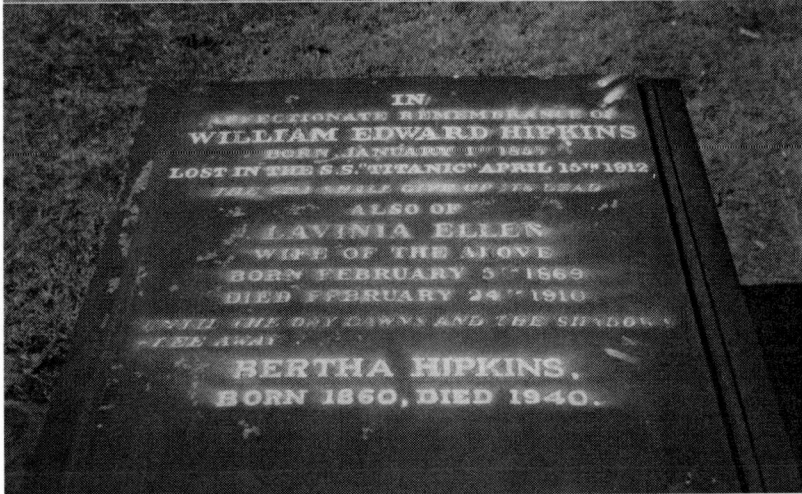

Hipkins' Family plot at Warstone Lane Cemetary,
Birmingham *(Author's collection)*

Wiiliam E. Hipkins in 1912
(Avery Historical Museum)

R.M.S. "Titanic" (Auhtor's collection)

On the night of April 9th Hipkins double-checked everything; it was late and he wanted to be assured that all was well. He telephoned Beadie and spent a quarter of an hour talking about nothing in particular and checking that she was feeling better; her cold had left her rather chesty. He got into bed and sipped his hot chocolate, in the morning he would be aboard the world's largest liner on her maiden voyage. He was excited at being a part of a moment in history. He felt that as he was a leading businessman only the largest liner would suffice for the crossing, especially as he was doing business with the Americans, they would be suitably impressed with his choice of ship. He read late into the early hours, eventually falling asleep after several chapters about Napoleon.

Next morning the motor cab dropped him at Waterloo Station; he paid the driver and dropped him a small gratuity. A porter tipped his hat and took Hipkins' bags placing them on a trolley and led him to the platform where the *Titanic Express* was waiting. It was 9.15am. The steel and glass roof of Waterloo looked magnificent; the station had recently been renovated. Hipkins only gave it a cursory look as he walked to Platform 12. The London and South Western Railway train was waiting, the freshly cleaned green livery of the T-9 locomotive stood gently steaming with a rake of chocolate brown and cream coaches coupled behind, their doors open inviting the passengers to board.

Hipkins boarded and sat down in the soft blue seats of the first class compartment and opened his newspaper; just another business trip had begun.

The first class express had many passengers on board destined to meet the *Titanic*. Father Frank Browne, for example, was travelling on the maiden voyage only as far as Queenstown in Ireland, purely for the experience and to take many photographs. Hipkins may have seen the priest on the platform clicking away as William Waldorf Astor posed smartly. Numerous press photographers had gathered too, hoping to capture that all important image of a known face.[3]

Promptly at 9.45 am the train pulled out of Waterloo station to race the 79 miles to Southampton docks. The sinuous route forced the locomotive to work hard as it passed through Vauxhall, a name familiar to Hipkins as there was a Vauxhall station in Birmingham not far from where the family business had been set up. On past Queen's Road, Clapham Junction, Earlsfield, and Wimbledon, the slate roofs of the ever diminishing number of houses catching the early sunlight. The suburbs of London and the outlying towns gave way to open countryside as the train raced on towards Woking, a vital part of the network. Hipkins could see the extensive goods sidings and the large orphanage completed just three years previously. The fireman stoking hard in the single firebox as the train gathered speed crossing over the junctions at Brookwood. One of these junctions led to Bisley Camp, familiar to Hipkins as in the Summer months the line was busy taking sportsmen and soldiers to the target shooting range.

The train entered into 'Deepcut' a deep and wide cutting leading out into the open line running next to the old Basingstoke Canal, which suddenly turns south just before Pirbright Junction and crossing the mainline on a substantial viaduct with enormous arches. The train rattled over the complex junction at Pirbright with Laffan's Plain lying to the South—a regular training ground for the army. The moors of rough grass and heather stretched on either side of the tracks, broken up by woodland of spruce, birch, and oak trees. It was a lovely sight as along the southern horizon the long ridge of Hog's Back came into view. The train was climbing past Farnborough, Bramshot Halt, Fleet, Winchfield, and Hook crossing over the large Fleet Pond and on past Basingstoke. Through Worthing Junction opening up onto a high speed stretch of ten stationless miles, entering into Litchfield tunnel near the summit of the long climb and into the twin Popham Tunnels. Just to the north huge excavations of chalk could be seen much of which was used in the West Docks at Southampton.

Now racing downhill, Hipkins watched Micheldever race past and then all darkness as the train entered Wallers Ash Tunnel. Then out into bright sunlight past Winchester and Shawford running along side the River Itchen and entering into Eastleigh with its large locomotive and carriage works. On past Swathing as the train slowed passing Saint Denys and entered into Southampton, slowly passing through the small station attached to the South Western Hotel. The traffic on Canute Road was halted as the train crossed over entering into Southampton Docks, coming to a complete stop at the platform opposite the quay with the *Titanic* waiting in the new deep water dock recently enlarged for *Titanic* and her sister.[4]

Hipkins left the carriage and walked the short distance to the gangway. He stopped and looked at the liner. The largest moveable object made by man, 882 feet 9 inches long, 92 and a half feet at her widest point, 46,328 gross tons (66,000 tons displacement) her four funnels painted White Star buff glinted in the morning sunshine. Hipkins was impressed; she was nearly twice the size of the last ship in which he had crossed the

Atlantic—the S.S. *Baltic*—a year ago—and a far cry from the SS *Tarifa* on which he sailed into Boston in 1873. He was always impressed by the largest, the biggest, the highest, and in 1912 the *Titanic* fitted all of these statements and more besides. Not only was she the largest but also the most luxurious liner afloat, attracting the very best clientele, the type of people who were the big players in the world of politics and business, the kind of people with whom Hipkins did business.

He walked up the gently sloping gangway to the first class passengers' entrance on B Deck where he was greeted by Chief Steward Latimer and his staff. Hipkins handed over his ticket and boarding card which was checked by Purser's Clerk Ernest King against his list. He looked flustered; passengers had been coming aboard in quick fashion. Hipkins' ticket, number 680 which had been allotted to room C39 was duly ticked off the list. A steward grabbed hold of Hipkins' carry-on bag and led him through the doors leading to the B deck entrance hall and staircase. They went downstairs to C deck; Hipkins was impressed by the fan shaped spread of the oak staircase with wrought iron scroll work somewhat after the style of Louis XIV.[5] The steward hurried ahead, it was a busy day and Hipkins followed turning left at the bottom of the stairs and walking towards the Purser's Office. A small passageway separated the Purser's office from room C39 and the steward entered the room, placed Hipkins' bag on the floor, and went through the usual pleasantries quickly showing Hipkins all the facilities. Hipkins was accustomed to quality accommodation on board ships, as he had experienced on the *Baltic* and the *Oceanic,* and his room on *Titanic* didn't disappoint.

The room could accommodate three persons although on this trip he had it to himself. The decoration wasn't as ostentatious as the B deck suites, but it was bright and comfortable with a WC and bath that was shared with rooms 35 (unoccupied) and 37 (occupied by Roberta 'Cissy' Maioni the Countess of Rothes' maid).[6] He looked out of the starboard side porthole and saw the calm water. On the Port side crowds had gathered staring at the ship. Lines of passengers were still boarding and Hipkins pondered if any business opportunities would present themselves on the voyage. He picked up his bag and placed it on the bed and began removing a few items to be placed in the dark wood chest of drawers, the brass handles sparkling and new. He didn't pause when he opened a drawer yet many years ago his father produced such brasswork in the old works in Ashted, and the brasswork here had come from Birmingham.[7]

Hipkins noticed on the top of a dresser was a collection of items supplied by courtesy of the *White Star Line*. There was a list of First Class Passengers and a plan of the first class accommodations and facilities. He looked at the plan. He was very conveniently located. The main staircase was only a few feet from his room, the Purser's office was next door, the first class dining saloon was a flight below and two flights above was the upper promenade deck.

He finished emptying his case placing a writing folder on the dresser along with a photograph of his departed wife. He checked his gold pocket watch that had once belonged to his father. 11.50, it would soon be time to depart. He checked that the connecting door to the bathroom was locked and then left for the deck. He walked up the stairs eventually reaching A deck with its marvellously decorated entrance with carved oak panelling, and from the bottom of the stairs he looked up to the topmost landing where a great carved wooden clock 'Honour and Glory Crowning Time' was fixed into the panelling. To top the whole staircase was a magnificent wrought iron and glass dome. He walked up the stairs and looked closely at the exquisite carving of the clock before moving on to the boat deck.

Many people were rushing about, others were standing looking over the side or admiring the ship. Some young boys were excitedly running about exploring, a cacophony of noise with people talking, shouting, motor engines, various whistles, horns all signified a busy dock—although' due to the coal strike' it was *Titanic* that would be leaving while a number of other ships stayed moored up like forgotten pets outside a shop.

At midday the ship's horn sounded' lines were cast off and the largest ship in the world slowly began to move away from the dock. People on board the ship were waving and shouting to unseen friends and family lining the quayside, people on the quayside were shouting and waving to the *Titanic*. The ship made her way forward as people ran alongside, the moored liner *New York* stirred slightly as the *Titanic* passed. She pulled at her mooring lines the strain growing when, suddenly, they snapped! The *New York* pulled clear of her stern moorings and was being dragged into a certain collision with the *Titanic*! If Hipkins saw this incident he would have been fascinated, he was one time Managing Director of J. & E. Wright Limited rope and cable makers. It was possible that it was their cables that had snapped and he would have known the breaking strength and thus the force required to pull the 10,508 ton ship from her moorings.

Calamity was, however, averted. The *Titanic* quickly came to a halt and the tug vessel *Vulcan* attached a cable to the *New York* pulling her away from the liner. A close shave, they missed each other by only ten feet, a minor if slightly nerve racking incident that only resulted in an hour's delay to the *Titanic*.

Hipkins responded to the bugle call to luncheon and he went down to D deck walking through the reception room and into the immense dining saloon—the largest room on ship being 92 feet wide and 114 feet long. Decorated in a style adopted from Jacobean English of the early seventeenth century with the designers carefully studying the architectural details at Hatfield and Haddon Hall as well as many other great houses. However instead of the sombre oak so characteristic of the period the walls and ceilings were painted white. The ceiling was richly moulded in a style typical of the very best Jacobean plasterers' art with curved sections supported by decorated columns. Large leaded glass windows in a style of a mansion behind which sidelights had been fitted. The room could seat 532 diners per sitting with the tables being arranged in a typical restaurant fashion with small tables some of which set into recessed bays for private parties or family groups.

Hipkins sat at his table and looked at the menu for April 10th it was a choice worthy of the White Star Line:

LUNCHEON
Consomme Jardiniere
Hodge Podge
Fillets of Plaice
Beef Steak & Kidney Pie
Roast Surrey Capon

FROM THE GRILL.
Grilled Mutton Chops
Mashed Fried & Baked Potatoes
Rice Pudding
Applesattan Pastry

BUFFET
Fresh Lobsters Potted Shrimps
Soused Herrings Sardines
Roast beef
Round of Spiced Beef
Virginia & Cumberland Ham
Bologna Sausage Brawn
Gelantine of Chicken
Corned Ox Tongue
Lettuce Tomatoes

CHEESE
Cheshire, Stilton, Gorgonzola, Edam
Camembert, Roquefort, St. Ivel. [8]

While Hipkins enjoyed his meal the *Titanic* steamed on to Cherbourg. The weather was fine, a pleasant April day and after luncheon Hipkins walked the deck before going back to his room to read through papers and prepare notes for his meeting in Milwaukee.

The *Titanic* arrived at Cherbourg in the evening dropping anchor outside the port with mail and passengers arriving at the ship via a tender. It was here that some of the *Titanic*'s most illustrious passengers would board including John Jacob Astor, a millionaire businessman, Benjamin Guggenheim a millionaire mining tycoon, and Sir Cosmo and Lady Duff-Gordon. As far as is known Hipkins was not personally acquainted with these people, he was, however, on speaking terms with Charles Hays head of the *Grand Trunk Railroad* since Avery's had been actively seeking contracts with United States railroad companies.

First class travel on trans-Atlantic liners in the early twentieth century was a lifestyle all of its own—especially on a *White Star* liner. The shipping line headed by J. Bruce Ismay had courted the very best clientele, and it was during dinner that the brightest stars in the business constellation shone. Hipkins saw himself as one of these stars joining an exclusive club. With Avery's position in the world and the new Milwaukee factory he was making an impact, and voyages across the Atlantic offered excellent opportunities to discuss business.

The first class al-a-carte restaurant, or 'Ritz' as it was referred to was a meeting place for the very sophisticated and Hipkins easily felt comfortable among the Astors and Guggenheims. One wonders who Hipkins talked with at that first dinner of the voyage, dining in the most opulent of surroundings onboard a liner. For a Francophile the room was to Hipkins' taste styled in the period of Louis XVI panelled from floor to ceiling in beautifully marked French walnut of a delicate light fawn brown colour, the mouldings and ornaments being richly carved and gilded. In the centre of the large panels hung electric light brackets, cast and finely chased in brass and gilt holding candle lamps. On the right of the entrance there was a counter with a marble top of fleur de peche, supported by panelling and plasters recalling the design of the wall panels.

The room was well lit by large bay windows which were a distinctive and novel feature giving a feeling of spaciousness. These were draped with plain fawn silk curtains with flowered borders and pelmets richly embroidered. Every detail down to the fastenings and hinges had been carried out with regard to purity of style even the plates had a special pattern in keeping with the décor. Hipkins appreciated such style and attention to detail.

The lavish meal was presented by the very best in waiter service, and Hipkins would have eaten only lightly avoided anything too rich. At the meal's conclusion the gentlemen would normally retire to the *First Class Smoke Room* located on A deck. It was here that many business deals could be discussed. Politics too especially as the likes of Astor, Guggenheim, and Hays would be concerned of any attempts by the US President Taft to reduce the freedoms of big companies or of the possible change in UK policy on free trade. The views of Major Archibald Butt would have been sought, he was President Taft's Aid de camp and no doubt over cigars and brandy heated discussions took place.

Like everything else about the *Titanic* the surroundings into which Hipkins found himself were of immense scale and luxury. The Smoke Room had panelled walls of the finest mahogany carved in the style of the Georgian period relieved everywhere with inlaid work of mother-of-pearl. A glorious fire-place made the room very homely, above which was a large painting 'Approach to the New World' by Norman Wilkinson. The room was surrounded by stained glass windows depicting ports and beauty-spots of the world. As a man who appreciated the finest things in life and one who respected success, the *Titanic* was Britain's greatest maritime success to date.

To most the voyage was routine, and for Hipkins the environment gave him time to work in peace and relax in comfortable surroundings. One wonders who he spoke to and if he made use of the gymnasium fully equipped with an electric horse, rowing machine, and static bicycles. Maybe he used the racquets court or took time in the *Turkish Bath*—it is likely he visited here as Avery's had supplied a weighing machine that printed out the weight of the sitter—a useful addition to the baths where passengers could see if they were losing weight!

Standing on the deck I wonder if he thought about his 1873 voyage, and I wonder if he gave a thought about when he was a boy from the deck of the *Tarifa*. There were some similarities in the passenger compliment. *Titanic*'s third class contained immigrant passengers seeking a better life in the New World, and these included a family from West Bromwich not far from Soho Foundry. West Bromwich was well represented; the ship's orchestra included John Wesley Woodward from Hill Top, and I wonder if he recognized Hipkins' accent? In all likelihood the mixture of people from all parts of Britain went about their business oblivious to most of the passengers and crew.

Sunday April 14th would have seemed like any other day onboard ship. Religious services were held, stewards raced about—although their boat drill had been cancelled. The Captain's inspection had kept everyone on their toes. The ship's designer, Thomas Andrews, was on board with a shakedown crew from Harland and Wolff of Belfast. He was also inspecting the ship looking to see if any improvements could be made. In the radio room the two Marconi operators were working hard sending passengers' messages, but also receiving some from other ships. These included weather reports, greetings for the Captain, and some reports of icebergs being seen drifting in the shipping lanes. Captain Smith had ordered a course change taking the ship further south; another order included the lighting of boilers that had remained cold—normal practice on a maiden voyage—whether this decision to light them had been influenced by the White Star Line Chairman Bruce Ismay no-one can be sure, but certainly it would add to the excitement of passengers running a sweep on the ship's daily run.

That Sunday evening was cold as the temperature was falling, the sky was perfectly clear and after the Sun had gone down the most beautiful night sky could be seen; millions of stars came out almost as if they all wanted to see the world's largest ship on her maiden voyage. The sea was dead calm like a mill pond. and the only wind was that formed by the ship racing to New York.

Many passengers did not, however, stay on deck to admire the celestial show; the cold forced them inside to their rooms, the lounge or the smoking room. Hipkins probably turned-in around 10pm to read as was his usual practice. He may have ordered a hot chocolate drink to help him sleep but certainly at 11.40pm he would have been awake reading as usual. Forward and above him on the bridge First Officer Murdoch was on watch, staring into the dark night.

Hipkins may have been stirred as a slight vibration ran through the ship; he may have looked out his porthole in time to see a white mass pass by—mistaken by some as a windjammer; he may have noticed the ship had come to a stop, but as there was no immediate alarm he would have returned to his book. Other passengers were not so calm. Many, on realising the ship had stopped, left their rooms to find out what was going on. Hipkins may have heard the commotion of people especially as female passengers started to line up outside the purser's office—near Hipkins' room—to claim their jewels from the safes. Hipkins would not have left his room to investigate; he would have waited until the knock came to his door and into the room entered a steward who would have politely asked him to put on warm clothes, his lifejacket, and come on deck. He would have asked what had happened, and was probably told that the ship had bumped a bit of ice and that it was simply a precaution to go on deck with lifejackets.

After putting on his clothes and lifejacket he would ensure he had his gold pocket watch that had once belonged to his father and went on deck via the Grand Staircase. On his way he would have seen the gathering of ladies at the Purser's office, and the confusion as some passengers had been ordered from the boat deck down to A deck.

On the boat deck he was confronted by seamen swinging-out the lifeboats with passengers standing by watching curiously. On the Port side Second Officer Lightoller called for "Ladies and children," on the starboard side Murdoch was preparing to load the boats, and Bruce Ismay, shocked at the news from the captain that the *Titanic* was doomed, shouting instructions to Third Officer Pitman. Amongst all this shouting ragtime music could be heard as the band was playing, West Bromwich man Woodward among them.

Hipkins was a typical Edwardian gentleman carrying with him the values of service, good manners and discipline. It would have been typical of him to have helped ladies and children in the direction of the boats—as many first, second and third class men did that night, but I have no record of him from any survivors.

As rockets fired high into the starlit night sky he would have been all too aware of the danger and as the arguments between husbands and wives about entering a lifeboat raged, he would have to make a decision as to what to do. Boats were being launched half-filled and it seemed that, given the number of people on deck and the number of boats left, there would not be enough room for everyone. Like many on board he had to finally make the decision as to whether to stay or try for a boat.

Benjamin Guggenheim, along with his secretary, in evening dress went for a last drink, John Jacob Astor after placing his young wife in a lifeboat stood back. Hipkins probably went back to his cabin, but we will never know. I can, however, imagine him walking down the staircase, crossing the floor and entering into his room; sitting down at the small dresser looking at the photograph of his late wife Lavinia, thinking perhaps of all he and his family had come through. How his mother had carried on even when she had lost her husband and brother-in-law in the space of a month; how he had risen from the small brassfounders to run the largest weighing company in the world. Here he was on the eve of his greatest triumph and it was about to end; he may well have recalled a quote from Napoleon:

"We are strong, when we have made up our minds to die"

He would have heard the creaks and groans of the ship's structure as the stern slowly rose and the bow disappearing under the cold water. The crashing of breakables disturbed from their shelves falling onto the tiled floors. I can imagine him taking from his pocket his trusted copy of Napoleon's Maxims, always a source of strength, now it would help him prepare for the end of his life. Hipkins was not a man to give up but from that little book of Napoleon's doctrines he found one suitable:

> *"There is but one honourable mode of becoming prisoner of war. That is, by being taken separately; by which is meant, being cut off entirely, and when we can no longer make use of our arms. In this case there can be no conditions, for honour can impose none. We yield to an irresistible enemy."*

That irresistible enemy was the North Atlantic ever increasingly filling the ship, compartment by compartment. Even Hipkins with all of his will to overcome difficulties, was powerless against the laws of physics. He looked at his pocket watch that had once belonged to his father, it was 2.10am.

The *Titanic* slipped beneath the North Atlantic at 2.20am, April 15th, 1912. William E. Hipkins was still on board.

CHAPTER 19

THE EMPORER IS DEAD

Better not to have been born than to live without glory.
                                        —Napoleon.

The news of the loss of the Titanic was slow to materialise. There had been whisperings of the loss on April 15th, but officials at the White Star Line had dismissed the notion that the largest ship in the world had foundered. Even reports in the press suggested that the great ship had indeed hit an iceberg but was still afloat and being towed to Halifax Nova Scotia.[1] Avery's Board wanted clarification with Walter Chamberlain and Arthur Gibson both trying to ascertain the truth; they received assurances from White Star that the ship and its passengers were safe.[2] Charles Beakbane President of the Avery Scale Company, was making enquiries of his own. The White Star Line office at 9 Broadway New York was receiving a lot of enquiries. The company's Vice-President Philip Franklin was calmly telling everyone not to worry and that he believed the ship was unsinkable. Beakbane should have felt reassured but he knew when he was being fobbed off. Franklin was stalling. The time difference between the U.S. and UK wasn't helping. On the morning of the 16th, British newspapers were repeating the news that the Titanic had struck an iceberg but was being towed to safety; the Daily Mirror reported:

> *Everyone on board world's greatest liner safe after collision with iceberg in Atlantic Ocean. Titanic's wireless signal brings vessels to scene Helpless giant being towed to port by Allen Liner.* [3]

Beadie would have been aware of the story and on hearing the reports that everyone was safe simply thought how William would have enjoyed the drama.

Within twenty-four hours after the first reports, however, the optimistic remarks from White Star Officials had turned to expressions of regret. In an age when communication over long distances was by Morse telegraph, accurate information was often difficult to come by. The Birmingham Daily Mail of April 16th was reporting a very different story based on reports they had from New York at 8.45pm:

Titanic Founders
Feared Appalling Disaster in the Atlantic
875 Survivors: 1,483 Persons Unaccounted For [4]

A special board meeting was convened with Walter Chamberlain, Arthur Gibson & Alfred Lloyd. The meeting was short and no official mention of Hipkins and the disaster appears in the minutes, but it is clear why it has been called. In the event Hipkins had died, then the company would have to move fast to ensure all ran smoothly.

When James Bevan heard the news he physically shook. Apart from William he knew someone else on the ship as well.[5] James knew he would have to go to Birmingham to be with Beadie. Beadie herself was notified by Arthur Gibson who called upon her. Beadie collapsed on hearing the news, and although Gibson did say that William could be one of the survivors, there was a sense that he was not.

Thousands of miles away in the North Atlantic the Cunard liner *Carpathia* was steaming to New York with the 705 survivors from the Titanic, William was not among them but the world had to wait for the news, and with a lack of news there was speculation. The Milwaukee Sentinel of April 16th carried reports of Milwaukeeans on board the ship and mentioned William:

> *Grave apprehension is feared for the safety of W.A. (sic) Hipkins of Birmingham, England, and a member of the Board of Directors of the Avery Scale Company of Milwaukee, of which C.F. Beakbane, 594 Farewell avenue is president.*

Mr. Beakbane received word from Mr. Hipkins stating that he was about to sail on the Titanic. Mr. Beakbane fears that he may have perished with the hundreds who went down with the boat.[6]

Beakbane in the States and Chamberlain in the UK awaited news from White Star. The news when it came was bad, although hope was offered in that the officials had yet to receive a complete list of survivors. The Birmingham Daily Mail published a list. Chamberlain and Gibson scanned it, there was no listing for Hipkins. The report also added that Benjamin Guggenheim, John Jacob Astor, Major Butt and Isador Strauss had also survived, but this information was incorrect. There were also reports that other survivors may have been picked up by other ships, which highlights the level of misinformation around soon after the disaster. Charles Beakbane remained in constant communication with White Star Line Offices in New York, Philip Franklin cabled Beakbane to give him the news he had been dreading, but half expecting:

"Regret to inform you that the SS "Titanic" foundered on April 15th at 220am. From the list we have received from the SS "Carpathia", Mr. W.E. Hipkins name is not among the survivors."[7]

Beakbane sent a cable to Walter Chamberlain and the news was official. Arthur Gibson took the bad news to Beadie at her home where she was being consoled by James Bevan and her servants.

The loss of the *Titanic* was the subject on everybody's' lips. The shock that hit the UK had never been previously experienced and there was a sense of disbelief. The shock was bad enough for members of the Avery's workforce, but it reached a new level when on Wednesday April 17th the various departments at Soho were called together for a special announcement. At the same time across the country at the various branches, workers were called to hear a special announcement from the Avery Board of Directors. At Digbeth in Birmingham, Cardiff, Leeds, Sheffield, Newcastle, Nottingham, London and Manchester, workers and staff gathered together to hear the Branch Managers read the four-line announcement. In Liverpool and Belfast the workers were already reeling from the news of the *Titanic* disaster, as a number of members of staff knew people serving on board. The Belfast Branch had a close relationship with *Titanic's* builders Harland and Wolff, having supplied and maintained weighbridges and other weighing machines at the shipyard. Mr Richardson had already briefed his Belfast office staff; he looked tired and he had had little sleep due to the fact some of his neighbours were worried about relatives on the *Titanic*. R.W. Darby in Liverpool wondered how much lost time there would be after the announcement. Some his workers had been absent as they tried to find out about friends and relatives on the great liner. In Glasgow, George Allinson was to read the announcement, he was visibly shocked and his hands trembled. The Glasgow workforce were a hard tough bunch, they noticed how the little piece of paper shook in Allinson's hand. None of the workforce was sure what it was about. Some thought that yet another directive from Hipkins was about to be announced, others that work was to be transferred to America. At Glasgow one workman joked that Hipkins' message was so strong it had even made old Allinson shake in his boots! In each area of Soho Foundry managers stood and waited for the gathered workforce to stop talking. At Newcastle, F. Gibson-Hill stood impassively as the hard Tynesiders gathered, some grumbling as to "what is it this time?" Charles Berry in Sheffield thought about the casting of the head for the 15 ½ ton anchor that was sent to Noah Hinckley's in Netherton. His branch had supplied weighing equipment for the job. In Cardiff H. Bloomfield tried to hurry along the workers so he could get the announcement over and done with. Joseph McGrath in London was still struggling with the news. As Avery's London Manager he had handled the order for two weighing machines for the *Olympic* and *Titanic*. He had even been the last Avery man to speak with Hipkins, a meeting that he had gone over and over in his mind since the news of the sinking had come through. Hipkins had left instructions with him and told him that he would see him on his return. At Digbeth, Francis MacKenzie looked as white as his freshly starched shirt collar, Hipkins had been good to him and he was visibly shaken by the news.

On the Engineering Department floor it was Gibbs who delivered the message, even the tough Gibbs found it hard to articulate. In the offices the company Secretary, Alfred Lloyd, gave the news. In the Foundry the Foundry Manager read the announcement to the gathering of men in leather gowns. All across the Avery Empire at 10 o'clock the message was read:

"It is with great sadness that I have to announce the death of our Managing Director Mr. W.E. Hipkins, who lost his life in the tragic loss of the SS "Titanic" last Monday. On behalf of you all the firm will pass on our condolences to Mr. Hipkins' family. We will be taking a collection which will be presented to the Titanic Relief Fund for the families of those lost in this tragedy." Walter Chamberlain. [8]

There was a stunned silence for a few seconds, as if nobody knew what to do. One of the foundrymen spat onto the ground and said "Right lads back to work". In Glasgow the workforce looked at each other, the maritime city always felt a loss with any ship that met with disaster. In Belfast there was a wave of emotion as the *Titanic* claimed a victim close to home. Most of the staff and workers were shocked and saddened but there were some, many of the older hands, who had resented the change in working practices who not only shed no tears but openly commented "Good riddance". For Beadie, however, it was a tragic loss. She had lost her mother, sister in law and brother in just a few years.

The Birmingham Gazette and Express of April 18th published an updated list of survivors, and also listed the names of Midlands' passengers who were missing. W.E. Hipkins name was there in the missing column. Arthur Gibson penned a brief biography for the paper which was duly printed on the 19th. Now there was no doubt.

The Avery's Management publicly kept the matter understated and businesslike. On April 27th the managers of the various branches sent a letter to the Avery Board with a copy to Beadie:

April 27th. 1912

The lateW.E. HIPKINS Esq.

Gentlemen,

We the undersigned, desire to express to you our very deep regret at the loss of Mr. Hipkins in the terrible disaster which overtook the "Titanic".

We cannot but feel shocked that he should have been taken away in such awful circumstances and in the fullness of his energy and abilities.

The loss of such a man, of keen perception and integrity of purpose, has undoubtedly inflicted upon the Company and all concerned, a very heavy blow which by its suddenness comes with increased severity.

We would therefore wish you to place upon record, the sorrow which we all feel and which we have endeavoured to give expression to in this mark of respect and esteem to the memory of one, the untimely end of whom we all deplore.

We beg to remain Gentlemen,
Yours faithfully,

J.Mc Grath	*Manager, London Branch*
A. Richardson	*Manager, Belfast Branch*
H. Bloomfield	*Manager, Cardiff Branch*
F.F. MacKenzie	*Manager, Digbeth Branch*
Geo. H. Allinson	*Manager, Glasgow Branch*
J. Lachford	*Manager, Leeds Branch*
R.W.Darby	*Manager, Liverpool Branch*
Rowland Smith	*Manager, Manchester Branch*
F. Gibson-Hill	*Manager, Newcastle Branch*
A. Archer	*Manager, Nottingham Branch*
Charles Berry	*Manager, Sheffield Branch* [9]

The business style approach continued from the Board, as the board meeting of May 1st 1912 showed:

Minute 3061 Directors place on record their deep regret at the loss of Mr. Hipkins when the "Titanic" foundered in the Atlantic Ocean after collision with an iceberg on 15 April 1912. [10]

The last act from the company's point of view was to settle the outstanding salary of Hipkins. A cheque was prepared for Beadie for £58 6 shillings and 8 pence, the due salary from April 1st to 14th 1912—not the 15th as William had not completed a full day. His few personal effects from his office including his Napoleon crested paperknife, was returned to Beadie and the reign of W.E. Hipkins was officially over. [11]

Although the Board seemed to show little feeling—somewhat surprisingly—some of the Avery's staff were genuinely sad to see the loss of their Managing Director. George Allinson, the Manager of the Glasgow Branch, was dismayed that Avery's were not planning a special memorial service and he was more shocked when his suggestion that Avery's should produce a memorial booklet fell on deaf ears. He decided to prepare one himself, at his own expense. In what can only be seen as a remarkable act of loyalty to the man who had promoted him, Allinson set about the task of researching the life of William Hipkins. He spoke to Beadie and to James Bevan; he also spoke with managers of Avery's, as well as Professor Ashley of the University of Birmingham. He lovingly prepared a small volume and distributed it to the managers of the various branches as well as the board of directors, James Bevan and William's sister Beadie. The book was distributed on September 2nd 1912 with a card insert which read:

IN MEMORIAM

I respectfully ask each of you to accept the accompanying Booklet.

It was primarily written for, and is addressed to, the Branch Managers, but I later decided to also ask the Chief Officials at Soho to accept a copy. The Booklet is a private production and carries no official authority, and is given to you personally.

After starting the task I realised that I had been presumptuous, and that I had neither the time nor the talent to worthily execute it, and now all that I can claim is that it is a sincerely reverent and yet faithful tribute and I ask you to accept it as such.

Yours faithfully,

GEO. H. ALLINSON [12]

Allinson tries not to lament on the virtues of Hipkins, a man to whom he gave absolute devotion and loyalty—as all of his branch managers did—but lament he does. The book was hastily put together and a general outline of Hipkins' life comes through the forty odd pages with additional material by James Bevan and Professor Ashley. Allinson's foreword sums up his feelings:

Four months have been woven from days and nights since that blackest tragedy, when, on the ice cold waters, men surrounded by their declarative triumphs over nature, heard her call to death and smiles, for at long last death was baffled by barriers contrived through all the centuries of pitiless conflict; every peril of the sea and the wind, nay, every peril of creation itself was at last impotent. Nature had been tricked out of her secrets; she was disarmed, subdued by her own renegade powers.

Alas, eternally, "Red in tooth and claw," rising from the dark ocean to prove again her omnipotence, she loosed the wrath of her primeval passions in a Satanic vengeance cut deep into the living heart of the world.

THAT NIGHT THE ANGEL OF DEATH LEANED ACROSS TWO THOUSAND MILES OF HEAVING SEA AND BEREAVED US, AMONGST MANY, SLEEPING, AND UNAWARE.

In the week of the disaster, in the blackness of irreparable loss, I felt a desire, deep and indeed imperative, to pay some tribute, however humble it might be, to the memory of our dead chief.

You hold this memory in such lasting respect that no written "In Memoriam" is needed, but I fancied I would inscribe a little booklet, portraying the man as I knew him, or as I conceive I knew him, and perchance my work might reveal an image greater and fuller than some of you knew. If any revelation is possible it can but increase reverence, and so accomplish simple justice to the dead. It would give me the keenest gratification to feel that I had rendered the slightest service to that justice.

What is my title to write this booklet? Respect and admiration mounting almost to affection! The title is sufficient for any of us!

I can pretend to no scholarship—else would I fashion each word and phrase with the loving care of a scholar, until I should build an epic worthy of the theme. But I speak only the plain language of business, and as you are business men, perhaps you will understand the better.

> *I would wish this "In memoriam" to be faithful and true,*
> *otherwise it would be unworthy of whom it is written, therefore*
> *I waited until time had quietened emotion, and now I know that*
> *emotion had but focussed the deliberative views of years.* [13]

There was, however, one final act by Avery's regarding Hipkins. The Avery Staff Social Society asked the board for permission to place a memorial tablet at the side entrance to the offices as a memorial to their late Managing Director. Permission was granted in January 1913 and a brass plaque was duly set in place.

Bertha Hipkins was the beneficiary from William's Estate, although she did give his motor car to Arnold Boothroyd. She remained at Augustus Road for a short while before moving to 29 Chantry Road in Moseley, and then finally settling in Great Malvern. She never married and lived happily caring for her garden with her companion Lillian Darby, James Bevan was in regular contact until he died in 1930. Beadie passed away ten years later and was buried in the family plot in Warstone Lane Cemetery. Once again united with her mother, father and sister-in-law.

William's body was never recovered and in all likelihood his personal items still lie in cabin C39 on board the *Titanic*, over twelve thousand feet below the Atlantic Ocean.

CHAPTER 20

AVERY'S WITHOUT HIPKINS

Glory is fleeting, but obscurity is forever

—*Napoleon.*

The premature departure of William E. Hipkins as Avery's Managing Director did throw the old firm into a managerial vacuum; albeit a brief one. Hipkins had ensured that the managers below him were well trained. However, with there being virtually no middle management the need for a new general who could drive the firm forward was essential, especially as Pooley's, Day and Millward and half a dozen other firms saw an opportunity to take advantage of their rival's managerial problem. The level of control Hipkins had can be seen from the way the Avery's Board reorganised to cope with his loss. Walter Chamberlain filled the gap, temporarily, with Arthur Gibson continuing his usual role. Although Chamberlain did not operate the same strict weekly and monthly meeting regime with the managers of the main branches—he simply didn't have the time. He set up three committees to cover Hipkins' work dealing with sales, the works, and finance, with each containing Walter Chamberlain as Chairman assisted by another director. Walter W. Wiggin was asked to join the board to add his industrial experience to try and plug another gap, but what was needed was a new commander in chief. It seems no-one inside Avery's was considered. Gibbs, the works' manager, might have been considered or even John Athill, both were overlooked. The Board decided to appoint a managing director from outside the firm. Gilbert Christopher Vyle was appointed as a director on June 18th, 1912 and a month later was given the post of Managing Director—although this does appear to have been a probationary appointment as it was not until July 1913 that Vyle's position was made permanent albeit backdated to July 16th, 1912.

Vyle was born in Hereford in 1870 studying in London, Glasgow and Nottingham specialising in electrical and general engineering. His first employment was with the *Post Office* followed by a stint with the *Colonial Office* as an engineer. He ran his own business for a time before moving to the *General Electric Company* in Nottingham; from there he moved to Manchester where he ran his own engineering consultancy firm. He then moved to Birmingham becoming a manager at the umbrella rib manufacturers *Wright, Brindley and Gell*. It is not known how Vyle became the man to replace Hipkins; he seems not to have had any previous connections with the company, although he was well connected with many in the business life of Birmingham as well as in the country as a whole.

Vyle was a physically big man with a personality to match, very different from Hipkins in many ways. In essence, a cross between W.B. Avery and Henry Avery. He had to get to grips with the company quickly, especially as the trading conditions changed sharply from late 1912. Avery's rivals at Pooley's were watching carefully to see if there would be any changes in the manner of the management. There was none—in the short term at least. Hipkins had started the process for legal action against Pooley's in March 1912 over a patent infringement; Vyle made sure this was pursued. He abolished the sales and finance committees but extended the works' committee to include the entire board of directors. The next issue was the Avery Scale Company in Milwaukee, it was to this factory that Hipkins was heading when he lost his life. The contract for the weighing machines for the US navy was going well. However, an increase in price of raw materials in the United States was causing problems. In November 1912 Vyle approved a loan of £1,000 to the factory and the President of the American side, Charles Beakbane, was *requested* by cable to return to England by the end of the month. John Athill was then to go to Milwaukee in order to look at the books and see what was happening, arriving in New York on board the SS *Carmania* on December 1st. With the departure of Hipkins, the great web he had spun across the branches had been broken, and Vyle, being a little more laid back, had unwittingly allowed some of the more far flung branches to be too independent leading to financial problems. Although, the American plant had already suffered from financial issues. Beakbane arrived at Soho Foundry and whatever transpired between him and Vyle the result was that Beakbane offered to tender his resignation as President, Director and Trustee of the Avery Scale Company. This had been accepted and Avery's would purchase the ten $100 dollar shares he had in the company. Beakbane returned to the United States in December. Whatever the problems at Milwaukee they were certainly taking up a great deal of Vyle's time. Following the results from the order figures supplied in January 1913 he appointed a new sales manager. On the first anniversary of the death of Hipkins a board meeting was held where it was agreed that Vyle would be appointed the *agent of W. & T. Avery Limited for the purpose of attending the meetings of the Avery Scale Company a corporation organised and existing under the laws of the state of Wisconsin* in which Avery's held a portion of the capital stock, and to vote the shares of this company upon all questions which may come before such meetings. Vyle was taking personal control of the American firm, realising that a firm hand was needed; the type of hand that Hipkins had always employed. Regardless of the internal problems at the American factory the trading conditions in the United States had made life very difficult. There had been a backlash from American scale makers over the awarding of the naval contract to Avery's, and it was still difficult to obtain suitably skilled labour to complete the order. By April 1914 it was clear Vyle was looking to rid Avery's of the American company. Arrangements with a Mr. Goodman to take over the management of the Avery Scale Company on certain lines were discussed. It was further suggested that in the event of this falling through, Messrs. *E. & T. Fairbanks & Company* should be approached through Mr. L.G. Bromwich, and that he should be authorised to sell the existing assets for a sum not less than $50,000. The sales figures in June 1914 were at a record high, yet Bromwich was given additional powers to negotiate on behalf of Avery's to sell the company. A month later and Vyle resigned as President of the American company and proposed that the powers pertaining thereto should be vested in John Athill who was now elected as President. Athill was despatched to Milwaukee arriving in New York on the 21st on board the SS *Baltic*. Athill consulted with the company's attorney L.G. Bromwich for the winding up of the company and the realisation of the whole of the assets. By August 18th the consultations had gone well with Athill reporting that all the salesmen had been dismissed. *Allis Chambers And Company* had been appointed agents for Avery's in the United States, and a single man had been kept at Milwaukee for repair work. By October, J.R. Robinson had been sent from Soho to prepare the pattern tools for shipping to Soho, and it was expected the whole factory would be closed by the end of November. The final accounts were calculated by February 1915 which showed a loss of £8000 for the past year. By then the Great War had started and with Milwaukee being an area occupied by a large German-American population, there was a great deal of animosity to the British company; this added to the problems—many of which cannot be clearly identified.

Athill carried out the final act of the Avery Scale Company by parcelling up the records and some machines and sending them to New York for shipment to the UK. The consignment was placed aboard the next available British passenger liner—the Cunarder R.M.S. *Lusitania*. On May 7th 1915 the *Lusitania* was struck by a torpedo fired by the U20 off the Old Head of Kinsale, Ireland. The great liner sank with a large death toll. The records of Avery's American adventure rested, like Hipkins, at the bottom of the Atlantic.

W. & T. Avery Limited as a company grew from strength to strength under Vyle, although some of the efficiencies that had been put into place by Hipkins were missing, which did cause some financial issues during the interwar years. The great rivalry with Pooley's came to an end in 1914 when both companies discussed merging, a response to the remarkable success of another old scale firm *Day & Millward (*which itself would be swallowed up by Avery's through *Charles W. Brecknell* in 1935). The merger was completed in 1915, and in order to avoid any embarrassment a large number of documents relating to Hipkins were destroyed. These documents related to the trade war between the two companies; Hipkins nemesis at Pooley's, Laurence Jacob, became a member of the Avery board.

Yet much of what Hipkins had started at Avery's was continued and even expanded upon. His suggestion scheme remained in place well into the 1960s, and the training and education ideas he championed were expanded to the point where anyone who carried apprenticeship papers that had been completed at Avery's could find a job anywhere in the country. The concept that businesses should advise universities regarding the training of future businessmen is now universally employed. Avery's continued to develop new cutting edge products with load cells, electronic counter scales, and stock control, ensuring that when one thinks of a scale one automatically thinks of the name Avery. Hipkins emphasis on the customer and a continued after-sales relationship has been expanded upon and copied the world over.

However, the great irony is that W. & T. Avery Limited is now *Avery Weigh-Tronix*, having merged with an American company famous for the development of the weigh-bar, which in turn now forms part of the great American company *Illinois Tool Works* (ITW). The United States is no longer a competitive nation but a partner in a global company. I wonder what William would have thought of that?

There are many business leaders and captains of industry who are well known to the general public, the likes of Boulton, Tangye, Docker, Chamberlain, and Cadbury. In some instances they became household names. William Edward Hipkins did not seek public acclaim, he simply dedicated himself to the business in hand and in the process changed forever the face of industry. His methods and ideas have often been copied but never credited. Had he survived the *Titanic*, perhaps, his would be a name that would be spoken alongside those whose self promotion was as important as their business acumen.

His story is an example of just how we all live our lives in the balance.

CHAPTER NOTES

Chapter 1 The Iron Men Cometh

1. William Camden (1551-1623) also visited Birmingham and wrote of his visit to *Bermingham* in 1538 stating that the town was ". . . swarming with inhabitants and echoing with noise of anvils".

2. *A History of Greater Birmingham Down to 1830* p39.

3. *The History and Antiquities of Staffordshire* Volume II p119.

4. The steel worm appears to have been developed from a similar shaped tool used for the removal of shot and unused charge from gun barrels (Stephen J. *Thomson A New Twist For Collectors*). This fits in well with the gun trade in Birmingham where such a tool would have been produced and developed by any number of artisans.

5. *Corkscrews of the Eighteenth Century* pp157-159. Boulton was already producing un-patented models since the late 1760s. In his notebook number 9 dated 1765 he makes a note of items that "We should make" and the list include corkscrews.

6. *British Corkscrew Patents From 1795* by Fletcher Wallis.

7. Edward Thomason would later be Knighted and was one of the 19th century's greatest inventors covering a wide range of products including marine power, plated coinage, riding whips and toasting forks to mention but a few. Other Birmingham manufacturers who took out patents for corkscrews up to 1852 were Charles Osborne (1839), Alexander Southwood Stocker (1843) and John Loach (1844). Ref: *Birmingham Inventors and Inventions* pp155-156, 211, 216-217.

8. It is probable that they had another daughter—Ann. Max Hipkins a genealogist from Australia suggests this to be the case. However with the lack of documented evidence I have omitted this from the main text.

9. The University of Aston In Birmingham now stands on the site.

10. Earliest record of Samuel Cotterill in a Birmingham Trade Directory is the entry in *Wrightson's Directory* of 1821.

11. *Birmingham and the Midland Hardware District* p83.

12. Ibid p85.

13. They were married on November 8th 1849 at The Parish Church at Norton.

14. On Sarah Houghton's death certificate it states she was the daughter of John Houghton. On Rebecca's marriage certificate there is a blank in place of her father's name.

15. Advertisement in *Slater's Directory of Warwickshire* 1850 describes Hudson & Hipkins as *Sole manufactures of Cotterill's Patent Single and Double-Action Door Springs, Patent Latches, and Bolts, of every description, Shutter and Door fastenings, Hinges, handles, Knobs, Bells, Knockers &c.*

16. Brassfounder's Ague was " . . . observed in Birmingham" especially and was referenced as a disease in medical textbooks and guides for general practitioners. Workers suffoured from constriction or tightness of the chest, shivering and profuse sweating. Treatment was by the taking of milk and quinine plus avoidance of zinc fumes Source: *Index of Diseases and their Treatment*, by Thomas Hawkes M.D., F.L.S. 1866.

17. *Birmingham and the Midland Hardware District* pp696-700. A quarter more men working in the metal trades died at age 45 compared with other trades. At age 55 a third more and at age 65 two and half times more died.

18. *Birmingham and the Midland Hardware District* pp694-695. Diphtheria death rates in Birmingham from 1851 to 1860 were 0.07%, this grew to 0.3% between 1861 and 1870. Cholera death rates were 0.22% from 1851 to 1861 and 0.2% from 1861 to 1870. The increase in deaths due to Diphtheria was the highest in the country. (source : *How We Die In Large Towns* a lecture by Balthazar Foster M.D., Temperance Hall Birmingham February 1875).

19. *Birmingham and the Midland Hardware District* p690. Infant mortality for those under 5 years of age in Birmingham between 1851 and 1860 was 9.4% of these a high proportion was due to diarrhea and lung decease. These rates remained fairly constant until 1870. (source : *How We Die In Large Towns* a lecture by Balthazar Foster M.D., Temperance Hall Birmingham February 1875).

20. Sheffield, Leeds, Bristol, Liverpool and Manchester, were statistically unhealthier overall although in certain categories such as diphtheria and scarlet fever Birmingham had more deaths than Leeds and Bristol.

21. Patent Number 1692, July 18th 1855 *Applying Springs or Weights for the Purpose of Closing Doors or Resisting Shocks, Strains or Pressure.*

22. For more detailed description of the bell hanging industry *The Birmingham and Midland Hardware District* by Samuel Timmins.

23. Patent Number 428, March 4th 1858 *Constructing & Attaching Knobs & Spindles; Connecting Knobs to Doors, Drawers and Other Articles.* He did not proceed with the application and only received provisional protection.

24. *London Gazette* 1855. Under the 1842 Act the status of being a bankrupt was confined to traders owing more than £50. Those who were not traders were classed as insolvent debtors and subject to common law proceedings which could lead to indefinite imprisonment. The legal definition of a 'trader' included all those who bought materials and worked on them which included all skilled craftsmen (farmers were specifically excluded). Thus in order for many to avoid the awful fate of an insolvent debtor gave their occupations as *Dealer and Chapman* a rather vague description enabling them to be treated as a trader. (Source: *Public Record Office Information Sheet on Bankruptcy Records*, and Caroline Burton of *The Insolvency Service*). In George Hipkins' case he was buying in raw materials to work on and resell.

25. *London Gazette* February 1856.

26. Patent Number 736, April 2nd 1855 *Improvements in the Manufacture of Corkscrews.*

27. According to trade directories for the Birmingham area a Charles Hipkins was producing corkscrews in Birmingham in 1829; Robert Hipkins in 1854 and of course George's father William was making them prior to 1813.

Chapter 2 The New Commander In Chief

1. Meteorological reports in the *Birmingham Gazette* January and February 1857.

2. St. Phillip's Church Records held on microfilm in the Birmingham Central Library list many Hipkins' christenings.

3. Advertisement in the *Birmingham Directory* by J.S.C. Morris 1862 p248.

4. Restorative soups were made to aid recovery especially after a loss of appetite. A typical soup was made with 1lb of newly killed beef or fowl, chopped fine and added to soft or distilled water with four to six drops of hydrochloric acid, and common salt. The mixture was passed through a sieve. Distilled water was then passed over the residue in the sieve. The reddish coloured liquid thus obtained was served cold to the patient. Lime water and milk was given when the patient found it difficult to hold food down.

5. James Oliver Bevan stated in 1912 regarding Rebecca's reaction to the news as "Her own sorrow had crushed her almost to the limit of her endurance." *In Memoriam* p39.

6. Inscription on grave in Warstone Lane Cemetery states his age as 42, he was actually born on September 30th 1818 making him 44 when he died. Any ages stated on a gravestone should always be considered as approximate as people's ages were often not known, guessed and even lied about. All dates on such stones (and in fact in census records where in the earliest records ages were rounded off) should be considered to be +/-5 years.

7. George F. Hipkins last Will and Testament.

8. Burgess Roll 1863.

9. Post Office Directory of Birmingham 1863.

10. There are a number of notable cases of women taking over their husband's businesses on their deaths, such as Elizabeth Rabone an ivory box-rule maker; Lucinda Evetts a brassfounder; Elizabeth Gill a gun maker and Susannah Parkes a gilt toy and watch chain maker. These were merely a few of the many women running businesses in Birmingham in the 19th century. (source: *Our Mom—An Old Birmingham Special* by Dr. Carl Chinn).

11. Rebecca Hipkins traded as G.F. Hipkins and in the trade directories there is no distinction made between her and her late husband. The Burgess Rolls/Rate books do clearly identify Rebecca as a corkscrew maker, brassfounder or manufacturer. This almost hidden identity of the owner of G.F. Hipkins has misled several attempting to trace the history of the business.

12. Other riots took place in 1793, 1795 and 1799 where soldiers in the barracks were called upon to quell them.
13. Although it is possible that she was dyslexic.
14. Letter from James Oliver Bevan to William Edward Hipkins October 22, 1869.
15. *In Memoriam* p43.
16. *The Birmingham and Midland Institute* p34. The Class of Spring 1856 had 134 pupils, the Autumn Class had 156. The Autumn class was held on Wednesdays and Albites also presented lectures on the history of French Literature (Modern Birmingham and its Institutions Vol 1 p 269).
17. Obituary to Achille Albites in the Birmingham Post June 10, 1872.
18. In Allinson's publication *In Memoriam* p8 it is stated that William and his sister went to Paris to study French under Achille Albites. William and Bertha went to France following William's period at King Edward's School 1869-1872 which meant they visited France in 1873. Albites died in Birmingham on June 8, 1872 of a heart attack and thus could not have taught William and Bertha in Paris. Allinson incorrectly made the connection between the Hipkins' visit to Paris and their French tuition under Albites.
19. Crockford's Clergy list 1930.
20. King Edward VI's School Admission Register 1870. Entry Number 355.
21. Ibid.
22. Charles Barry went on to design the House of Commons.
23. *King Edwards' School Birmingham 1552-1952* p120. Description originally taken from *The Analyst* 1836.
24. *No Place For Fop or Idler* p78.
25. *Fresh Herring* was the name given to boys in their first year, this later became corrupted to *Sherring*.
26. *King Edward's School Birmingham 1552-1952* p48.
27. King Edward VI School List December 1870.
28. King Edward VI Governor Order Book No. 2055 October 31, 1866.
29. King Edward VI Governor Order Book No. 2255 May 20, 1870.
30. *In Memoriam* p14.
31. Willie's school results as published in King Edward VI School List for July 1871, December 1871, July 1872 and December 1872.
32. *In Memoriam* p8.

33. *New Street Remembered* by Donald J. Smith p17.

34. William Hipkins' personal copy of *Murray's Handbook Of* Paris which is suitably annotated. References to his other activities in Paris are also annotated in this book. Sadly no equivalent was found for the other places his visited in Europe.

35. The usual crossing took one and a half hours, the larger slower steamer took between two and a half and three hours. The passage was also smoother as the smaller mail boats were more akin to cargo vessels and passenger space was more rough and ready.

36. *Murray's Guide To Paris* p2.

Chapter 3 Emperor's Europe

1. Originally 3000 flags hung from the roof but when Willie visited the church a much lesser number were on display most of which had been captured in Africa and Sebastopol including one British flag. The rest of the flags were reportedly burned by Joseph Napoleon in 1814.

2. Generals Jourdan, Moncey, Oudinot, Mortier, Duroc, Grouchy, Bugeaud and severla others.

3. *I wish that my ashes rest on the bank of the Seine, among the French people I have loved so much.*

4. *A Holiday Tour In Europe* p188.

5. Willie would have known the town as *Aix-la-Chapelle*.

Chapter 4 Atlantic Odyssey 1873

1. A plaque commemorating Peter Oliver exists on one of the north piers in St. Philips' Cathedral (the same building in which William E. Hipkins was christened).

2. Elihu Burritt was US Consular Agent to Birmingham from 1865 to 1869 although he remained in Birmingham for several months after his appointed time had ended. Of his many books one is of great importance to midlands industry, entitled *Walks In the Black Country and its Green Borderland* published in 1868 in which he describes in some detail the whole region, its industries, history and people.

3. Autobiography of Elihu Burritt pp59-60.

4. William Morris' description of Liverpool before he set sail on the SS *Moravian* in 1874.
5. *Lloyd's List of Shipping* July 27th 1873
6. *Merchant Fleets In Profile*—Volume 2 *Cunard Line* p33; and *Lloyd's Register* 1873.
7. The historian John William Burgess reported on a voyage he made on the S.S. *Tarifa* in the 1870s, and his information has provided details of the vessel.
8. Bill of Faire S.S. *Tarifa* 1873.
9. Ship's Provisions List S.S. *Tarifa* 1873.
10. *Lloyd's List of Shipping* July 28th 1873.
11. Thomas Guest's diary 1873.

Chapter 5 Learning The Trade

1. The name 'Tompson' has been associated with malting in Birmingham since at least 1829.
2. Tompson, Berry and Tompson knocked down number 203 and erected a new building on the corner of Dartmouth Street/Ashted Row with work beginning in 1872 with the site becoming known as the *Birmingham Vinegar Bewery*. Three years later Tompson, Berry, Tompson had become John Tompson & Company and eventually merged with Collens' old firm Swann and Company. In the 1880s the Ashted facility became well known as *Holbrooks* after a highly successful brand of sauce produced on the site. The brewery was seriously damaged by an air raid in 1940, and in the 1950s the firm moved its production completely to Stourport. It became part of the Sarsons Vinegar group and then British Vinegar and is now apart of the Nestle group. Sources: *Brum And Brummies 3* pp99-101; *Post Office Directory of Birmingham* 1856,1864, 1872, 1875; *White's Directory* 1855,1876; *Dix's Directory of Birmingham* 1858; *Wrightson & Webb's Directory of Birmingham* 1847; *Pigot's Directory of Birmingham 1841.*
3. Crockford's Directory.
4. The *Brassfounder's Manual* was written by Walter Graham and published by Lockwood and Company forming part of the *Weale's Rudimentary, Scientific and Educational Series* of books which covered

all forms of engineering and science subjects. The first edition was printed in 1861 and many editions followed. It described extremely well the techniques and tools required to operate a brassfounders. The book was aimed at all levels from the workman up to the owner.

5. *Brassfounder's Manual* 1875 edition p8.

6. The pre-formed core boxes came in three standard shapes, 1. Square cores formed by a wooden board with sliding bars. 2. Tapered cores using a tin mould. 3. Cylindrical cores formed in a metal box. More complicated cores had to have specially made moulding boxes. Core material mix often used was 1 part plaster of Paris, 2 parts brickdust and water added as required for the mixture.

7. A mixture of Copper, Tin, Zinc, lead and iron.

Chapter 6 G.F. Hipkins & Son

1. According to his application form for the Institute of Mechanical Engineers he started in the drawing office in 1880, however his patent application of August 1879 suggests he joined the drawing office earlier. The form contains a number of errors and reference to his joining the Institute is made later.

2. Patent Number 3167, August 6th, 1879 *Corkscrews*. The author owns a good example.

3. Patent Number 2892, July 13th, 1880.

4. The Chamberlain in the firm's title was Joseph's father.

5. Ironmonger November 29, 1884 pp696-7.

6. The Hipkins moved house on several occasions always improving the quality of the property. From 37 Calthorpe Road they moved to *The Birklands*, 7 Westfield Road in 1882 and then to 34 Wheeley's Road in around 1886.

7. Earliest entry in Kelly's Directory of Birmingham in 1884, the firm could have begun trading sometime in 1883.

8. *The Avery Weigh* p428.

9. Sansome, Teale and Company had a substantial stand at the Annual Stanley Cycle Show held in London.

Chapter 7 New Money For Old Rope

1. *Birmingham Mail* February 22, 1934
2. Ibid. He scored 55 before being caught and bowled by William Barnes.
3. Ibid.
4. *Birmingham Daily Mail* February 29, 1908 letter by William J. Twining *and Pinmakers to the World* p13. D.F. Tayler and Company had originated in London in around 1809 when Daniel Foote Tayler led a team of craftsmen making pins in the clock-making centre of Clerkenwell. Tayler formed a partnership with Henry Shuttleworth and moved to Stroud setting up the Lightpill Mill in the late 1820s.
5. Ibid and *Pinmakers to the World* p15. Pins required a vast quantity of paper for packaging with one ton of pins requiring 35,840 sheets of printed paper.
6. *Birmingham Daily Post* February 28, 1908.
7. *Rope a History* p105.
8. A detailed description of rope making may be found in Samuel *Timmins' Birmingham and the Midlands Hardware District*, with the chapter on rope making being written by John Turner Wright (senior).
9. *Rope* by William Tyson pp105-106.
10. *The Wire Rope and Its Applications* by W.E. Hipkins p5.
11. *The Wire Rope and Its Applications* by W.E. Hipkins pp10.
12. *The Wire Rope and Its Applications* by W.E. Hipkins pp10-11.
13. *The Wire Rope and Its Applications* by W.E. Hipkins p91 advertisement.
14. *Rope a History* p106.
15. *Rope* a History pp106-107.
16. *The Ironmonger* December 20, 1890 p567. These additional subscribers were also well known to the group. Wilfred Williams was married to William Hughes' sister.
17. *The Wire Rope and Its Applications* by W.E. Hipkins p91 Advertisement.
18. There was a strong tradition of rope manufacturers co-operating although there were some bitter disagreements. Glass, Elliot and Company collapsed due to a variety of internal and external problems, which at one point seriously jeopardised the production of the 1865 Atlantic cable. In John Horsefall's account of the firm of Webster and

Horsefall (*The Iron Masters of Penns*) a chapter is dedicated to the 1865 Atlantic cable highlighting the problems of Glass, Elliot and Company. No mention is made of John and Edwin Wright Limited owning the Patent for the cable which is somewhat surprising, in fact a number of publications about Birmingham Industry that mention the cable omit references to Wright's. Primary and secondary source material that may have been used, often omits the fact as well which may point to some ill feeling towards Wright's by other cable firms. Not only did Wright's have the patent they also produced materials for the cable. According to William Tyson the Millwall branch may well have been set up to support Glass, Elliot and Company's works, later to become the works of the Atlantic Telegraph Company following the former's collapse.

[19.] Bevan wrote quite a number of books throughout his life including *Voices of Earth, Whispers of Heaven* (1863); *The Birth and Growth of Toleration* (1909); *Egypt and the Egyptians* (1909) and many others.

[20.] *The Ironmonger* December 24, 1892 p523 & May 20, 1893 p300.

Chapter 8 Weighing The World

[1.] *Weighing the World, (1930)* p7. It is also stated in a pamphlet of 1894 created by William Henry Avery *A Short History of the Rise and Progress of W. & T. Avery* and this publication appears to be the source of all subsequent references. Letterheads of 1880 bear the statement *Established 1730* although John Barton who had taken over from Ford had been in operation since 1728 which suggests that there may have been some personal link between the Avery family and James Ford the nature of which has not been recorded. Alternatively it could simply have been an error and the actual origin of the company line was not truly known. With the knowledge that Barton who lived at 11 Well Street buying out Ford who had been trading since 1730, thus William Henry Avery assumed (wrongly) that Ford had been at Well Street.

[2.] The name James Ford first appears in L.H. Broadbent's *Avery Business* (1949) p.9-11 prior to this only the surname is mentioned. Broadbent obtained the name James from the parish register of St. Martin's Church, Digbeth. In the 18th century a Richard Ford a jobbing smith of 58, Smallbrook Street Birmingham took out a patent (935) in 1769 for

'Stamping as a means of raising scales, sauce etc', the same Richard this time of 27 Great Charles Street, Birmingham advertised in Aris' Gazette August 24, 1772 as producing a variety of scales. The earliest physical evidence for a Ford is that of a weight which is marked 'Ford, Bir' that has been dated to around 1722, now in possession of the Avery Historical Museum and as Barbara Smith states the Ford who made the weight may well be the Richard Ford advertising in the Gazette.

3. *The Avery Business*, (1949) p9.

4. *The Avery Weigh* (1967). Barbara Smith investigated the origins of Avery's in some detail and found there was little historical foundation for the traditional view of the founding of the firm.

5. *One Hundred Years of Fairbanks Scales* (1930) pp1-2.

6. Patent 6479, October 5, 1833 *Construction of Weighing Machines*. Taken out in the name of Miles Berry acting as agent for Thaddeus and Erastus Fairbanks.

7. Thomas Avery obituary, Birmingham Weekly Post 24, February 1894.

8. *Smethwick Telegraph*, 1, April, 1950.

9. *The Avery Weigh* p.58.

10. Patent 11,754 June 16, 1847 *Weighing Machine* became Pooley's first patented design.

11. Patent 214, January 24, 1857.

12. *The Avery Weigh* p.217.

13. *Avery 50 Year Men* p.5 Mr. Alfred Groom the son of Thomas Groom wrote about his experiences after working at Averys for 58 years. His father died in 1910 aged 76 after 66 years service having joined the company in 1844. His brother Arthur worked for the firm for 60 years. Alfred finished his days working on large brass beams.

14. Pooley's first branch was set up in London sometime after 1834 and prior to 1875 they had established branches in Manchester, Newcastle-on-Tyne, Derby, Newport Mon., and Glasgow. They had avoided setting up a branch in Birmingham due to their co-operation with Averys.

15. William Allen, His personal experiences of working at Averys filed in the Avery Historical Museum.

16. *The Avery Weigh* p135.

17. France and Austro-Hungary 1882, Switzerland 1884, Germany 1885 and Italy 1888. A more in-depth look at the tariff situation and its affect on Averys is discussed in a later chapter.

Chapter 9 The New Emperor

1. Notes of the meetings and discussions taken from the papers of William Beilby Avery, Walter Chamberlain and Wilfred Williams.
2. Board minute 185, 7 Aug 1895. Resolved that WE Hipkins be invited to join board for 12 months from 1 Aug 1895 with a salary of £300 per annum.
3. *The Evening News*, Glasgow February 12, 1932.
4. In Memoriam p.11.
5. William Allen, His experiences of working at Averys filed in the Avery Historical Museum
6. William Hipkins to George Allinson paraphrasing Napoleon who gave instructions to his Aide-de-camp Philippe de Sejur *"This officer must set down nothing by here say. He must see everything with his own eyes report nothing but what he has seen; and when he is obliged to report something he has not seen say he has not seen it"* August 1803.
7. *The Avery Weigh* pp.473-474.
8. Hipkins was quoting Napoleon's order to Marshal of France Massona before the attack on Eckmühl on 17th April 1809.
9. *Rope A History* p107.
10. Ibid. Avery was not it seems happy to wait another 12 months before retiring which would have allowed Hipkins to take over after Turner had arrived back from India. The Avery's board were also keen to start work at modernizing the company; the loss of Henry had seriously threatened the viability of the entire firm.
11. Avery Directors' Board Minute 235, December 1895. It was agreed to William Hipkins taking the appointment on the following terms:
    a. He shall be sole managing director.
    b. He shall execute the full power of a director having a vote.
    c. Remuneration £1000 per annum and a commission of 10% upon trading profits above £15000.

d. He undertakes not to be interested in any other weighing machine business for 10 years after ceasing to hold the appointment.

e. Appointment to commence from January 1 1896.

f. He shall be at liberty to remain a director of J & E Wright Ltd for 12 months.

[12.] I interviewed Martyn Vaughan who was at the time Managing Director of Alstom Transport in Birmingham to get a view on how the role of a Managing Director has changed over 100 years. It is clear from his comments that the modern Managing Director of a large company is limited to directing his site in line with the policies laid down by the company's board. In fact his role appears more of a works manager than that of an M.D. in comparison to Hipkins. Mr. Vaughan (and no doubt other M.D.s) had far less room for maneuver and influence over the company as a whole where as Hipkins' position was one of virtual Emperor.

[13.] Private ledgers and Avery Directors' minutes: 997, June 28, 1898; 1666, November 6, 1900; 2883, November 16, 1909.

[14.] Avery Directors' Minutes 1896 pp.101 & 127.

[15.] Note in Personal file of G.H. Allinson.

[16.] *Ironmonger*, August 9, 1895.

[17.] In Memoriam pp12-13.

[18.] Watch Committee records August 1896.

[19.] Avery Directors' Minutes 1896 pp 122,127,130.

[20.] *Birmingham Daily Mail* August 6, 1896.

Chapter 10 The Spirit of Soho

[1.] Dickinson H.W, & Jarvis R.(1927) *James Watt and the Steam Engine* Encor Editions.

[2.] *The History and Antiquities of Staffordshire Volume 2 Part 1*, J. Nichols & Son.

[3.] *Aris' Birmingham Gazette*, February 1, 1796.

[4.] Avery Directors' Minute 151, May 7, 1895.

[5.] Avery Directors' Minute 151, June 5, 1895.

[6.] Avery Directors' Minute 151, September 15, 1895.

[7.] W.L. Awdry's Application form for the *Birmingham Association of Mechanical Engineers* 1899.

8.   Walter Awdry on his application for the Birmingham Association of Mechanical Engineers refers to the Soho Foundry as 'The Sacred Site'.

9.   Hand-written note by William E. Hipkins to Alfred Lloyd, Company Secretary.

10.   Letter Head in author's collection.

11.   Letter Head in author's collection dated 1904, shows a drawing of the Foundry as it looked in 1899 following completion of Hipkins' reconstruction programme.

12.   *Birmingham Daily Post* November 1, 1895.

13.   Actual cost on completion in 1898 was £7,467 (Avery Directors' Minutes p.301).

14.   *The Canadian Trade Review* p.48, May 20, 1898.

15.   T. Payne's example appears in the Avery Director's minutes, 1899 pp.26, 30. As new machines were introduced the same policy was adopted as in 1901 when piece rates were reduced following the purchase of a Buck and Hickman Thickening machine.

16.   Avery Directors' Minutes 1898 p.301.

17.   Superintendent Tozer of the Birmingham Fire Brigade had been asked to inspect the cupolas at Soho as a fire risk and to make general comments on fire safety. His report called for the smithy and the foundry walls to be whitewashed, the smokestacks of the hearths to be altered and spark arresters fitted to the cupolas along with the provision of fire fighting equipment. (Avery Directors' Minutes 1897, p.173, and *The Avery Weigh* pp529,530).

18.   *Birmingham Daily Mail* May 27, 1898.

Chapter 11 The Home Revolution

1.   Avery Directors' Minutes 1897 pp224, 227, 228

2.   Willard Bundy founded the *Bundy Clock Company* in 1875. He was in business as a clock maker and jeweller in Auburn, New York in 1885, and he designed and made a successful "Watchman's Detector". In 1890 a Mr. Harlow organised the *Bundy Manufacturing Company* to produce these time recorders, and registered patents both in New York and London under the *Bundy Clock Company*, and the *British Bundy Clock Company* respectively. In 1894 J. L. Willard and F. A. Frick of

Rochester, New York, formed the *Willard and Frick Manufacturing Company* as the first card time recorder company in the world. The *International Time Recording Company* (ITR) was established in 1900 following the mergers of the *Bundy Manufacturing Company*, *Willard & Frick Manufacturing Company* and *Standard Time Stamp Company*. Following a period of significant growth the firm left Birmingham NY and relocated in Endicott, New York. ITR swallowed up other companies such as the *Dey Time Register Company*. In 1902 Willard Bundy left ITR, moved to Syracuse and founded *WH Bundy Record Company*. It appears that he sold Bundy recorders and clocks until the *Simplex Time Recorder Company* acquired the company in 1916. In 1911 ITR merged with the *Computing Scale Company*, (well known to Hipkins) and the *Tabulating Machine Company* of Hollerith, and was renamed the *Computing-Tabulation-Recording-Company* (CTR). In 1924, the company was once again restructured and the *International Business Machines Corporation* (IBM) was born.

3.   Avery Directors' Minutes 1898 pp247, 257a, 294.

4.   Each time-recording machine cost £30.

5.   J.T. Burford *How The Factory is Changing*, article in *Efficiency Magazine* January 1937. Burford is particularly caustic as regards the Hipkins' era of management commenting that ". . . this period in the history of the firm . . . was the blackest so far as injustice to workpeople is concerned." Burford certainly reads as a very bitter man towards certain elements of the Avery management, how much of this is the result of genuine mistreatment and how much is due to the effects of the changes on him personally that he simply did not like I do not know.

6.   *Birmingham Daily Post* August 24, 1899.

7.   *The Avery Weigh* pp.527, 528.

8.   Avery Directors' Minutes 1898 pp.226-227. Burford also received the extra payment in the following year although by then he would not have been incurring extra expense. This seems to contradict his own statement in 1937 that the excepted rates of pay were not being applied by Hipkins, indeed he seems to actually do well here.

9.   Avery Directors' Minutes 1897 p200.

10. In Memoriam pp12-13.

11. The companies who had to pay out were Northern Insurance Company (2 policies), Liverpool and London and Globe, Manchester Fire

Insurance, Royal Exchange Assurance, London & Lancashire Fire Assurance, Norwich Union Fire Insurance Company and the Scottish Union National Insurance Company. With the Mill Lane Works empty and Soho renovated the insurance money must have come in useful, certainly it offset some of the costs of the move to Soho.

12. *Birmingham Daily Post* June 30th, 1899.

13. First fire occurred on August 26th 1878 at Mr. Dennison's Sweetshop in Digbeth, the second on January 11-12 1879 when the Birmingham Library was destroyed. In the Spring of 1879 the Brigade was reorganized. Source: *Fire Fighting In Birmingham* by Stephen Price.

14. *Avery Fire Brigade*. A small outline of the brigade written by an employee and dated July 15, 1932 currently in the Avery Museum Archives.

15. Avery Directors' Minutes 1900 p84.

16. Hudson's Whistles supplied numerous firms with Fire Brigade insignia including Avery's neighbours Tangyes (source: Hudson's Whistles).

17. The Avery Fire Brigade became members of the National Fire Brigade Association and had expanded by 1932 to 14 men and two fire engines. Good Conduct and Long Service medals were occasionally awarded, paid for it seems by the Brigade Captain.

18. *The Avery Weigh* p532.

19. *Sunday Telegraph* November 11, 1900.

20. W. & T. Avery's Suggestion System Poster 1904.

21. Avery Directors' Minutes 1904, p269.

Chapter 12 Invasion

1. *The Avery Weigh* p476. Barbara Smith adds that it is not known from the records what decision as made over the issue.

2. Part of the payment was made in Avery Shares and the Parnells became employees of Averys.

3. *The Avery Weigh* p516.

4. The Avery Museum still has a vast collection of weighing machine and scale catalogues from many firms covering the 19th and 20th centuries.

5. Records of such actions were rarely kept and many years later in 1914 any existing records of these covert activities were destroyed. Only

two documents remain which talk about the actions one is a brief history of an employee's time at Averys and Pooleys the other is a note from Gibbs to Hipkins confirming the appointment of the plant in Pooleys.

6. *Dictionary of Military Quotations* p300.

Chapter 13 The Tariff Problem

1. *Tariffs Levied by the Great Powers* compiled by C.T. Grant of the Glasgow Chamber of Commerce 1903.
2. *Birmingham Daily Post* December 11, 1903.
3. *Tariffs Levied by the Great Powers* compiled by C.T. Grant of the Glasgow Chamber of Commerce 1903.
4. *Birmingham Daily Post* June 30, 1904; Birmingham Gazette June 30, 1904; Hardware Trade Journal July 8, 1904; Birmingham Daily Mail June 29, 1904; Birmingham Dispatch June 29, 1904.
5. Birmingham Gazette July 9, 1904.
6. Birmingham Gazette July 6, 1904.
7. Evidence in Closed Record in Causia The British Moneyweight Calculating Scale Coy., Limited Against W. & T. Avery Limited, pages 5-7 January 17, 1905.
8. Birmingham Daily Post July 18, 1905.
9. I.G. Farben was a conglomeration of Bayer, BASF, Agfa, Hoechst, Cassella and Kalle forming 'Interessengemeinschaft' (Community of interests).
10. Birmingham Gazette July 5, 1905.
11. Ibid.
12. Dispatch July 4, 1905.

Chapter 14 Arming For The Future

1. W. & T Avery Board Minute 2439, April 18th, 1905 Hipkins given permission to join the board of BSA.
2. The fourteen firms were Bentley & Playfair, Joseph Bourne, Cook & Son, Cooper & Goodman, Hollis & Sons, King & Phillips, Pryse

& Redman, Joseph Smith, Swinburn & son, Tipping & Lawden, W. Tranter, Joseph Wilson, Woodward & Sons, and Charles Reeves.

3. *The Rifleman* December 1906. At the Avery Board Meeting of June 19, 1906 Hipkins reported the formation of the rifle club with a membership of 486. (Board Minute 2581).

4. *The Book of the BSA Air Rifle* 1911 pp40-41 mentions the formation of rifle clubs and reproduces Hipkins' letter.

5. *The Educational Times*, December 1st 1904.

6. W. & T. Avery Board Minutes 1904 p 269.

7. *Birmingham Daily Post*, July 13th 1906.

8. *The University of Birmingham Its History and Significance* p25.

9. Birmingham University established a course in 'Transport Economics' to meet a specialist need.

10. The Chamber of Commerce 'urgently' pressed upon the Executive Committee formed to promote the formation of Birmingham University to establish as part of the University a 'School of Commerce'. The Chairman (F.B. Goodman) and Vice Chairman (H.C. Field) of the Chamber subsequently met with the council of the Mason University College to discuss the formation of such a body. A year later Alderman F.C. Clayton Chairman of the Council of Mason University College forwarded an outline of a scheme to form a 'Faculty of Commerce' suggesting the subjects to be included. As an interim measure the Chamber of Commerce joined with Mason College, King Edward's School and the Birmingham School Board to organise an 'Evening School of Commerce' at the Birmingham and Midland Institute. *The Chronicles of the Birmingham Commercial Society* pp398 & 406.

11. Lord Strathcona had once been a lecturer at the Josiah Mason College. *The First Civic University Birmingham* 1880-1980 p148.

12. *The University of Birmingham Its History and Significance* p 139-140.

13. Docker amalgamated Metropolitan Amalgamated Carriage and Wagon Company, Oldbury Carriage and Wagon Company, Lancaster Carriage and Wagon Works, Brown Marshalls, and Ashbury Railway Carriage and Iron Company.

14. BSA Directors' minutes of meeting held September 5th 1906, note in book 2 pp15-16.

15. BSA Directors' minutes of meeting held February 1st 1907. Minute number 3137 refers to the Hipkins-Docker report. The board instructed

Hipkins and Docker to negotiate with the Eadie Manufacturing Company.

16. Taylor was also held directorships at Rudge-Whitworth Company Limited (cycle makers), Lanchester Motor Company Limited, Midland Employer's Mutual Assurance Limited and of the Central Insurance Company Limited.

17. Examples of typical visits to manufactories included W. &. T. Avery's Derby works; Birmingham Power Station; B.S.A., and Hamstead Colleries in 1911. Hickman's Steel Works in Bilston and United Brassfounders (Martineau, Beames and Madeley Limited) in 1912.

18. *Birmingham Daily Gazette* November 12, 1907.

Chapter 15 Sanctuary

1. William Hipkins' application form for the Institute Of Mechanical Engineers May 7, 1898. William's subscription was £3 per year plus £2 entrance fee.

2. Rate Books 1899-1912, Birmingham Central Library.

3. William bought Emily and Beadie 100 shares each in 1896, Emily bought an extra 200 at the same time. This gave them a half year's interest of £1 18/8 and £5 16/8 respectively. Beadie purchased a further 500 shares in 1898. Source: W. & T. Avery Cash books.

4. Comment made by Beadie to George Allinson in 1912 and quoted in *In Memoriam*.

5. Annie Mary Hipkins married John Boothroyd at the Parish Church, Edgbaston on August 20th, 1879. John Boothroyd's father was a butcher.

6. John Boothroyd's death certificate (February 28th, 1942) states he was a commercial traveller for a scale-makers. A record of his employment with Averys is in the W & T Avery Archive.

7. Items of Vertu refers to a variety of types of quality items such as high-grade steel toys.

8. Samuel Phillip's service record at the PRO outlines some of his career history. He is mentioned in *Campaigns and History of the Royal Irish Regiment* by Lieut. Colonel G. Le M. Gretton (1911).

9. The attendees were likely to be only Arthur Gibson, and Reginald Robinson giving the whole ceremony the feel of a business deal . . .

10. I have to add that he would be free from the prying attentions of biographers.

Chapter 16 Over The Tariff Wall

1. *Birmingham Gazette* July 5, 1905.
2. Based on data from the US Immigration/Passenger records.
3. Richardson arrived in New York on October 19, 1903 travelling on the R.M.S. 'Cymric'. He brought with him his wife and children moving into accommodation at 300 Gregory Ave, Passive NY.
4. Herbert Godfrey arrived in New York on January 9, 1904 and stayed with Richardson.
5. *The Avery Weigh* p455. Godfrey's occupation listed in Immigration/ Passenger records of 1906 describes himself as a *Company Secretary*.
6. Wilfred sailed on the R.M.S. 'Celtic' from Liverpool to New York arriving on October 24, 1904.
7. Hipkins may or may not have found it interesting to note that the Milwaukee German-Americans raised funds for Germany during the Franco-Prussian war that removed Bonaparte III and led to Hipkins' French teacher Archilles fleeing back to Birmingham!
8. J. Burrows and a Mr. Dunn had apparently reported Beakbane's incompetence—*The Avery Weigh* p458.
9. Beakbane sailed on the R.M.S. 'Caronia' from Liverpool to New York arriving on November 11, 1905. His trip would also include a visit to Montreal in Canada to negotiate sales of Avery scales.
10. Simeon sailed on the S.S. 'Kaiser Wilhelm II' from Southampton to New York arriving on January 17, 1906 to help set up the board and deal with the financial arrangements of the new company.
11. Wilfred Bland sailed on the R.M.S. 'Carmania' from Liverpool arriving on June 12, 1907.
12. *Birmingham Mail* August 28th, 1908. The 'informant' was William E. Hipkins as noted in his scrapbook.
13. *Birmingham Daily Post* November 4th, 1908.
14. Minutes of W. & T. Avery Limited, Annual General Meeting March 1909.

Chapter 17 Lost Love

1. Symptoms taken from modern description.
2. Personal weighing machine in possession of descendant.
3. *The History of the Birmingham Medical School* p.67.
4. Daily Telegraph February 25th 1910, Daily Post February 26th 1910. Cuttings found in William Hipkins' scrapbook.
5. Letter dated January 29th 1912 from C.F. Beakbane to W. & T. Avery Board.

Chapter 18 Atlantic Odyssey 1912

1. 1873 SS 'Tarifa' Liverpool to Boston; 1910 SS 'Oceanic' Southampton to New York; 1911 SS 'Baltic' Liverpool to New York.
2. Bradshaw's Railway Timetable and Guide 1912.
3. The photograph depicting William Waldorf Astor has been reproduced in many books and most incorrectly refer to William as John Jacob Astor, who could not have been on the station as he joined the 'Titanic' at Cherbourg.
4. Description of the Waterloo to Southampton journey taken from *The Maiden Voyage* by Geoffrey Marcus.
5. Descriptions of the interiors of the 'Titanic' taken from 'Shipbuilder' magazine 1911.
6. Details of the rooms and occupants comes from a list of passengers in first class recovered from the jacket pocket of a steward.
7. Details of Birmingham and the Black Country suppliers to the 'Titanic' are from the author's research to be published as *Titanic the Midlands' Connections*.
8. Menu from Titanic's first day of voyage April 10th 1912.

Chapter 19 The Emperor is Dead

1. Newspaper report in *The Evening Sun*, New York April 15th 1912.
2. Cable to Walter Chamberlain from White Star Line Offices Liverpool.
3. *Daily Mirror* April 16th, 1912.

4. *Birmingham Daily Mail* April 16th, 1912

5. Henry Forbes Julian a distinguished metallurgical engineer from Redholm in Torguay, Bevan and Julian had been friends since 1880 with Bevan last meeting him just a month before he sailed on the 'Titanic'.

6. *Milwaukee Sentinel* April 16th, 1912.

7. Cable from Philip Franklin of White Star to Charles Beakbane Avery Scale Company April 16th, 1912.

8. Statement prepared fro Walter Chamberlain read to the workforce by branch managers and works' managers April 17th, 1912.

9. Letter to the Avery Board of Directors dated April 27th, 1912.

10. Avery's Directors' Minute Book.

11. Details of salary paid to W.E. Hipkins on a monthly basis along with his bonuses and commissions can be found in a ledger at Birmingham Archives and Heritage.

12. A copy of this card is to be found in one of the copies of *In Memoriam* located at the Avery Historical Museum.

13. *In Memoriam* Foreword.

14. Avery Directors' Minutes Book, minute 3122 7 January 1913 Memorial Tablet. This tablet remained in place until it disappeared in the late 1980s or early 1990s.

Chapter 20 Avery's After Hipkins

1. Avery's Directors' Minutes Book. Minute 3048 Mr. Hipkins reported that Pooley's having infringed one of the company's patents he considered it necessary to commence an action against them.

2. November 5 1912 Avery Scale Co.3100 Mr. Vyle reported a further loan of £1000 since last meeting.

Bibliography

Books

Anonymous (1874) *Handbook for Visitors to Paris*. John Murray.

Anonymous (1907) *A Handbook for the War Office Miniature Rifle*, Birmingham Small Arms Company Limited, Birmingham.

Anonymous (1938) *Soho Foundry Then and Now* W & T Avery Limited.

Anonymous (1948) *W & T Avery A Record of its History and Scope* W & T Avery Limited.

Anonymous (no date) *Historical Associations* W & T Avery Limited.

Albutt, Richard; Flynn, Martin; Bassett, Philippa & Inman, Jackie (1995), *Contrasts In A Victorian City—Birmingham*. Birmingham City Council Department of Leisure & Community Services.

Allinson, George H. (1912). *In Memoriam—William Edward Hipkins*. Allinson Glasgow.

Archibold, Rick & McCauley, Dana. (1997). *Last Dinner On The Titanic*. Weidenfeld & Nicolson.

Ashley, Anne, (1932). *William James Ashley A Life*. P.S. King & Son.

Biel, Steven (Editor) (1998) *Titanica The Disaster in Poetry and Verse*. Norton.

Boyd-Smith, Peter (1994) *Titanic from Rare Historical Reports*. Steamship Publications.

Briggs, A. (1982). *The Power of Steam*. Michael Joseph London.

Briggs, A. (1952). *History of Birmingham Volume 2*. Oxford University Press.

Brinnin, John Malcom (1986 2nd). *The Sway of the Grand Saloon* Arlington Books.

Broadbent, L.H. (1949). *The Avery Business*. W & T Avery Limited.

Bryceson, Dave, (1997). *The Titanic Disaster as Reported in the British Press*. Patrick Stephens.

Burritt, Elihu, (1868). *Walks in the Black Country*. Sampson, Low, Son and Marston.

Burstall, F.W. & Burton, C.G., (1930) *Souvenir History of the Foundation & Development of the Mason Science College and of the University of Birmingham 1880-1930*. Mason Science College.

Butler, Daniel Allen, (1998). *Unsinkable The Full Story*. Stackpole Books.

Caren, Eric & Goldman, Steve (1998*). Titanic The Story of the Disaster in the Newspapers of the Day* Castle Books.

Cook, Chris, (1999). *Britain In The Nineteenth Century 1815-1914*. Longman.

Cook, Joel, (1879). *A Holiday Tour In Europe*. J.B. Lippincott & Co.

Cornwell, John (2003). *Hitler's Scientists*. Viking.

Davenport-Hines, R.P.T., (1984) *Dudley Docker the Life and Times of A Trade Warrior*. Cambridge University Press.

Dickenson, H.W. & Jenkins R. (1927 reprinted 1981) *James Watt and the Steam Engine* Encore Press.

Dodman, Frank E. (1955). *Ships of the Cunard Line*. Adlard Coles Limited.

Drake, Peter (compiler) (1998). *Images of England—Handsworth, Hockley & Handsworth Wood*. Tempus.

Dunham, Kieth, (1955), *The Gun Trade of Birmingham*. Birmingham Museum and Art Gallery.

Eaton, John P. & Haas. Charles A. (1994 2nd Ed). *Titanic Triumph & Tragedy*. Patrick Stephens.

Englander, David Editor (1997). *Britain & America Studies in Comparative History 1760-1970*. Yale University Press.

Flanders, Judith, (2003). *The Victorian House*. Harper Collins.

Forestier-Walker, E.R. (1952). *A History of the Wire Rope Industry of Great Britain*. Federation of Wire Rope Manufacturers of Great Britain.

Gale, W.K.V. (1952). *Boulton, Watt and the Soho Undertakings*. City Of Birmingham Museum & Art Gallery, Dept of Science & Industry.

Gale, W.K.V. (1948). *Soho Foundry*. W & T Avery Limited.

Gill, Conrad (1952). *History of Birmingham Volume 1*. Oxford University Press.

Giulian, Bertrand B. (1995). *Corkscrews of the 18th Century*. Whitespace Publishing.

Gracie, Archibald (1913 reprint 1985). *A Survivors Story*. Alan Sutton.

Grant, C.T. (1903). *Tariffs Levied By The Great Powers*. James Harper & Co.

Greenhill, Basil & Giffard, Ann (1972). *Travelling by Sea in the Nineteenth Century.* Adam & Charles Black.

Gretton, Lieut. Colonel G. Le M. (1911). *Campaigns and History of the Royal Irish Regiment.* William Blackwood & Sons.

Haws, Duncan (1979). *Merchant Fleets In Profile Vol.2* Patrick Stephens Cambridge.

Hipkins, William E. (1896). *The Wire Rope and its Applications*. D.F. Tayler & Co. Birmingham.

Hood, A.G. (Editor) (1911 Reprint). *The Shipbuilder Vol VI Midsummer 1911 Special Number The White Star Liners Olympic & Titanic.* Patrick Stephens.

Horsfall, John (1971). *The Iron Masters of Penns.* Kineton: The Roundwood Press.

Hunt, Jonathan. (1989). *Pinmakers To The World.* James and James.

Hutton, T.W. (1952). *King Edward's School Birmingham 1552-1952*. Basil Blackwell, Oxford.

Hyslop, Donald; Forsyth, A. & Jemima, S. (1994). *Titanic Voices*. Southampton City Council.

Ives, Eric; Drummond Diane; Schwarz Leonard, (2000). *The First Civic University Birmingham 1880-1980.* University of Birmingham Press.

Kidner, R.W, (1983). *The Waterloo-Southampton Line*. The Oakwood Press.

Langford, John Alfred. (1868). *A Century of Birmingham Life Volumes 1 & 2.* William Downing, Birmingham.

Leech, Margaret, (1959*). In The Days Of McKinley.* Harper & Brothers

Leigh-Bennett, E.P. (1930). *Weighing The World.* W & T Avery Limited.

Lord, Walter (1956). *A Night To Remember*. Longmans.

Lord, Walter (1986). *The Night Lives On*. Morrow.

MacInnes, Dr.Joseph (1992*). Titanic In A New Light*. Thomasson-Grant.

MacMorran, James L. (1973). *Municipal Public Works & Planning in Birmingham 1852-1973.* City of Birmingham Public Works Department.

Marcus, Geoffrey (1969). *The Maiden Voyage.* Viking Press

Marsh, Peter T. (1994). *Joseph Chamberlain Entrepreneur In Politics.* Yale University Press.

McCluskie, Tom (1998). *Anatomy of the Titanic.* PRC.

Platt, D.C.M. (1968). *Finance, Trade, and Politics in British Foreign Policy 1815-1914*. Clarendon Press.

Roberts, Kenneth D., (1976). *Tools for the Trades & Crafts an Eighteenth Century Pattern Book of R. Timmins & Sons, Birmingham*. Ken Roberts Publishing.

Russell, W.H. (1865). *The Atlantic Telegraph*. Day and Son.

Ryerson, Barry (1980). *The Giants of Small Heath*. Haynes Publishing.

Samways, Charles R.( ) *Industrial Birmingham*. Birmingham Chamber of Commerce Journal.

Sanders, L. (1960). *A Short History of Weighing*. W & T Avery Limited.

Scrivenor, Harry, (1854). *History of the Iron Trade*. Longman, Brown, Green & Longmans.

Shaw, Stebbing (1798-1801). *The History and Antiquities of Staffordshire Volume 2 Part 1*, J. Nichols & Son.

Shill, Ray (2002). *Birmingham's Industrial Heritage 1900-2000*. Sutton.

Skipp, Victor (1980). *A History of Greater Birmingham Down to 1830*. Brewin Books.

Skipp, Victor (1983). *The Making of Victorian Birmingham*. Heron Press.

Smiles, Samuel (1878). *Lives of the Engineers—Boulton & Watt*. John Murray.

Smiles, Samuel (1878). *Industrial Biography Iron Workers and Toolmakers*. John Murray.

Smith, Donald (1984). *New Street Remembered*. Barbryn Press.

Sproule, Anna (1978). *Port Out Starboard Home*. Blandford Press, Poole.

Timmins, Samuel (1866). *The Birmingham and Midland Hardware District*.

Timmins, Samuel; Lapworth, C.; Hughes, W.R.; Matthews, W. Editors (1886*). Handbook of Birmingham issued to the Local Committee of the British Association*. Hall & English.

Trott, Anthony (1992). *No Place for Fop or Idler* James & James.

Tyson, William (1966). *Rope A History*. Wheatland Journals London.

Wade, Wyn Craig. (1979). *Titanic The End of a Dream*. Weidenfeld & Nicolson.

Vincent, Eric W. & Hinton, Percival (1947). *The University of Birmingham*. Cornish Brothers.

Wallis, Fletcher (1997). *British Corkscrew Patents From 1795*. Vernier Wallis.

Waterman, Margaret Irene (Editor); Jenkins, Charles; Shoebridge, Michelle; Van Zyl, Patricia (1992). *Birmingham Athletic Institute Remembered*. Brewin Books.

Watts, Duncan (1992). *Joseph Chamberlain and the Challenge of Radicalism*. Hodder & Stoughton.

Wilkinson M.D., K.D. Editor (1925). *The History of the Birmingham Medical School 1825-1925*. Cornish Brothers.

Wright, G. Henry (1913). *Chronicles of the Birmingham Commercial Society and Chamber of Commerce A.D. 1783—1913*. Birmingham Chamber of Commerce.

Study Cases/Theses

Preece, V.A. (?). *Duddeston & Vauxhall Gardens*. Birmingham Central Library.

Smith, Barbara M.D. (1967) *The Avery Weigh* University of Birmingham.

Waterman, Margaret Irene. (1969*). The History of the Birmingham Athletic Club—Birmingham Athletic Institute 1866-1918*. Birmingham Central Library Archives.

Directories

Birmingham Directory compiled by J.S.C. Morris 1862.

Chapman's Directory of Birmingham 1800, 1803.

Corporation Directory of Birmingham 1861, 1863, 1864.

Directory of Directors 1900, 1901, 1902, 1903, 1904, 1905, 1906, 1907, 1908, 1909, 1910, 1911, 1912.

General & Commercial Directory of Birmingham 1849, 1855, 1858.

Hart's Army List 1888, 1889.

Houghton & Company Post Office Directory of Birmingham 1882.

Hulley's Directory of Birmingham 1870, 1876-77, 1881.

Jones Mercentile Directory 1865.

Kelly's Directory of Birmingham 1868,1880,1881,1883,1884,1886,1888, 1890,1892, 1895,1896,1897,1898,1899,1900,1901,1902,1903,1904,1 905,1906,1907,1908,1909, 1910,1911,1912.

Lloyd's Register of Shipping 1869, 1870, 1871, 1872, 1873, 1874.

Morris & Company Commercial Directory, Gazetteer of Warwickshire with Birmingham 1866.
Pearson & Rollason's Directory of Birmingham 1777, 1780, 1781.
Piggot's Directory of Birmingham & its Environs 1818, 1819, 1820, 1828, 1830, 1842.
Post Office Directory of Birmingham 1854, 1856, 1860, 1867, 1871, 1875, 1878, 1879.
Post Office Directory of London 1805, 1820, 1828, 1841, 1842, 1846.
Pye's Directory of Birmingham 1785, 1787, 1791, 1797.
Rylands Hardware Directory 1894.
Rylands Directory of Iron Trades 1910, 1912.
Slater's Directory of Warwickshire & Birmingham 1850, 1852/3.
Thomson & Wrightsons Directory of Birmingham 1808.
White's Directory of Birmingham 1849, 1855, 1869.
Wrightsons Directory of Birmingham 1812, 1815, 1816-17, 1818, 1821, 1823, 1825, 1829-30, 183.1

Official Documents

Birmingham Burgess Rolls 1872-73, 1873-74, 1875.
Birmingham Census 1851, 1861, 1871, 1881, 1891, 1901.
Birmingham Rate Books 1849-1863.
Public Record Office Titanic Documents on CD ROM.

Newspapers/Magazines/Articles

Antiquarian Horology September 1982
Aris's Gazette February 4, 1796
Birmingham Argus 1896, 1899, 1901
Birmingham Daily Mail 1896-1912
Birmingham Daily Post 1895-1913
Birmingham Weekly Post February 24, 1894
Birmingham Gazette & Express July 22, 1896-1912
Boston Daily Globe April 16, 1912
Canadian Trade Review May 20, 1898
The Cyclist 1888—1893

The Cyclist Yearbook 1893
The Daily Chronicle April 1912
The Daily Mail April 18, 1912
Daily Mirror April 1912
Daily Sketch April 1912
Daily Telegraph 1895-1912
The Educational Times December 1, 1904
The Engineer 1896
Evening Dispatch 1902-1906
Express & Star 1912
Le Gaulois September 2, 4, 1902
Hardware Trade Journal 1904-1905
London Evening Standard August 16, 1895
London Evening Standard November 16, 1907
London Mail March 22, 1903
London Mail July 5, 1905
The Machinist and Contractor August 2, 1895
Midland Express July 16, 1902
Milwaukee Sentinel April 16, 1912
New York American April 17, 1912
New York Herald April 3, 1911
New York Times April 16, 1912
New York Tribune April 16, 1912
The Mermaid Vol 5 1908-09
The Mermaid Vol 6 1909-10
The Mermaid Vol 7 1910-11
The Mermaid Vol 8 1911-12
The Monthly Review September 1899
The Monthly Review March 1900
The Monthly Review December 1902
The Rifleman December 1906
The Star Johannesburg April 26, 1906
The Statist July 19, 1902
The Statist June 27, 1903

Institute of Mechanical Engineers Memoirs May 1912
Ironmonger 1883, 1884, 1890, 1892, 1893

Andrew P.B. Lound

Museum/Library Archives

Avery Historical Museum, Soho Foundry, Smethwick, West Midlands.
Avery Berkel
Avery Weigh-Tronix
Birmingham Archives and Heritage
Birmingham Central Library Local History Department.
Birmingham Central Library Patents.
Birmingham Medical Institute
Birmingham Museum and Art Gallery.
Birmingham Probate Office.
Birmingham University Library.
Coventry Central Library Local History Department.
Doncaster Archives.
Guildhall Library, London.
HBSC Bank Archive.
Institute of Mechanical Engineers Library, London.
Lambeth Palace Library, London.
The Lound Collection
Malvern Public Library.
Maritime Archives & Library, Liverpool Maritime Museum.
Milwaukee Public Library, USA
National Archives, New York, USA
The Patent Office, Newport, Wales.
Public Record Office (UK).
Sandwell Library Local History Department.
Sheffield Archives
Soho House Museum, Handsworth, Birmingham
Sutton Coldfield Library, Local Studies.
University College London Library Special Collections.
University of Wisconsin in Milwaukee, Golda Meir Library, USA
Wellcome Trust Library of Medicine

Contract Ticket List, White Star Line 1912 (National Archives, New York
    NRAN-21-SDNYCIVCAS-55[279]).

People to thank

Hugh Barham Carslake
Norman L. Biggs
Don Bull
Professor Carl Chinn, University of Birmingham
John Doran, The Avery Historical Museum
Ruth Fallon
Helen Fisher
Frederic Fouret
John Forbes
Regina (Forbes) Schraut
Bertrand B. Giulian
Max Hipkins
Howard Green, The Avery Historical Museum
Michelle L. Harrell, University of Wisconsin
Michael Horne
Keith Houghton
Wendi Kings
Lauren Leech
Val Loggie, Soho House Museum
John Lound
Tory Manning, Avery Weigh-Tronix
Keith Moore, Institute of Mechanical Engineers Library
Peter Moore
Brigitte Over, Director Alstom Transport, Birmingham
Janet Pickard
Harry Seabourne
Barbara M.D. Smith
Martyn Vaughan, Managing Director Alstom Transport, Birmingham
Linda Waite
Fletcher Wallis
Sarah Wickham, Assistant Archivist, Lambeth Palace Library
Laura Wilks, Avery Weigh-Tronix
Michelle Williams
Stuart Williams, Walsall Local History Centre

Societies

British Titanic Society
Cradley Then and Now Group
Friends of Soho Foundry
Handsworth Historical Society
International Society of Antique Scale Collectors
Quinton Local History Society
Smethwick Local History Society
Titanic Historical Society

Lightning Source UK Ltd.
Milton Keynes UK
UKOW051957191011

180604UK00001B/81/P